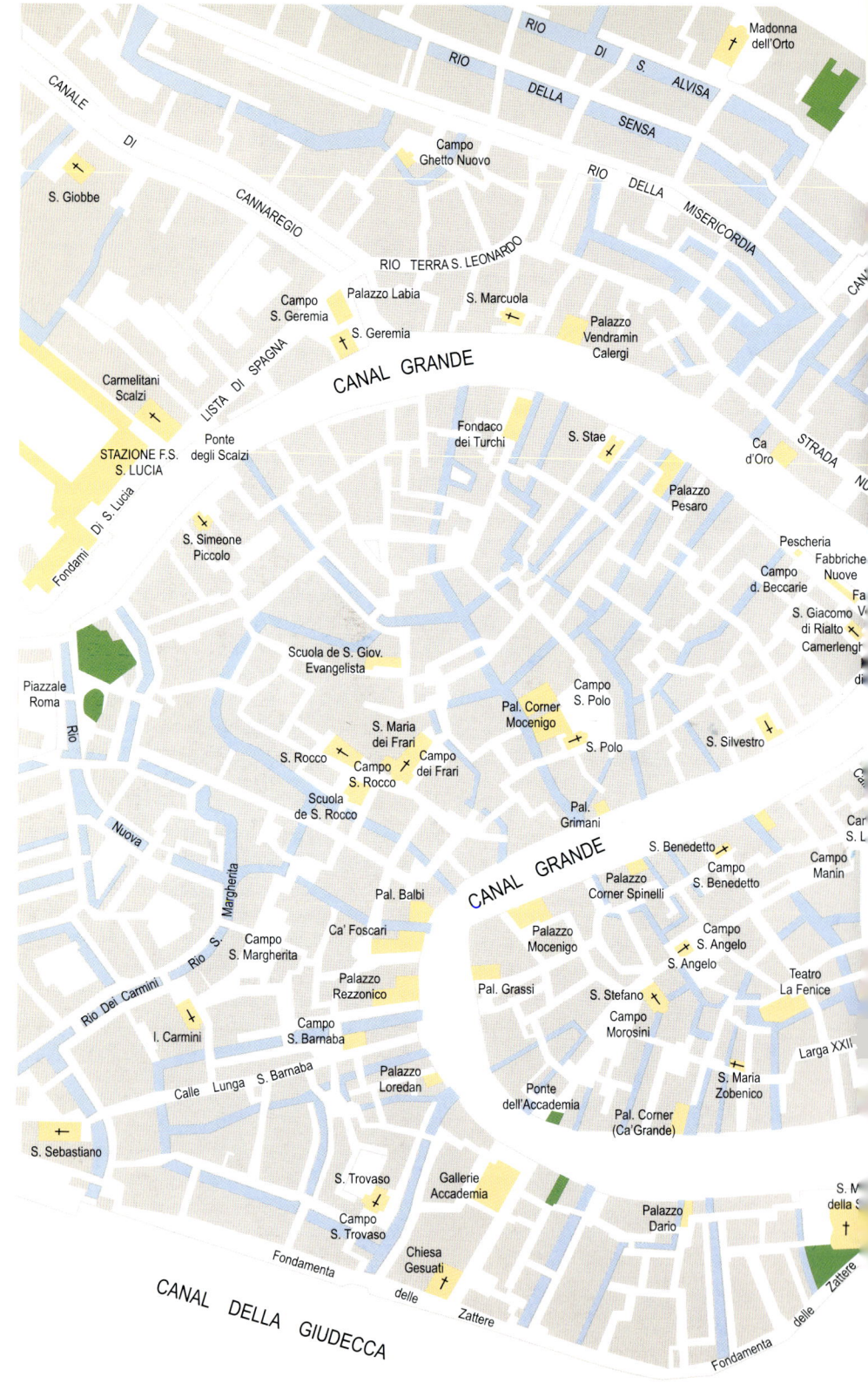

Isola di
S. Michele

North

Chiesa
dei Gesuiti

MISERICORDIA

Apostoli

S. Maria
dei Miracoli

Fondam. dei Mendicanti

Scuola di
S. Marco

S.S. Giovanni
e Paolo

S. Giovanni
Crisostomo

Monumento
a Colleoni

Campo
S. Zanipolo

Fondaco
ei Tedeschi

Campo
Bartolomeo

Palazzo
Priuli

Bartolomeo

Campo S. Maria
Formosai

Scuola di S. Giorgio
degli Schiavoni

. Salvatore

S. M. Formosa

MERCERIE

Pinocoteca
Querini-
Stampalia

S. Giuliani

ARSENALE

S. MARCO

S. Zaccaria

S. Giorgio
dei Greci

Torri
dell'Arsenale

Campo
S. Zaccaria

Pro.
Vecchie

Piazza
S. Marco

Ponte
dei Sospiri

Chiesa
Dalla
Pieta

PALAZZO
DUCALE

Prigioni

Pro. Nuovi

Piazzetta

DEGLI

Ponte
del Vin

Libreria

RIVA

Ponte
de Paglia

SCHIAVONI

VIA GARIBALDI

BACINO DI
S. MARCO

ISOLA DI S.GIORGIO
MAGGIORE

S. Giorgio
Maggiore

Venice *The Enlightened Traveler's Historical Guide*

John W. Higson, Jr.

Half **Full Press** Oakland, California

Cover and map design by David Hill, DK Graphics, Walnut Creek, CA
Book design by Stephanie Woo

Printed in China

ISBN 0-971-955-21-2

First Edition

This book is dedicated to my wife Eleanor,
who, over the past half century, has been
with me every day of the many months that
I have explored and studied the fabulous
city of Venice.

Santa Maria della Salute

Table of Contents

Part II:
THE CITY OF VENICE AS HISTORY 64

Illustrations

Foreword

Over the many centuries man has raised up untold millions of buildings and other structures upon the earth, from primitive dwellings and rural villages to remote castles and monasteries to complex urban centers. At the same time he has been possessed of a restless, destructive urge and has laid waste almost as much as he has created. What indeed of the built environment over the ages remains intact and unspoiled, having withstood the vicissitudes of history, war and natural disasters? The physical remains of the great Greek and Roman civilizations for the most part lie in ruins, as do those of other empires. Similarly the nation-states of Europe and the Mediterranean area that evolved during the Middle Ages obliterated as much as they built, with conquering armies and the relentless pursuit of change leaving little of their cities wholly intact.

In Italy alone the process has been inexorable and most of its cities have been badly scarred or largely demolished and rebuilt, as well as now being overrun with modern traffic and hemmed in by the stifling encirclement of sprawling suburbs.

Remarkably, however, one major exception, not just a village, but a capital center—the unique city of Venice—has come down to us in its historical entirety, untouched by large scale demolition and reconstruction, free of big industrial structures, housing projects, high-rise towers, adjacent suburbs, and free also of the automobile and its intrusive highways.

Even war, especially its modern versions, so devastating to many European cities, has left no trace in Venice. Neither of the two world wars caused any damage and no enemy in prior centuries ever succeeded in invading the main islands of the lagoon. Except for the wear and tear of time and the unending scouring of the sea tides, the city remains astonishingly as it was 500 years ago, the product of intrepid seafaring adventurers and the inspired artists and architects they employed. Maps dated to the 16th century show us buildings, squares, bell towers, canals, bridges, embankments, shipyards almost identical to the modern city.

However, it is not just for Venice's survival that we are blessed, but also because so much of it is singularly special—beautiful by any standard, stylistically and architecturally unique.

Fortunate as this may be, the future fate of Venice is far from certain. And not just its political or economic future, but its very existence. The world has been made painfully aware of the many problems the city faces—industrial encroachment on its lagoon, pollution of its air and water, a declining population, deterioration and neglect, subsidence of the underlying land strata, periodic flooding. Some of these problems, like the various causes of pollution, have been identified and steps taken to correct them, and many buildings and art treasures have been painstakingly restored, but a number of more fundamental dilemmas, especially high water inundations, have proven stubbornly intractable. Unless the world community can find solutions or the root causes, such as global warming, disappear on their own, Venice as it is today may not long survive.

This prognosis would be tragic for any historic city, but it is simply unacceptable for such a special place. It is the author's hope that a fresh look at Venice will help to remind the enlightened reader and traveler not only of the perils that threaten the city, but also of the reasons why its long history and remarkable survival merit every effort to save it.

In the meantime, Venice is there and waiting. Not for everyone, prudence suggests, as excessive tourism has its costs, but it is there for those who sincerely want to appreciate this extraordinary jewel in the crown of western civilization.

In similar format to my earlier book on Florence, I have attempted to simplify in one volume the many threads that combine to tell the city's story and, by employing strict selectivity and chronological interpretation, to blend Venice's history with descriptive commentary on its buildings, monuments and other works of art. That is, the major themes of the city's political, mercantile, military and social record, set against the background of the Mediterranean world, form a framework for more generalized comment on art and architecture, music and pageantry, finance and trade, morals and religion.

Over the last 50 years my wife and I have been in Venice innumerable times; yet, each arrival holds the same thrill and anticipation, as once more we board the *vaporetto* and steam along the Grand Canal with all its hectic activity and its magnificent palaces, or later in the evening glide in a gondola through the silent back canals. We hope and pray that the mystery, the intrigue, the exotic fantasy of La Serenissima will still be there for generations to come.

Author's Note

As the reader will soon deduce, this book is not a work of scholarly or original research, nor an in-depth, exhaustive account of the manifold components that make up one of the most fascinating cities in the world. Neither does it take the place of the many and admirable pocket guides which are organized around geographical areas of Venice to facilitate orientation and sightseeing and provide practical information on restaurants, hotels, waterbus schedules, etc.

Rather, this book is meant to cover a middle ground, to render an awareness and understanding of the city as it was and as it is today by way of a wide-ranging overview, to be read in the comfort of one's armchair either before, during or after a visit to Venice, or even, most assuredly, in lieu of a visit.

Accordingly, I have tried to summarize chronologically and selectively the most important aspects of the city's history as reflected in its monuments and works of art. It is naturally tempting for an author to inject his prejudices and personal judgments in selecting and appraising the material at hand, but it seemed wiser to be guided as much as possible by the general consensus and time-tested observations of the many perceptive scholars who have gone before.

While a short glossary is included at the end, mention should be made of the common Italian use of the terms *trecento, quattrocento, cinquecento* (dropping the prefix *mille* or one thousand) to indicate the 1300s, 1400s, 1500s; less confusing than our English "14th century" to refer to the 1300s, etc. Throughout the text, birth and death dates are shown for most historical persons, except in the case of the doges where the dates refer to their incumbency, e.g. Doge Francesco Dandolo, 1329–1339. (I point this out lest the reader think that the Venetians elected only children to their highest office.) The numerous footnotes may at first seem a burden, as my publisher tends to feel, but in many cases they may be more interesting than the referenced comments above.

Most of the buildings, *campi*, canals, bridges, etc. mentioned in the text can be found on the map, but not all. For those readers who want to explore the city more diligently, detailed maps, like those found in the pocket guides, are indispensable. These travelers will, however, be at a disadvantage compared to the author, who was fortunate to have enjoyed the companionship, advice and knowledge over the years of two invaluable friends, Gino Macropodio, well-known gondolier and descendant of an ancient line of Venetians and Vinny Lorenzi, musician, lawyer and long-time resident of the city. To them our thanks.

PART I: The Foundations of Modern Venice

No place on earth in appearance, character or essence remotely resembles Venice. Pictures of the city inevitably convey a singular impression. They communicate an unmistakable message that can only issue from that watery refuge on the lagoon, a message forever repeating that special ambience that may be confused with no other and that remains, in a word, Venetian.

And this is true not only of its topography—its buildings, squares and canals—but of its other attributes as well—its art, government, institutions, social arrangements—all of which developed a unique distinction. The reasons for this are clear, though hardly simple, as Venice from the beginning has been a complex mixture of diverse, if not conflicting, forces. Partly of the land and partly of the sea, half occidental and half oriental, a focal point of trade between Teutonic northern Europe and the peoples of the sunny Mediterranean, Venice has always combined and digested a myriad of influences that together have created its special character.

No other European city was destined to play this role, to act as a bridge between east and west. At the beginning of the Middle Ages, after the Roman Empire, and later the Christian world, had divided itself in two, it was through Venice that contact was maintained between Western Europe and the Byzantine realm, and between Catholic and Orthodox regions. Still later, when the Crusaders funneled across Europe to recover the Holy Land — forever after confirming the pattern of Muslim-Christian relations—Venice played a vital role as a point of departure and as a supplier of men and ships. And with the increase in world commerce that followed, it was Venice that became the great trading emporium—merchant, shipper, banker—second to none. Finally, when the humanist revolution and the art movements of the Renaissance and baroque periods began to work their influence on Europe, it was again Venice that was able to combine the new western ideas with the older traditions inherited from Byzantium to create a unique culture, perhaps one of the most brilliant and colorful the world has ever seen.

1 OVERVIEW OF VENETIAN HISTORY, GOVERNMENT AND SOCIETY

The disruption of the Roman Empire by the first barbarian invasions in the 5th century A.D. set the stage for the city's existence. Even earlier, the empire had been split in half for administrative purposes and its principal capital moved by the Emperor Constantine from Rome to the old city of Byzantium, which was largely rebuilt (324–330 A.D.) and renamed Constantinople. At the time this seemed reasonable, since the eastern provinces were wealthier, less vulnerable to attack, and, with Constantine's conversion to the new religion (312), more thoroughly Christianized than those of the west. Later, when western Europe was overrun by German tribes, the decision to move the capital proved to be decisive in the defense and preservation of the eastern portion of the empire. In fact, while the west disintegrated, the eastern or Byzantine Empire prospered, especially under Justinian (527-565), who was able to reconquer portions of the lost western territories, including the Italian peninsula. His successors, however, were unable to defend such an extensive area and were gradually forced to give up North Africa and the Near East to the Arabs and most of Italy to the Lombards, the last of the barbarian invaders. Thereafter, what had been the Western Roman Empire, once an administrative and political whole, was permanently shattered into a chaotic patchwork of diverse, decentralized states that developed along feudal lines and to which the genius of Charlemagne (742-814) and his heirs gave only a temporary and imperfect unity.

It was in this context that refugees from the neighboring mainland communities, fleeing from the successive waves of invaders, became the earliest permanent inhabitants of the Venetian Lagoon. A long period of development followed through the early Middle Ages, which saw the gradual shaping of a political entity, with the building of the city itself, its protective sea walls and its fleets and commercial business. Throughout this period the Venetians generally looked to the east, avoiding entanglements with mainland regimes and seeking political and economic cooperation with the Byzantines. At first in a subordinate role, but later as an equal, Venice linked itself with Constantinople, the only surviving city of consequence from the Classical Age, the guardian of civilized life, art, law, religious traditions and the hub of what survived of long distance trade between east and west.

Thus did the Venetians, a people ethnically and linguistically western, absorb during their formative centuries strong cultural, economic and political influences from a much older eastern civilization that was more sophisticated and unified than their neighboring feudal communities on the mainland. In time, the larger polities of France, Spain, Poland and Hungary gradually formed themselves into a semblance of their present national confines, but throughout the Middle Ages, the core of Europe, embracing modern Germany and Italy, long remained merely a conglomeration of many small principalities, dukedoms, bishoprics, free cities, etc. These often antagonistic states, although in theory owing a shadowy allegiance to the German or Holy Roman Emperors (heirs to Charlemagne's title[1] if not his authority) were on the whole backward and divided and presented fewer trading and cultural opportunities to the Venetians.

Build Up of Venice's Trading Empire

The vast majority of the European people at the time lived a precarious existence on a subsistence level, consuming almost the entire volume of their production. Capital was slow to accumulate and wealth consisted primarily of land. Basic vocations remained the same generation after generation, and agricultural and mining methods had changed little since classical times. Almost everyone lived under rural conditions or in small villages, and aside from the necessities of life turned out by local artisans and weavers, little manufacturing existed. The exchange of goods—wine for grain, wool for iron, etc.—was largely regional and luxuries, rare or imported products from a more sophisticated culture, were scarce and hard to obtain. It was to satisfy this potential demand that the Italian merchant companies came into existence, especially in Venice, and commenced to revolutionize the world's trading patterns.

The growth of towns during the 11th and 12th centuries aided this process by maintaining a pool of labor for manufacturing (e.g. metal workers in Milan and wool workers in Florence) and at the same time creating market

---

[1] Although it is commonplace to say that it was neither holy, Roman nor an empire, there was some sense to the title. It was holy in that the pope sanctioned the office and often sponsored and crowned the occupant; it was Roman in that it claimed direct descent from the Caesars through Charlemagne; it was an empire in that its jurisdiction spread out over many subordinate states.

centers for exchange and capital accumulation. Further, with the advent of the Crusades in the 11th century, knowledge of and demand for foreign products were stimulated by new contacts abroad. Luxury goods, those from the East especially, which until then had only trickled into Europe, began to flood through such ports as Venice in increasing quantity. These included silks and brocades, tapestries and carpets, gems and jade, as well as the so-called spices, a term that embraced a great deal more than such condiments as pepper, nutmeg, cinnamon, saffron, ginger and cloves, but also included all manner of special products unavailable in the west: dyes, mordants, incense, gums, scents, artists' pigments, medicinal drugs. In return, Europe paid for this by exports of wool and woolen textiles, timber, grains, furs, and metals such as gold, silver, lead and iron.

Venice was not the only vital trading center, but none other was in the same category. By the 12th century, towns like Paris, Cologne, Milan, Genoa, Florence and Naples were beginning to feel the first stirrings of a revival of trade, but they were still small, whereas Venice had already achieved a population and wealth unrivaled in western Europe. The Venetians were the most strategically located and their port, where maritime cargoes from the East could be unloaded closer to their final destination, became the logical focal point of a great deal of east-west, north-south trade. Goods flowed over the mountain passes of the Alps going to and from northern Europe, while one of the most fertile valleys in the world, the Po, had its natural outlet at the head of the Adriatic.

Moreover, by a policy of deliberate aggression, the city gradually acquired a string of islands and outposts stretching down the Adriatic to the eastern Mediterranean and then across the Aegean to the Black Sea, where contact was made with the ancient silk and spice routes coming out of India and China. Some of these overseas settlements were only fortified castles or protected harbors and ports serving merchant convoys. Others were trading stations of varying size. At Alexandria, Egypt, for example, where some of the camel caravans terminated, the Venetians maintained two large walled complexes. These bases included storage depots, living quarters with their own kitchens and oven facilities, baths, gardens, courtyards and churches—all of which were on a grander scale than any of their Genoese, French or Spanish competitors. Still other Venetian settlements were substantial territorial holdings, such as Negroponte (Euboea) off the Greek mainland, Nauplia, Monemvasia, Modon and Argos in the Morea (Peloponnesus), as well as many of the islands in the Cyclades, the North Sporades and the Dodecanese chains (e.g. Mykonos, Tinos, Aegina). A few, in later centuries, were true colonies, like the large islands of Corfu, Crete and Cyprus. No uniform system of administration applied to these dependencies. Some had varying degrees of local autonomy, but each had its governor, bailiff, rector, castellan or other overlord, usually a Venetian patrician appointed by the government.

Once so positioned, with its main avenues of trade sustained by treaties with the eastern potentates and protected by its growing fleet, Venice generated a sizable volume of commerce and profit earlier than its mainland neighbors.

Prosperity Crests

Not surprisingly, Venetian civilization developed its most distinctive character in the 13th and 14th centuries, as its prosperity was simultaneously cresting. Yet to come was the expansion of the city's mainland territory in the Veneto and the 16th century golden age of art, but the earlier period saw the consolidation of the basic character of the Venetian nation—a synthesis of east and west. During those years the city's fleets, overseas colonies and trade reached their apex, both in numbers and in comparison to the other powers. Moreover, Venice had achieved a singular independence. It was no longer subordinate to the Byzantines and was practically free of the squabbles and turmoil within the Holy Roman Empire, under which mainland Italy never ceased to chafe. Accordingly, La Serenissima,[2] having established itself as a reliable and efficient conduit for world trade free of interference from competing authorities, attempted, and for a while succeeded, in making itself indispensable to the commerce between Europe and Asia. In the process its unique institutions of government, business and social life firmly emerged, along with its own special artistic and architectural achievements.

The fact that the Greek Orthodox Church and the Roman Catholic Church remained divided apparently did little to hinder Venice's alliances or cultural development. Though always a member of the western communion, Venice maintained a clearly defined independence from Rome and, in those early centuries, a much closer relationship with Byzantium.

---

[2] Literally "the most serene," but in its feminine form, "The Republic of Venice," which its citizens considered an oasis of peace amidst the disorder of the medieval world elsewhere.

Maritime and Commercial Rivalry

This is not to say the Venetians had all things their own way. There were continual struggles with the Byzantines, first as commercial rivals and later as naval adversaries, with the Muslims, and with the other western maritime states, Genoa in particular, all of whom had widespread interests in the Mediterranean. But for several hundred years, Venice managed to more than survive, even though it was operating from a relatively modest base. By the 15th century, however, the widening territorial conquests of the Ottoman Turks and the final collapse of the Byzantines forced the Venetians to shift their main concern and involvement away from the eastern Mediterranean and toward Europe. Not only were their Aegean colonies overrun one by one and their trade disrupted, but also it became increasingly difficult for a small nation, physically in such close proximity, to remain isolated from the affairs of Italy as a whole. Accordingly in the 15th and 16th centuries, to compensate for its loss of influence and maritime supremacy in the East, Venice reluctantly but consciously undertook an expansion on the mainland—the *terrafirma*. In the process its ruling class found itself gradually transformed from a long line of seafaring merchants into a land-owning nobility. Fortunes earlier won in world commerce were systematically employed to acquire and improve landed estates. This development occurred at a time when the strength of the Venetian state, economically, financially and militarily, was on the wane in relation to the growing populations and wealth of other western nations. It managed, however, to maintain its *terrafirma* possessions for several centuries and to remain independent—at least in theory—until the time of Napoleon, but Venice's great days as a major power were over and its people lived in a continual state of anxiety and insecurity.

The wealth of Venice had never been based on natural resources or on the extent of territory the city controlled. Neither did it come to depend so much on manufacturing, as did Florence for example, though shipbuilding was of course important. Instead, the city's influence and strength rested on its naval traditions and on the far-flung trading apparatus it controlled. This included the most numerous merchant fleet, the largest shipyards, the best warehousing facilities and the most vital trading enclaves in the Mediterranean. With these advantages, the Serenissima had early developed an unrivaled volume of commerce, which was all coordinated by a large number of overseas consuls and merchant representatives permanently posted in the colonies, trading centers and naval stations linked to the mother city. Moreover, the patrician merchants who controlled this network also ran the government. All the facilities of the state—the convoy crews, the armed war galleys, the state-owned cargo ships chartered to private entrepreneurs, the colonial outposts, the customs officials, the court system—were at their ready command. Little wonder that they developed a special relationship and deep reverence for the sea upon which their fortunes depended.

Evolution of the Constitution and Social Classes

Also contributing to the city's commercial success were the stability and continuity of its social system and political institutions, both of which were so admired by other nations. Though customarily referred to as a republic, Venice was never one in the modern sense, and even less so was it democratic. On the other hand, the city never succumbed to the yoke of a tyrant or other one-man rule, nor did it pay homage, in theory or in practice, to either the pope or the western emperor, as did the rest of Italy and much of central Europe. The government was in fact an independent oligarchy, ruled by the privileged few, but with certain singular characteristics.

The Venetian constitution, like the British one, was unwritten. It consisted of laws, precedents and long-established customs that evolved gradually over the centuries. From a very early period, the power of the highest official, the doge, had been limited and circumscribed, and by the 13th century, the office became more or less symbolic. Real power often lay with a few of the wealthiest and most prestigious nobles, but they in turn answered to the Great Council made up of male members from the leading families (the Patriciate) whose names, once inscribed in the Libro d'Oro, acquired a semi-hereditary status.[3] These families were generally not considered part of the European nobility in the formal sense, at least by other nations, as their status and dignity stemmed not from papal, imperial or royal declamation but from their own recognition, and their wealth not

---

[3] The membership of the Great Council ranged from several hundred in the early days to more than 2,000 by the mid-16th century (or roughly 6% of the total adult Venetian male population). Thereafter it declined, ultimately to about 1,100 in 1797 at the end of the Republic as Venice itself and its population declined.

from land (the traditional and acceptable source) but from trade. The use of titles had always been proscribed and armorial coats-of-arms on buildings were prohibited by law at an early date. Accordingly the Venetian patricians had no connection with the feudal gentry, which were associated with chivalry, knighthood and landed preoccupations, but were actively engaged in the day to day affairs of politics, business, finance and the merchant marine. Large fortunes were accumulated, but primogeniture, the practice of passing an estate to the eldest child, was not customary in Venice, as it was in most of Europe, and a patrician might divide the inheritance arbitrarily between his various sons, all of whom were expected to earn their positions on their own. Many became expert administrators and diplomats, as well as successful traders, bankers and ship-owners. As such, the patrician class commanded respect over many centuries, not only from abroad, but, even more remarkably, from their fellow citizens, who, though possessing no political power whatsoever and unable to cross the dividing line of class, were for the most part content to uphold the status quo. The system did manage to last for more than 1,000 years.

Contributing to this balance was a small middle class group—about 10% of the population—know as *cittadini,* made up of notaries (lawyers), members of the chancery and other civil servants, military officers, the lesser merchants, industrialists and such. Although they lacked political representation, the *cittadini* enjoyed an intermediate and privileged status between the patricians themselves and the mass of the Venetian proletariat— laborers, craftsmen, servants, mariners, etc. Surprisingly little friction existed among these classes, and riots and civil turmoil, such common occurrences in cities like Florence, were rare. This was due in part to the absence of feudal divisions—the patricians did not gallop by on horseback but mixed daily with the people on foot—and in part to the fact that the welfare of the entire population depended on the cooperation of all in the general commercial enterprise, the lifeblood of the community. In addition, the privileges of the nobles were for a long period well earned, for aside from the economic risks they were forced to assume, the governing class was saddled with many political and military duties and responsibilities (which many tried in vain to avoid) that lessened the envy of those below. Numerous contemporary comments in the writings of foreigners confirm the existence of this respect and tolerance, a certain informality and forbearance, between the rulers and the people.

Divisions within the Patriciate

This apparent unity, however, did not extend within the Patriciate itself, where, especially in the later centuries, repeated frictions and divisions erupted, though these conflicts were carefully screened and hidden from the outside by a policy of secrecy that permeated all levels of government. In addition to the natural differences in approaching political, military or economic problems, there were a number of other underlying factors adding to these internal divisions within the Patriciate. For one, a special aura of superiority clung to a small group of some two dozen families whose ancestors had taken an active role in government in the early years of the Republic; those admitted to a comparable status at a later date did not enjoy the same prestige. For another, a sizable number of noble families, at least by the 16th century, had lost all or most of their wealth in the checkered course of events, yet remained by birthright part of the ruling class. Naturally this placed them at some disadvantage and with a divergent point of view. More important, since membership to the Great Council was automatic for all adult male members of a patrician family, there almost always existed a difference of opinion between the young and the older members. This was further aggravated because, unlike a state like Florence that encouraged youth, Venice was traditionally ruled by the elderly and there were always hundreds of ambitious younger nobles excluded from high office.[4] Factionalism was always a concern, but because the Great Council had as many members as it did and because many offices were filled by a combination of election and the drawing of lots, power remained diffused and no single clique was ever able to grasp the key levers of control for very long.

One potential source of division within the Great Council was, however, absent. This was the church hierarchy, which often played a role in high ministerial posts in other countries and cities, but which was specifically excluded from political office in Venice. Even the highest clerical dignitary, the Patriarch of Venice, did not have his seat at San Marco, the center of

---

[4] It has been calculated that the average age of the doges between 1400 and 1570 was 72 and other high officers were of a similar age. It has also been said that since the Venetians elected their doge for life, they preferred him old so that his days in office were numbered.

government, but instead presided at the somewhat remote San Pietro di Castello on the island of that name. He and other high clergy were selected and taxed by the Venetian Senate, not by the pope, and if charged with a crime, tried in state, not ecclesiastical, courts. Similarly, at the lower end of the church hierarchy, local priests were elected by the city parishes. In short, papal influence in Venice was secondary and political factionalism did not depend upon it.

Again veering away from the trends of feudal Europe, Venice did not develop a military class, nor an army of any size. The city, for the most part, utilized foreign mercenaries and a citizen's militia during and after the Middle Ages, a practice that helped to prevent the establishment of martial loyalties to any one political clique.

The Republic's System of Government

The influence of the highest state officer, the doge, varied over the centuries and with the personality of the incumbent, but the office came to symbolize primarily the unity and authority of the government. Some early doges earned a princely aura or maritime fame and exercised substantial political authority, but in later years their real powers came to be strictly limited. By the 13th century the Great Council had assumed control and the process of setting limits on the dogeship followed in due course. So at the height of Venice's prosperity, the doge, though still the head of state, no longer enjoyed much freedom of action. He was not, for example, permitted to receive or consult foreign ambassadors or emissaries in private; he could conduct no personal business nor engage in any unauthorized communication. Neither could members of his family fill the higher offices. He could not leave the city except on very special occasions, nor could he receive any gifts. He could not even abdicate if he wished to lay down the burdens of office. However, whatever the doge lacked in power or freedom was made up in ceremonial pomp and circumstance, the cost of which was trivial in return for the benefits of unity, patriotism and concord to which the dogeship contributed.

On all other levels of government, power was constrained by a system of checks and balances. Terms of office were limited, councils and committees, to which no two members of the same family could belong, were designed with overlapping jurisdiction or responsibility, and notaries were appointed to oversee and record deliberations. Little final authority was left solely in the hands of one or two individuals.

Also lending stability was the Venetian system of justice, which stemmed from a body of severe but relatively impartial laws that were codified as early as the 13th century. Justice, whose figurative symbol appears often on the city's buildings, was not an abstract idea, but an agreed-upon relationship between the governors and the governed. Throughout the history of the Republic, a sincere attempt was made to minimize legal privilege, to maintain accessible lower courts, and to extend these rights beyond the city into the subject territories. This was true in spite of Venice's later reputation for its notorious spy system, its starchamber procedures in trying suspected traitors and its secret executions.

These police-state methods, repeatedly pointed out by rivals, have undoubtedly tarnished the Republic's good name, but they were not peculiar to Venice. Most European governments in the 17th and 18th centuries employed agents, spies and counterspies to infiltrate other regimes. Venice did so, too, and with good reason. Several serious plots involving both foreigners and citizens to overthrow its government and even its sovereignty were discovered and frustrated, the conspirators apprehended and hanged. Given the inherent military weakness of the island community relative to its neighbors, diplomatic maneuvering and negotiation became its main weapons of survival. These in turn depended on political intelligence that could only be obtained through intrigue and paid informers. It was not that Venice was alone playing this game, only that, for a time, it was the most successful.

The Scuole

Throughout the 13th and 14th centuries, the great mass of the population, especially the middle class, remained content to live without political representation and was even supportive of the regime. One reason for this was the existence of those quasi-official institutions known as the *scuole,* where a degree of self-government could be practiced. Sometimes translated literally into English as "schools," these bodies, of which there were some 14, were really lay confraternities devoted to a particular spiritual cult and/or ethnic group within the city.[5] All were essentially mutual aid societies with religious affiliations, patron saints and elaborate rituals. Each had its own elected officers, constitution, by-laws, civic obligations and member participation. In addition to looking out for its own in sickness and misfortune, each undertook some charitable objective or sponsored a religious cause, and each developed its own privileges and traditions. These *scuole* provided not only a focal point for participation by the common citizens, but also created rivalries among themselves, so that they seldom presented a united front against the government. Finally, since the *scuole* admitted members from all ranks of society, from laborers to *cittadini* and even nobles on occasion, and since much of their charity benefited the poor, they served as a means for keeping a cross-section of the population in close touch with one another and as a conduit of welfare for the needy.

Most of the *scuole* have long since disappeared as active organizations, but they are remembered today for the works of art they sponsored and for the architecture they left behind. These legacies constitute a vital part of the total artistic heritage that forms such a major ingredient in the Venetian civilization.

---

[5] The larger, more important—the scuole grande—were: dei Carmini della Misericordia, S. Maria della Carita, S. Giovanni Evangelista, S. Marco, S. Rocco, and S. Teodoro. There were also two other noteworthy scuole established by immigrants to Venice: S. Giorgio dei Greci (Greeks) and S. Giorgio degli Schiavoni (Slavs).

2 VENETIAN ART AND ITS VARIED STYLISTIC TRADITIONS

Certainly, if Venice is remembered for nothing else, it will be remembered for the incomparable wealth of fine art in all its forms that issued forth from the city, especially during the golden age of the 16th century. Not surprisingly, the long history of the city's artistic contribution closely parallels the city's political and economic relationships. While Venice was living within Constantinople's sphere of sovereignty, Byzantine ideas prevailed, but later, when this tie had been weakened, western cultural influences—successively Romanesque, Gothic and Renaissance—increasingly made themselves felt. In the end Venice succumbed, like the rest of Europe in varying degrees, to the baroque, rococo and neoclassical styles, but throughout it always retained some measure of its own unique traditions, some thread of its peculiar admixture of east and west.

The Byzantine Influence

The art style known as Byzantine emanated from the capital of the empire, Constantinople, which from its establishment until the 13th century was the richest, largest and most cultured city in Christendom. Its population reached well over half a million at its peak, when even the largest European cities of this time—Venice and Salonika for instance—seldom exceeded 100,000, while Paris and London were mere villages. Not only was Constantinople the hub of an empire, it was also the focal point of the eastern Mediterranean trade routes. Most importantly for art, it was also the seat of the Patriarch, the head of the Orthodox Church. Unlike the Roman pope, who managed to remain independent of the secular powers, the Greek patriarch was appointed by the emperor and subordinate to him. Church and state were one in the eastern empire and art existed primarily to serve both. Accordingly, the wealth and influence of the court and the aristocracy filtered via the church establishment into the arts, which were largely controlled for official purposes.

Over the centuries the parameters and power of the empire gradually contracted, but the status of Constantinople hardly changed, and its culture developed a marked stability. Accordingly, Byzantine art, originally stemming from a fusion of Greek and Asiatic forms employed for Christian purposes, acquired and retained a distinctive style, whether pictorial, decorative or sculptural, based on conservative tradition and standardized rules. Nevertheless, it underwent several evolutionary cycles. At first, the Hellenistic strain, characterized by compositional balance and harmony, three-dimensional solidity and careful modeling, remained important, but gradually this was diluted by eastern influences emphasizing abstract, decorative patterns and the repetition of accents in rhythmical designs. In the process the special Greek understanding of spatial relationships and the illusion of reality gave way to flat, two-dimensional concepts, which were more in keeping with the transcendental nature of the new religion. Whereas the pagans had placed value on man's earthly life and hence on the beauty of the human form, Christianity, with its hope centered on the next world, emphasized the spiritual side of man and the salvation of his soul. Less importance was attached to the physical body and it was seldom shown by the Byzantines in the nude. Instead of studying life from nature, artists imitated one another using set formulas and designs, tending toward the abstract. The realistic, living aspects of human figures, so beautifully expressed in the Classical era with their noble, monumental bearing, were progressively and subtly transformed into more lineal, stylized ones. Proportions became less than ideal and the human form was used not to depict physical reality but rather spirituality, suffering and mortification. Robes and draperies became simplified, no longer enclosing a real body, but falling in abstract patterns. Solid objects appeared flattened, shadowless, elongated.

An other-worldly or sacred ideal as expounded by the church demanded an emphasis on the essentials, not on the extraneous; the holiness of a religious personality was important, not his human qualities. Hence, realistic facial characteristics disappeared in favor of serene, two-dimensional, stereotyped countenances with large, staring eyes suggestive of the supernatural. In depicting Christ, emphasis had to be placed on His Godlike or king-like aspect rather than the human. Following in the eastern tradition, He was more often portrayed in an abstract, distant or regal attitude: the concept of Christ Pantocrator. And, as Christianity grew more orthodox and concerned with the hereafter, natural backgrounds and perspective in pictorial art gave way to abstract fields of color or gold. Spatial relationships disappeared, time became eternal and even proportion and size were arbitrary, as in depictions of Christ's figure, which often appears larger than the others. In the process formulas and methods became fixed, repeated over and over. It has been said that Byzantine art well suited the Christian dogma developed by the Orthodox church, since it grew, in the Greek tradition, out of an intellectual rather than humanized interpretation of the Bible.

Even before the so-called Iconoclastic Controversy (726–843), these Asiatic influences on the art of Byzantium had all but triumphed throughout the Mediterranean world. However, this event induced the final step in the direction of dehumanizing art. The Iconoclasts ("Image-breakers") took literally the Biblical caveat against worshipping graven images, which had originated from the discredited pagan practice of idolatry. This interpretation, demanding an end to such veneration and embracing almost all representational art, became, despite strong opposition, the official policy of the empire. As a result a vast number of sacred objects (icons, cult statues, pictures, etc.) were deliberately destroyed and what little creativity remained was stifled. Moreover, of the art still allowed by the authorities (mainly mosaics), the already dominant tendencies were formalized into rigid rules and strictly enforced.

Even so a defiant undercurrent of resistance persisted among the masses, so that eventually the Iconoclastic prohibitions were relaxed and by the 10th century this extreme ascetic formalism had somewhat given way. Certain Hellenistic characteristics—composition reordered around a central theme, semi-modeled figures, the three-quarter view of the head, Greek architectural elements, landscapes—again reappeared, and the human side of Christ, the suffering mortal of the Passion, was reintroduced. The two tendencies finally reached an accommodation, a fusion, and it was from this time on that the Byzantine style—sometimes decadent, sometimes inspired—began to work its influence on the art of Venice.

The Romanesque Style

Meanwhile a parallel development was underway in western Europe: the slow emergence of the Romanesque style resulting from the interaction of the remains of late Roman architecture and sculpture with the native art forms of the Celtic and Teutonic peoples. The latter introduced something entirely new into the western tradition: an artistic expression based on an organic liveliness, a dynamism, a fantasy of form quite different from the symmetry and balance of classical art or the rhythmic repetition and ordered formalism of Byzantine art. This style made its earliest appearance in manuscript illumination, enamel and metal relief work and later in wall painting, stained glass and sculptured stone. The representation of the human figure, for example, did not appear in a natural or idealized form (Greek or Roman), nor did it appear static, other-worldly and impersonal (Byzantine or Asiatic). Instead, it assumed an infinite variety of intense human attitudes and shapes, agitated movements, individualized expression and personality, all devoid of modeling or illusionism. Firm contours and a marked sense of pattern dominated pictorial art, whether a wall mural, tapestry or illuminated manuscript. In sculpture especially, a distortion of the figures, human, animal or mythical, was characteristic. To a degree this was because Romanesque sculpture was conceived as an integral part of church architecture and served not only to instruct the faithful, but to decorate the various structural parts of the building. As such the sculptures had to be literally carved out of and into columns, capitals, arches, lintels and window frames. But primarily, the distortion arose from the artists' need to express emotion and involvement with the episode at hand, an intensity of feeling so different from the aloof, self-contained, calm figures of Byzantium.

By the 11th century these native artistic tendencies had coalesced over most of western Europe into the style we call Romanesque. Despite their diversity, the various peoples occupying what had been Roman provinces on both sides of the Alps had by then reacquired a common culture and a degree of unity as the Dark Ages receded. Trade and communications were on the increase, towns were growing, and a new urban middle class was forming, while at the same time new wealth was accumulating. And pervading all was the potent and unifying influence of the Roman church, invigorated by a resurgent Christianity, which expressed itself in the great 11th century religious revival, the endless shrine pilgrimages and the beginning of the Crusades.

This spirit, besides influencing pictorial and sculptural art, also found expression in a vast building program of churches and cathedrals throughout Europe, some of great size in order to accommodate the increasing number of the faithful, which, in the Middle Ages, included almost the whole of a growing population. Earlier, monastic and parish churches had been built on a smaller scale, and, though customarily constructed of masonry, were often roofed over by ceilings of wooden beams and rafters and other combustible materials. Fire was always a concern, however, so whenever possible some simple type of stone vaulting was attempted. In its most elementary form, this was no more than a barrel or tunnel vault—that is, a continuous series of transverse arches of heavy stone down the nave. As European churches began to be built wider and larger, the piers and parallel aisle walls were of necessity heavier and stouter to support the increased weight and thrust of the roof vaulting. Windows were accordingly narrow, which left the interior dark. To remedy this, Romanesque builders adopted the groined vault—simply the intersection of a lateral one at right angles to the barrel vaulting of the nave. By building a series of these across the nave, clerestory windows could be opened up at the end of each transverse vault, letting in more light. This was an improvement but did nothing to relieve the tremendous weight and lateral thrust of the roof, which still required thick walls and ponderous buttresses. The resulting massiveness and bulk of the buildings not only limited interior space but often caused irregular settling and subsidence.

To overcome this difficulty, the ribbed vault was introduced. Instead of simply joining two barrel vaults at right angles, stone ribs were constructed along the lines where the vaults would have met—the groins—and the intervening triangular spaces filled in with a sheathing of lightweight material. Not only was the weight of the roof reduced, but its burden was transferred and channeled down the ribs, which acted as a kind of skeleton, to specific points—the piers—which could be buttressed independently. This in turn permitted the nave walls in between, no longer bearing the weight of the roof, to be constructed of light stone or be opened up into large windows of stained glass.

The Gothic Style

Following this development, which marked the transition from Romanesque to Gothic building methods, church interiors became progressively more complicated—square bays were elongated into rectangles, ambulatories added around the apses, etc.—often requiring that the arches and ribs assume a pointed shape in order that they crest at a common height. So appeared the most distinctive feature of Gothic architecture—the ogive or pointed arch. Structurally more stable, this carried the roof ever higher, producing a vital ingredient in the verticality of the new style. The central characteristics of Romanesque architecture—thick walls, narrow windows, groined vaults and round arches—gradually gave way to those of the Gothic—thin walls, large windows, ribbed vaults and pointed arches. Later, as the possibilities were more fully realized, other Gothic hallmarks made their appearance: taller piers and higher ceilings, spires and crockets, flying buttresses and more complicated tracery.

These are the most obvious manifestations of the Gothic style, but the essence of it lies in the European environment out of which it grew: a more orderly social context emerging from the primitive and anarchic conditions of the earlier era. As trade increased during the 12th and 13th centuries, a new communal spirit appeared, increasingly independent of the feudal system and the monastic orders, and centered on town life, the guilds, the local bishop and especially on the building in his charge, the cathedral, now to be built ever higher, reaching toward the heavens. Compared to the more solemn Romanesque period, there developed a new optimism, a new religious fervor and desire to create artistically something splendid to the glory of God, with whom the people felt a closer, more personal relationship. The inordinate dread of the hereafter slowly gave way to the hope and the possibility of an accommodation between man's earthly and spiritual needs.

Manifestations of this new sense of confidence, sustained by the growing wealth of the trading communities, appeared not only in architecture but in all other forms of art. Monumental sculpture, for example, long merely an incidental part or embellishment of a building, again acquired, for the first time since antiquity, a separate identity of its own, progressively independent of its frame. Figures literally detached themselves from reliefs, columns and other building members to become statues in the round, as they were in classical times. Moreover, they began to assume an element of realism and serenity, later even a stylized elegance, that was no longer distorted and inhuman and no longer subordinate to the themes they illustrated, but stood on their own as reflections of man's renewed self-assurance and hope for salvation.

Italy, as much as any place in Europe, felt the effects of these social, religious and artistic forces, but the Gothic style and its attributes, primarily a creation of people north of the Alps, was never totally accepted. Rather it was selectively adapted to local tradition. In Venice especially, only those aspects that best suited its conditions were utilized, and then only as modified by Venetian taste. In architecture this meant that many Gothic motifs and decorative elements were employed, but with a special Venetian stamp. The new Gothic structural methods were largely adopted (it was important in a city built on pilings to lighten heavy walls and to divert and radiate weight over a greater area), but with reservations. For example, in many Venetian churches the practice of reinforcing arches with heavy wooden horizontal tie beams was never abandoned, though their use is jarring to the eye and is contrary to the Gothic principle. Other features—fan vaulting, flying buttresses, soaring spires, extreme verticality—all the culminating glories of many northern buildings—were generally disregarded completely.

In painting, certain Gothic characteristics—a new kind of three dimensional picture space, the naturalness and humane intimacy of the figures, and the realism of particulars—were readily imported, while the older Byzantine-Venetian artistic traditions continued. It is particularly significant that no native school of fresco painting, which was so integrally a part of other Gothic environments, ever developed in Venice. This was probably due to the Venetian preference for the mosaic medium in wall murals and also, once the hierarchical Byzantine approach had given way to the humanization of religion, for smaller individual works of art in the iconic tradition, especially carved, gilded and brightly painted polyptyches to decorate their church interiors. Only in the sculptors' art, where there was less of a strictly Venetian tradition, did Romanesque and Gothic influences and later those of the Renaissance, almost completely dominate.

The Church of San Marco

Something of this long interaction of art and history can be conveniently studied in a single building, the most important in Venice: the Church of San Marco. Glimpsed from the far end of the Piazza, its unique ensemble of shapes and styles, its glorious encrustation of marble, mosaic and gilding, create an impression that few other buildings can equal. Dedicated to the Evangelist Mark, whose bones, tradition insists, were stolen from his tomb in Alexandria, Egypt by Venetian mariners and carried back to Venice, the church was built to house the saint's relics and to enshrine his memory as patron of the city. From the beginning San Marco was the official place of worship of the doge and his government; his election was proclaimed here and religious sanction was conferred upon him. San Marco has always been more closely associated with the state than with the papal hierarchy, from which it has remained relatively independent. The doge, not the pope, always appointed its primarius, or chief priest. And it is fundamentally a Byzantine

The Byzantine façade of San Marco with its later Gothic additions.

building in conception and details, a testimony to early and continuing resistance to the influence of Rome.

San Marco's structural framework of brick, which replaced an earlier smaller church, dates from 1063, but many elements of the architectural decoration—pilasters, columns, capitals, carvings—which have been so beautifully incorporated into it, are much older. Many are fragments from ancient Byzantine, Greek, Syrian and Roman buildings—bits and pieces of foreign booty brought home from distant places. Venetian galley captains were instructed to include in their return cargoes spoils from rival cities and much of this booty found its way into the fabric of the building. Such a massive overlay of exotic decor might have left only an impression of ostentatious display and vainglory, but somehow it conveys a profoundly religious feeling. Equally remarkable is that a diversity of so many parts could have formed such a unified and majestic whole.

The building's basic plan is patterned after the Church of the Twelve Apostles in Constantinople (since demolished after the Turks captured the city), which had a classical Greek-cross floor plan of four equal arms, a dome over each and a fifth larger dome over the crossing. The façade of San

Marco, however, has no counterpart, but is heavily overlaid with Byzantine elements. Perhaps its oldest components are also its most famous: the four magnificent bronze[1] horses. These horses are masterpieces of proportion, vigor and idealized form, and are sometimes said to have been cast during Nero's time (1st century A.D.) to grace a triumphal arch in Rome, although they are probably of Greek inspiration. Constantine moved them to his new capital on the Bosporus, where they are thought to have stood in the Hippodrome for some nine centuries before being carried off by the Venetians after the conquest and sack of that city by crusaders in 1204.

There are many other theories on the origins of the horses. One theory postulates that long before Nero's time they were sculpted in Rhodes and yoked to a chariot by none other than Lysippus (second half of the 4th century B.C.) and presented as a gift by the people of Rhodes to the oracle at Delphi. There, a huge pedestal of exactly the right size and shape to accommodate the four horses and a chariot still stands in front of the Temple of Apollo. Whatever their actual origin, we know that the Venetians brought them to Venice in 1204 and placed them in their present positions.[2]

But there are many other decorative components of the façade that antedate the building itself: a rectangular relief carving of Hercules in the spandrel of the arch on the extreme left or north side (Roman, 3rd century); the sculptural relief of the architrave above the St. Alipius door on the left side (5th century) and another stone relief depicting 12 sheep (the Apostles) around the divine throne set into the wall just around the northern corner (Byzantine, 7th century). From the time of San Marco's consecration in 1094, Venetian ships continually brought back spoils from all over the Mediterranean: columns and capitals of Byzantine and classical origin, pierced Byzantine screened windows, marble slabs from ancient buildings,[3] and specifically, the two interesting carved reliefs on either side of the central arch depicting the two warrior saints usually shown in armor and drawing

---

[1] Now determined to be mostly copper (98 percent) plus tin (one percent) and lead (one percent).

[2] Air pollution has caused corrosion of the metal, requiring that they be housed inside and copies substituted in their place.

[3] The names of some of these beautiful marbles are as colorful as the stones themselves and as exotic as their origin: marmo Greco (Greek marble), red porphyry (from Egypt), breccia Africano (called roadstone), cipollino (veined), verde-antico (green), porpora (purple), diaspro sanquinoso (red jasper), serpentina, alabaster.

The ancient and famous bronze horses removed from Constantinople by Venetian crusaders.

their swords: St. Demetrius of the Orthodox church (Byzantine, 12th century) and St. George (13th century).

Toward the end of this period (about 1260), the famous mosaic over the St. Alipius portal was set into place and shows us in a stylized way what the façade looked like at that time. The four prancing horses can be seen in their places in the mosaic, as can the swelling domes, no different than today, but as yet no western influences appear in the façade. The first signs of these present themselves only after the date of the mosaic in the carvings on the three superimposed arches over the central doorway. This is the earliest identifiable work here by native Venetian artists, wherein Byzantine tradition is seen to be modified by the Romanesque (late 1200s).

Next in point of time come the three central bronze doors executed in 1300, one of which is signed and dated by the sculptor, "Magister Bertuccius Aurifex Venetus MCCC." Late in that century and continuing into the 1400s, Gothic influence appears in the many elaborate decorative motifs at the upper part of the façade—the cusps, pinnacles and statues—and in the vast central window, which was at that time divested of its Byzantine screening and opened up to lighten the interior of the church. Apparently, when the metal helmets were added on top of each of the domes a little earlier, some interior light sources were lost. This may have prompted the installation of this large glass expanse over the main door in the façade, as well as the Gothic rose window in the south transept. At the end of this period, figures were added to support the rain spouts between the arches of the upper tier. These so-called *doccioni* are attributed to Florentine sculptors; their style is still basically Gothic but shows the first signs of the Renaissance (early 1400s).

Since that time there have apparently been no material changes in the façade, with the exception of the mosaics under the arches. All the originals, except for the St. Alipius, were unfortunately destroyed and replaced in later centuries.[4]

Inside the church the same dominant Byzantine presence, even less diluted by western influence, strikes the visitor. Two colors overawe the eye—the rose of the marble and the gold of the mosaics—as one adjusts to the filtered light playing on the vast textured surfaces and upon the undulating, patterned floor. Here the deep roots and the ancient history of the city's past become manifest.

The mosaics are indeed impressive, covering practically the whole of the interior above the gallery level, and present an opportunity to study Byzantine art found in few other places in western Europe. And it is from the galleries that the visitor can best appreciate the mosaics as well as the pavement below. It is true that some of the iconography, subject matter and arrangement stem from the Latin church (e.g. the position of Christ enthroned in the apse, the personification of the Virtues in the central cupola, the symbols of the Evangelists in the eastern cupola) and that certain western influences are found in the mosaicists' pictorial approach (e.g. the Old Testament mosaics in the atrium). But on the whole, the inspiration, the models from which the scenes are drawn, and the overall stylistic effect are clearly Byzantine: the images in the Pentecostal dome, the Gospel Cycles on the vaults supporting the central cupola, the seated figure of Christ between the Virgin and St. Mark above the main entrance, the figures of Jesus and

---

[4] Those of the upper story in 1617–1618, the two over the right-hand doors in 1660, the one over the second door from the left in 1728, and the one over the central portal in 1836.

The soaring arches and cupolas of San Marco's nave looking toward the iconostasis.

Byzantine mosaic of Christ between the Virgin and St. Mark on the entry wall.

four prophets (left nave aisle) and the Madonna and four prophets (right nave aisle) are all of eastern origin. In fact, the main iconographic program throughout the building bears the clear imprint of the art of Constantinople in the 11th and 12th centuries in its developing phases, and is unique in western Europe.

The earliest mosaics—several in the atrium and some in the interior cupolas—seem to date from the last part of the 11th century and the early part of the 12th, when the building was first completed structurally. Others date as late as the 14th century, showing strong Gothic influence (e.g. those in the Chapel of San Isidoro), and some date even into the 15th century as in the Chapel of the Mascoli, whose vault mosaics, with their more sophisticated and worldly style, employ the then newly discovered techniques of shading, perspective and realism that reflect a less spiritual message and clearly reveal the approach of the Tuscan Renaissance.

Perhaps the Baptistry, entered from the right side of the nave, is a good

The mosaics of the Baptistry surround the font designed by Sansovino, who is buried here by the altar.

place to start as it incorporates something from almost every period and in as many artistic mediums. Its structural form follows that of the church itself, with a Byzantine cupola on pendentives. Aside from the massive granite block forming the main altar, upon which tradition claims Christ stood to preach in the city of Tyre, the oldest part of the embellishment is a 12th-century Byzantine fresco of the Madonna with arms raised against a blue background. This is followed, in point of time, by 13th-century mosaics of Jesus' childhood in the smaller adjoining room. Next is the relatively simple and unadorned tomb of Doge Giovanni Soranzo (1312–1328) set against a blue marble wall. Then come the famous mosaics commissioned in the mid–14th century by one of the best remembered doges and friend of Petrarch, Andrea Dandolo (1343–1354), whose tomb, a combination of classic and Gothic elements, is also here.

These mosaics, especially the one in the Baptistry's central cupola (Christ sending the Apostles to the Gentiles) well represent the last phase of Byzantine art, as do the four figures of the Fathers of the Greek Church in the pendentives. The same may be said of the mosaic above the altar of the crucified Christ with the Virgin and Saints Mark, John the Baptist and John the Evangelist, except for the kneeling figures of Doge Dandolo, the Dogaressa and the Venetian Chancellor in the lower part of the mosaic, which are a Gothic introduction. On the side walls are the well-known cycles of Salome, Herod's banquet and St. John's execution, a synthesis of the Byzantine and Gothic styles, as illustrated by the ornate court costumes and the animated gestures of the figures.

Lastly we have a touch of the Renaissance—the beautiful baptismal font by Jacopo Sansovino in the center with its figure of the Baptist and reliefs in bronze portraying his life—reflecting the great change in artistic approach that occurred during the 15th century.

Altogether the Church of San Marco remains the best example in Venice of Byzantium's mature and unique culture onto which have been grafted influences from western Europe. While there do exist a few other fundamentally eastern-inspired buildings, more or less modified by later styles, virtually all of the remainder of the city's monuments were conceived under Gothic, Renaissance or baroque inspiration, though always filtered through local tradition. Accordingly most of Venice's extant buildings are an expression of the city's last 500 years, a textbook of its more recent, westernized past, but with occasional footnotes to the earlier period.

3 THE LANDSCAPE OF VENICE TODAY

While, therefore, not a great deal survives intact and unmodified from the ancient Byzantine city, there is also very little modern construction, a claim few other urban centers can make. Fortunately Venice suffered little damage in World Wars I and II, and there has recently been a concerted effort to resist modernization and to preserve the city's character. Of course, some alterations and additions were inevitable with the advent of the industrial age. These reflect little credit on our own era and the best that can be said is that they were "necessary" in order to bring the city into the 20th century. For example, the coming of the railroad prompted the building of a rail causeway from the suburb of Mestre on the mainland to facilitate the direct entry of goods and passengers, which has forever ended the city's relative isolation and inaccessibility. This was followed by an auto road viaduct during the Mussolini years and modern constructions were built at the terminals of each. The railway station is fairly inconspicuous with a low profile and good design, but the ugly automobile garages of massive size are totally incongruous.

Arriving in Venice

These garages, together with the general tawdriness of the immediate surroundings, including the crowded Piazzale Roma with its sheds and bus platforms, provide an unfortunate first impression for those who arrive by motor vehicle. Better is an arrival by train, the terminal for which opens conveniently out onto a spacious terrace along the Grand Canal so that travelers need only to walk across to an awaiting *vaporetto* (waterbus) or gondola.

Best is an arrival by water, either by motoscafo from the nearby Marco Polo Airport on the mainland north of the city, or by ocean steamer from the open sea. And, of course, it was by water that all visitors made their approach to Venice in olden times. Some came either by way of the Adriatic or across the lagoon from Chioggia (as did the diarist John Evelyn), entering the city through its proper gateway, the Piazzetta. Most, however, had to come either by barge down the Brenta from Padua and then across the western lagoon to the Giudecca Canal (as Shakespeare's Portia did) or by carriage to Mestre and then across to the Canal of Cannaregio. The

Chioggia approach from that small fishing village to the south still has much to recommend it if one can take the time and the trouble, but to proceed along the Brenta today or to pass directly through Mestre or Marghera can be depressing. All this area on the western side of the lagoon has suffered a sad transformation over the past century as it has been inexorably converted from lonely tidal flats and peasant houses into one of the largest industrial complexes to be found in Europe. With its gigantic petrochemical plants and oil refineries, its warehouses and sprawling suburbs, it would be bad enough anywhere, but is especially obnoxious so close to Venice. Ironically, though, this development on the mainland has spared the city itself, which remains almost free of industrial buildings. Venice's problems therefore relate not to conscious destruction and rebuilding of areas within its perimeter, but to other consequences of a changing environment, most often the result of man-made and natural factors that endanger the physical existence of the city in its traditional form.

Problems Facing the Venetian Lagoon

Much has been written in recent years of the nature and extent of these problems—the gradual subsidence of the land, periodic inundations from the sea, the pollution of the lagoon and the atmosphere, a decline in population, and the general decay and deterioration of the very fabric of the city and its treasures. Though at first glance these misfortunes seem almost overwhelming, it is heartening to know that they at last have been recognized and defined and are being grappled with, not only by the Italian government, but by numerous other institutions formed for that purpose all over the world.[1] Much remains to be done, but at least a start has been made.

This is not, however, the first time the Venetians have been faced with serious environmental adversities. Their ancestors in the 16th and 17th centuries, too, were confronted with a set of gradually changing circumstances and had to make Herculean efforts to maintain the delicate equilibrium of the lagoon. At that time, probably due to the steady deforestation of the hill country in the Veneto and the draining changes made in the Po Valley by land reclamation, the rivers flowing into the lagoon began depositing

---

[1] The International Fund for Monuments and the Committee to rescue Italian Art in the United States, Britain's Venice in Peril Fund and other societies in Germany, France, Australia, etc.

The port of Marghera on the mainland with its petrochemical plants and oil refineries.

increased amounts of silt. If the process had been permitted to continue, Venice would have found itself landlocked and surrounded by sand as did Ravenna earlier. At the same time, the protective *lidi*, those narrow strips of land forming the external perimeter of the lagoon, long since divested of their vegetation, were slowly being destroyed by wave action from the Adriatic. It was only a question of time before the city would be choked by the rivers' silt or overwhelmed by the sea.

But the Venetian Republic refused to bow to the inevitable. A body of Water Magistrates was established, second in importance only to the doge and his councilors, and given supreme power over all matters pertaining to the lagoon and its environs. Solutions were agreed upon and several projects were carried out at great expense. The most difficult of these was the diversion of the three principal rivers flowing into the lagoon—the Brenta, the Sile and the Piave—by a series of canals so that most of their contents were discharged into the Adriatic to the north and south, thereby halting the build up of silt deposits in the city's immediate vicinity. Next, the Venetians constructed a stout wall of massive stones on a stepped base along the entire seaward side of the *lidi* designed to break the force of the incoming waves and prevent the erosion of the soil. Finally, they restricted the volume of the tidal flow by extending the wall part way into the three *porti,* or openings, to the Adriatic. Of course, closing the *porti* was never an option, not only because Venice would do nothing to hamper the movement of its shipping, but also because, having no sewers, the city depended entirely on the daily flushing action of the tides through these openings. However, laws were passed to prohibit the deepening of the *porti,* or the ship channels running across the lagoon to them, so as to moderate the inflows from the open sea. By such means a balance was restored and the traditional environment preserved.[2]

Today, however, the balance has again broken down. Most pressing is a solution to the phenomena of *acqua alta* (extreme high tides) that have become more frequent and destructive in recent years. For decades scientists have noted a gradual subsidence of the land mass under the lagoon, and everyone was aware that even normal tides were rendering the lower floors of many buildings untenable, but little real concern was expressed. Then came the great storm of November 1966, which not only flooded Florence, but submerged Venice under five feet of water, the highest inundation ever recorded. Suddenly the world was put on notice that unless something was done, the city's days were numbered.

Part of the problem was the condition of the seawall, which had been worn away in many places, permitting the storm waves to surge over the *lidi.* In addition, excessive dredging in the *porti* and the lagoon channels to widen and deepen them for the passage of modern super tankers en route to Marghera permitted extremely heavy inflows. These factors, together with an unusual combination of circumstances—an exceptionally high tide, heavy rains and strong winds that built up a sea-surge from the Adriatic—were the immediate causes of the *acqua alta* of 1966. The seawall can, of course, be repaired and the government is indeed doing so. Also, a number of proposals have long been under study to construct some kind of moveable or submersible dams at the three entrances from the open sea. These barriers would normally be filled with seawater and lie flat on the channel bottom,

---

[2] One of the laws promulgated by the government read:
   This city was founded on water, is surrounded and protected by water instead
   of by walls . . .who so ever should cause damage in any way to the public waters
   will be condemned as an enemy to the nation and will be punished no less
   severely than he who has violated a sacred wall.

The church of San Giorgio Maggiore across the canal appears deceptively close as tourists casually accept *acqua alta* in the Piazzetta.

allowing for regular commercial use of the *porti*. When necessary, the water would be pumped out by forced air and the barriers would rise up to inhibit excessive inflows from the Adriatic.

Some claim, however, that if the world's oceans continue to rise,[3] these dams would have to be activated so often that shipping would be hampered and the daily flushing action of the tides would be interrupted, causing serious pollution problems. They argue that the deep channels, dredged to accommodate large tankers, should be restored to their earlier, relatively shallow depths for use by smaller craft only. At the same time, overland pipelines should be constructed between the refineries in Marghera and Mestre

---

[3] The awesome possibility of continued global warming, melting of the polar ice caps and the rising of the oceans remains an open question.

and new marine terminals on the Adriatic. Still another proposal would leave the shipping channels as they are, block off only the northernmost *porto*, and simultaneously seal off the northern part of the lagoon. A dike would surround Venice proper to protect the city from extreme high tides and sea surges. Discussion continues as it has for decades, but at this moment the moveable dams project appears to be going forward.

But there are other more basic causes also responsible for the current predicament, causes resulting from man's failure to preserve the equilibrium by which the lagoon was formed. In particular, industry on the mainland has further aggravated the situation by massive pumping of fresh water from artesian wells and by repeated landfill reclamations around the port of Marghera. The former practice has had the effect of gradually lowering the water table, and the ground itself, under the entire lagoon area, including Venice. At the same time land reclamation has displaced a large expanse of mud-flats that previously served to absorb the inflowing tide, but now act as a barrier, pushing the tide back higher around the city. Though it may be impossible to undo what has been done, new laws now prohibit the further pumping of wells (fresh water is now being brought by aqueduct from the Dolomites) and no additional landfilling will be permitted. Happily, since these steps have been taken, some scientists claim the situation has stabilized and further subsidence may have been arrested.

However, other less momentous problems remain. For decades, industrial wastes, chemical fertilizers and detergents have been flowing into the lagoon in larger quantities, killing marine life. Even worse are the effects of air pollution, particularly the effluence from high sulfur fuels—crude oil and coal—which combine with moisture to blacken and disintegrate fresco and painted surfaces, stone and marble. One source of this trouble has been corrected: all furnaces in the city must now burn the relatively harmless methane. However, industrial pollutants from the mainland are still largely uncontrolled. Almost as harmful to exterior surfaces have been the acid-loaded droppings from the thousands of pigeons, which were innocently introduced during Austrian rule, and until recently, ignored, if not encouraged, by the authorities. At last, in spite of some die-hard opposition, some have been netted and disposed of, but far too many still remain.

Final solutions to all these problems have been delayed by the classic confrontation between industry, environmentalists and the scientific community and the resulting impasse is further complicated by the Italian bureaucracy. Meanwhile, many private institutions have gone ahead with piecemeal restoration, even though many basic questions remain unresolved. Much of this effort has been directed toward the rehabilitation of individual buildings and their façades and works of art that have been deteriorating over the years. Hundreds of frescoes, paintings and pieces of sculpture, long neglected and in serious states of decay, have been painstakingly restored. Entire churches—their marble façades, interior surfaces and wooden ceilings—have been cleaned and refurbished, and even their foundations rebuilt and stabilized. The 38 large paintings by Tintoretto in the Scuola di San Rocco have been laboriously and beautifully restored after five years work and the entire fabric of the Church of Santa Maria del Giglio and that of the Scuola di San Giovanni Evangelista have been rehabilitated from top to bottom and their art treasures carefully repaired.

In both the latter cases, roofs had to be completely replaced and exterior and interior walls scraped and cleaned, re-plastered and painted. At the same time, marble cornices, capitals and door frames, as well as statues and paintings damaged by centuries of dampness, were methodically repaired. To correct the basic problem of excessive humidity inside the buildings, the marble floorings, heretofore resting on a permanently damp base, are now supported by a layer of aggregate and cement separated by waterproof material. Even more important were the improvements made to exterior walls, whose structural integrity had been seriously weakened by the capillary rise of sea water with its destructive crystallization of salt, which turns porous brick and mortar into crumbling sand. This required a layer of sheet lead at the ground level foundations to stop the capillary action, and the replacement of the brick above. But these efforts have paid off, and not only are those walls secure again, but the building interiors are at long last dry.

A concern of a different nature, but equally disturbing, is the continual drop in the resident population of the city, which has declined from about 200,000 at the end of World War II to less than 100,000 today.[4] Most of the Venetians who have departed have settled in Mestre, where they can find new and modern, if somewhat mean, accommodation in place of the old,

---

[4] The population of Venice, until modern times, has been relatively stable over many centuries, only growing from about 80,000 in the 13th century to about 190,000 by 1575, when the plague wiped out almost one-third of the total. After that it fluctuated between 100,000 and 160,000 until the 20th century.

decrepit, damp buildings in Venice itself. As a result there are hundreds of vacant structures in the city slowly deteriorating from lack of attention.

If and when solutions are ever found to safeguard the physical city, there still remains the question of how Venice will earn its living, how it will provide jobs and rehabilitate residential buildings in order to encourage people to return to live. Some see the city only as a tourist destination, while others hope it can once again become a financial and mercantile hub, or a cultural and educational center, or a beehive of artisans or perhaps a little of all of these.

A Unique City of Islands, Canals and Gondolas

The depletion of the resident population becomes more apparent in the winter months when all the paraphernalia of tourism has been put away and the tourists themselves are gone. Many hotels, shops and restaurants are closed and the city returns to those that are left. Fog, mist and rain, cold winds and a weaker light wrap the lagoon and its islands in a somber embrace. The old ambience of mystery, lost somewhat in the summer months, returns to the narrow streets and the twisting canals. This is the time to appreciate the city for what it was, to notice all the details—architectural features and carvings, well heads in the *campi,* little walled gardens, stairways, rooflines, doorways, gracefully arched bridges. These off-season months are also the time to notice the people—bundled up against the chill air, catching the warmth of a shaft of sunlight, patiently waiting for the *traghetto,* buying supplies at the outdoor markets and from the floating vendors, and generally going about their daily lives. Some areas are nearly deserted and one can wander aimlessly for hours, always discovering something new and not unlikely getting lost. But eventually most waterways and *calli* will lead, like so many veins, to that major artery and principal thoroughfare of the city, the Grand Canal, which confirms certainty of location and the assurance of transportation.

The Grand Canal is almost always busy and interesting, but there are few places to walk along its banks—only on those *fondamente* near the Rialto Bridge. Mostly, it is fronted by the façades of the great palaces, as this is where the patricians preferred to build their family monuments and where almost every architectural style from Byzantine to neoclassical is duly recorded. The canal forms a backwards *S* dividing the main part of Venice into two halves that

Portable walk-ways help out during winter storms and high water as St. Mark's lion stands guard.

Fresh produce and local color are provided by the floating vendors in all seasons.

are joined together in the middle by the Rialto Bridge. These two areas, each laced with many smaller canals, comprise the city proper, which traditionally has been subdivided into six *sestieri* for administrative purposes.[5]

Marcel Proust, writing at the turn of the 20th century in his book *Remembrance of Things Past,* comments on a trip along the Grand Canal:

> We watched the double line of palaces between which we passed reflect the light and angle of the sun upon their rosy surfaces . . .seeming not so much private habitations and historic buildings as a chain of marble cliffs.

He also notes:

> The most beautifully dressed women, almost all foreigners, who, propped luxuriously upon the cushions of their floating vehicles, …turned to their guidebooks to find out the period, the style of the palaces…

To see and appreciate the various parts of Venice, one should set out

---

[5] They are Cannaregio, San Marco, Castello, San Polo, Santa Croce and Dorsoduro. A peculiarity of Venice is that buildings do not have street addresses but are numbered consecutively from 1 within each sestiere.

early on foot to a specific *sestiere* with comfortable shoes and a good pocket guide book. Ideally a full day should be devoted to each area, stopping around midday to rest and have lunch in one of the innumerable trattorias, and then either continuing on or, if weariness has set in, returning on one of the many convenient *vaporetti* (waterbuses). Alternatively this would be a good opportunity to hail a gondola for a more leisurely (and more expensive) trip back through the fascinating labyrinth of the smaller canals. There is no more pleasurable conveyance anywhere. Comfortably stretched out on the plush cushions, surrounded by the incomparable architecture of ancient palaces, one passes at an unhurried pace along the canals. The ride is smooth and silent, except for the occasional warning call of the gondolier echoing along the waterways as it has for centuries.

Even more romantic is the same experience at night. As you glide through the quiet waters and under the arched bridges, a few people move in the shadows, dark silhouettes of buildings loom above and the lapping of waves and the pulse of the oar are the only sounds. It is then that the mystery and the enchantment of the city and its past are recaptured for the moment.

The gondola evokes Venice in a unique way. Its origins are lost in time—the earliest recorded mention is from the 1200s—but its design and construction have apparently changed very little. Always a sleek, gracefully shaped craft, the gondola acquired some elegant additions for a time during the Renaissance. Carvings, inlay work and gilding appeared, as did the *felze* (a covered canopy), placed in the center of the gondola for privacy, and often made of damask, velvet or other fine material. Even the traditional dark paint was replaced by brighter colors. But this soon provoked a reaction, leading to government regulations not unlike the rules against ostentatious dress that controlled the extent of decoration, type of materials, color (mandated to be black thereafter), etc.

Today the *felze* has all but disappeared, but the boats are still built painstakingly by hand in one of the *squeri* (open boatyards of which only a few remain), with the finest woods (oak, walnut, elm). They require continual maintenance to keep their black-lacquered decks and other surfaces gleaming. The decorations on the modern gondola are few, with only a golden seahorse on either side and an axe-like metal fixture on the prow called the *ferro*. The history and purpose of the *ferro* are uncertain, but the six teeth extending below are said to represent the six *sestieri*. To row the craft, the gondolier stands on the left stern, the side of which is about 10 inches wider and the

The artist, like the gondolas, accommodate to high tides.

keel eccentric, so as to compensate for the gondolier's weight and keep the boat on a straight course.

A look at a map of the entire region shows that the city proper, which includes the two appendage islands of Giudecca and San Giorgio Maggiore, is central to and dominates the lagoon area. To the north is the cemetery island of San Michele and, at a little greater distance into the lagoon, the islands of Murano, Burano and Torcello. The latter is practically uninhabited today, though it was once a flourishing community of some 20,000 people. Except for the cathedral group and a few other adjacent structures, nothing remains—market gardens occupy what was once a town. It is believed that Torcello's buildings served as a quarry and were dismantled stone by stone for use in Venice proper. Even Murano and Burano, though still housing populations of about 7,500 and 5,300, respectively, are only quiet shadows of their former selves. Murano was once a favorite retreat of the patricians, who built a number of palaces with extensive gardens on the island. Only a few remain, one of which is the Palazzo Trevisan, a structure attributed to the 16th-century architect Andrea Palladio.

These places are frequently visited, however, unlike a number of other tiny islets scattered across the lagoon that seldom feel the tread of a traveler's

One of the open boatyards (*squeri*) where gondolas are built and repaired.

foot. Two of the islets are occupied by monasteries: San Lazzaro, with its distinctive campanile topped by an onion-shaped cupola and its complex of conventual buildings, which house a group of Armenian monks who are always happy to show off their library and collections; and the beautiful, remote San Francesco del Deserto, owned by Franciscan friars, which lives up to its name and its maxim engraved on the gate, "O Beata Solitudo, O Sola Beatitudo" (Oh Blessed Solitude, Oh Singular Bliss).

Then, of course, there is the long narrow island community to the southeast known as the Lido, which stretches toward Chioggia. The Lido is no longer the barren strand that Lord Byron knew and where he rode his horse, but is today filled with hotels and resorts. Many visitors, especially Italians, go there in the summer months, a reversal from the exodus once practiced by upper class Venetians and their retainers, who sought to escape the hot weather in the lagoon by migrating to their villas on the mainland. This was especially true during the late 16th through 18th centuries, when small rural houses originally owned and used for agricultural purposes were enlarged and improved as summer retreats. At first built primarily along the Brenta River, these country villas later materialized all over the Veneto, making an arc from Treviso to the Euganean Hills. Many were designed or influenced by the architect Palladio. Most had extensive gardens where feasting and merrymaking went on day and night by an aristocracy, at least in the 18th century, that had little or no serious purpose except to indulge itself and enjoy the villa life for that part of the year they were not celebrating Carnival in the city itself. With Napoleon and the fall of the Republic, many of these beautiful buildings were ransacked and looted, some completely destroyed, while others fell into protracted desolation and decay.

The Piazza San Marco

The commercial heart of the city grew up around Rialto, just as the political and religious center developed at San Marco, whose magnificent square is the only one in Venice dignified by the name *piazza*. All other open spaces are termed *campi*. Of these, the largest and most important are Campo Santa Margherita and Campo San Polo to the west, and Campo Santa Maria Formosa and Campo Santi Giovanni e Paolo to the east. In this last stands the church of Zanipolo (a Venetian contraction of Giovanni-Paolo), one of the two largest in the city. The other is the Frari in the western section and both surpass San Marco in size. For sightseeing purposes everything worth visiting, with few exceptions, is located south of a line drawn to connect these two churches and can be reached easily on foot, or, in the case of the Giudecca and San Giorgio islands, by a short *vaporetto* trip.[6] Safe to omit are the extreme western and eastern sections of Venice, the former containing railroad, bus and ship terminals, and the latter the incongruous postwar Biennale buildings constructed for International Art Exhibitions.

The magnificent Piazza San Marco, paved with marble slabs from the Euganean Hills, is, of course, the starting point of a visit to Venice. It is the heart and soul of the city where everything begins and ends. Here, the city's symbols of conquest, the booty from a hundred distant battles, have been gathered over the centuries. Here, the civic, military and religious rites, processions and ceremonies that have so enriched the life of Venice have been conducted and recorded by the painters and engravers. Here, from time immemorial, both citizens and strangers have congregated for social

---

[6] Those few exceptions are the Ca' d'Oro, the Palazzo Pesaro and a church or two north of that line.

Eighteenth-century view by the painter Canaletto of the Piazza looking west. The church at the far end was later torn down by Napoleon.

intercourse in what Napoleon later called "the drawing room of Europe." The most important buildings in the city are located around the Piazza: the Church of San Marco, the Doge's Palace, the Libreria Sansoviniana, the two Procuratie Palaces, the clock tower, the Loggietta and the city's tallest campanile. Such an assembly of world-famous monuments naturally attracts a dense throng of visitors at almost all hours, so one must be prepared to adjust to the situation. However, it has become an almost obligatory requirement that every visitor must at least once in the late afternoon or early evening take a seat at one of the open-air cafés,[7] order an aperitif in spite of the scandalous prices and the crowds, and settle down for an hour or two. Unfortunately our current relaxed attitudes of informality and acceptable dress leave the Piazza a little less attractive when compared to the

[7] The two most famous are Florian's and Quadri's, both of which date from the 18th century and were frequented by such personalities as Casanova, Lord Byron, George Sand, Wagner, among others.

colorful and often elaborate costumes once seen there and recorded in many Renaissance paintings and in 18th-century works by artists like Canaletto.

Perhaps the early morning hours, or alternatively after lunch during the siesta, may provide a quieter and less hectic opportunity to observe the details of the Piazza and its buildings. This is when the architecture should be studied, with close attention paid to the façades of San Marco (Byzantine), the Doge's Palace (Gothic), the Procuratie Vecchie (early Renaissance), the Procuratie Nuove (late Renaissance) and the so-called Napoleonic wing (neoclassical).

An even better way to escape the crowds is to ascend the campanile where not only the Piazza, but all Venice with its vast expanse of red tile roofs, towers and domes, can be taken in. And, should it be a clear day, one can see all the way to the distant Dolomites to the north, the plain of the Po to the southwest, and to the east, beyond the surf breaking on the Lido shore, the city's ancient partner, the Adriatic Sea.

This advice is hardly original. Thomas Coryat, an English traveler visiting the city in 1608, a time when few of his countrymen had been there, insisted that

> whosoever thou art that means to see Venice, in any case forget not to go up to the top of St. Mark's tower . . . for from everyside you have the fairest and goodliest prospect that is, I think, in all the world . . . this incomparable city, this most beautiful queen, this untainted virgin, this paradise, this temple, this rich diadem and the most flourishing garland of Christendom. . .

A bit much, we might say, but he had traveled widely and seen many places, so we can only guess at the degree of his hyperbole.

The campanile itself, whose bells once summoned the Great Council and Senate to assemble, is a reconstruction of the original, which collapsed in 1902 when its foundations gave way. A number of other campanili have crumbled to the ground and several others are presently leaning precariously. Fortunately, the one at San Marco gave warning of its impending doom in the form of several large cracks. As a result the area had been cordoned off and no one was injured. In fact its collapse into a great mound of rubble was so orderly and well timed that the people said *"se stato gentiluomo"* (it behaved like a gentleman). The only casualty was the Loggietta at its base, though parts of it were salvaged and later reconstructed along with the tower. At the

View to the north from the Campanile showing the façade of the Scuola Grande de San Marco in the foreground, the cemetery island of San Michele, the island of Murano, and in the distance the snow-covered Dolomites.

The Torre dell'Orologio, the work of several early Renaissance artists, was built at the beginning of *the cinquecento*.

time there were some citizens who thought it was unnecessary to go to the expense and maintained that the Piazza actually looked better without the campanile. But it was such a prominent fixture in the city that the majority decided it must be replaced *"com'era, dov'era"* (as it was, where it was). Accordingly it was rebuilt exactly, but on stouter foundations, and completed in 1912, one millennium, in theory, after the original construction.

Also worth noting is the Torre dell'Orologio built around 1500, and its famous clock, which records not only the time, but also the phases of the moon, the seasons and the signs of the zodiac; while high at the top, two giant statues strike the hour as they have done for some five centuries. Midway up the clocktower are two doors, which are opened only during Ascension Week so that four mechanical figures—an angel and three wise men—may pass across the front as they present themselves to a statue of the Virgin. Altogether the building is a happy combination of the efforts of several important Venetian artists,[8] who blended the then new Renaissance architecture with the traditional Byzantine-Venetian use of surface decoration and color. They carefully placed the structure itself at a key spot over the entrance to the always busy Strada delle Mercerie on the Piazza's lateral axis, thereby connecting it with the Piazzetta, which borders the Basin of St. Mark, the lagoon and thence the open sea. This smaller space, with its two massive granite columns, forms a wing of the main square, a kind of entrance court, and historically has served as the principal gateway to the city from the Adriatic. To the east from here, past the Doge's Palace, extends a broad, paved quayside, the Riva degli Schiavoni (Slav's Embankment), an always crowded thoroughfare alive with movement and upon which stands the venerable Royal Danielli Hotel. Once a private palace, this building looks much as it did half a millennium ago, which we know from a large engraved perspective map made in 1500 by the artist Jacopo de Barbari (1440–1515). The view from the Riva, opening out toward the isles of San Giorgio, the Giudecca and the magnificent baroque church of the Salute, is world famous and one that Canaletto was fond of painting.

---

[8] Mauro Coducci designed the tower; Pietro Lombardi, the wings; Alessandro Leopardi sculpted the Madonna; Giampolo Ranieri built the clock.

4 VENETIAN ART COLLECTIONS AND OTHER ATTRACTIONS

After the topography and architecture of Venice, not to mention its unique and incomparable ambience about which each visitor must come to his or her own conclusions, the collections are perhaps next in interest. Of these, three of the most important are located on the Piazza San Marco, all housed in the Procuratie Nuove building: the Museo Archeologico mostly contains sculptures from the Classical Age, while the Museo Correr and the Museo del Risorgimento together carry the story of Venetian civilization through its many centuries.

The Museums

Most of the finds in the Archaeological Museum were assembled by a Venetian family, the Grimani, in the 16th century, when the spirit of the Renaissance stimulated the upper class to search out the remains of Greek and Roman sculpture and to establish collections for reasons scholarly, artistic or pretentious. These ancient portrait busts, statues, reliefs, tomb carvings and vases provided the subject matter, poses and techniques that influenced Venetian artists of the Renaissance and beyond.

Adjoining this are the other two museums. The main entrance to them is in the Napoleonic wing, a structure built during Napoleon's control of the city in the early 1800s to connect the two Procuratie buildings at the west end of the Piazza. A grand staircase leads to several rooms, all decorated in the French-influenced neoclassical style, which display three early sculptures by Antonio Canova (1757–1822)—the last of the Republic's renowned artists—who left Venice for Rome and world fame to become one of the greatest exponents of that style so favored by Napoleon. In the rooms that follow, the Correr's main collections, devoted to the city's late medieval, Renaissance and baroque periods, contain memorabilia of every description, mostly from the 16th through 18th centuries: flags and symbols of the Republic, illustrations of its ceremonies, coins and medals issued continuously from the 12th to the 18th centuries, naval artifacts including ship cannons and models, souvenirs from the Turkish wars, and various ducal possessions, robes and portraits. Especially interesting are the rooms devoted to navigational instruments, sea charts (portolans), terrestrial globes, maps and cityscapes, including one by the aforementioned Barbari. This work gives a birds-eye view of Venice and illustrates in amazing detail almost every building then standing, many of which can still be identified today. On the floor above is the Quadreria (picture gallery), a chronological record of the evolution of Venetian art containing medieval Byzantine icons, late Gothic polyptychs and altarpieces, and early Renaissance paintings of the 15th century. The great Bellini family of painters, a strong influence on artists of the quattrocento, including Carpaccio, and their immediate followers are well represented here.

The same building also houses the smaller Risorgimento Museum. This collection of paintings, artifacts, weapons, prints and other documents illustrates the period between the overthrow of the ancient Republic by Napoleon in 1797 and its incorporation into United Italy in 1866.

From the Quadreria one has access to the Biblioteca Marciana that is housed in two impressive rooms in the adjoining Libreria Sansoviniana, which is situated opposite the Doge's Palace. Scholars are fond of pointing out that Venice, which preferred the visual and musical arts, was never a great intellectual or literary center, and that few great writers were nurtured here. Neither did it ever establish a great university. Even Petrarch's unique library, which he left to the Republic in 1366, was disgracefully allowed to disintegrate and be scattered after his death. But a subsequent gift in 1468 of a comparable library by one John Bessarion, a Greek refugee from the Turkish conquest of Constantinople, was carefully protected and appreciated. This bequest formed the nucleus of the Marciana, a rich collection of Byzantine and medieval codices and illuminated manuscripts. The Marciana also contains numerous examples of the city's most prestigious business enterprise during the Renaissance, the printing and publishing of fine books—contemporary works as well as the Greek and Roman classics—which were famous all over Europe.

Leaving the Piazza San Marco, one finds the other important museums along the Grand Canal, beginning first with the Accademia, located just over the wooden bridge of that name and easily reached by foot, and, going north, the Ca' Rezzonico, the Ca' d'Oro and the Palazzo Pesaro in that order, all more conveniently reached by *vaporetto.*

The Accademia, the city's principal art gallery, is housed in a group of interconnected buildings, originally a complex of church, monastery and scuola known as Santa Maria della Carita (Our Lady of Charity). Founded in the 13th century to help raise money to ransom Christian captives from the Saracens and pirates, these premises now display art works illustrating the history of Venetian painting from the 14th to the 18th century—that is, the beginning, climax and final maturity of the Venetian school. Residing here are the early polyptyches that mark the transition from the Byzantine heritage to the Venetian Gothic (especially in the works of Paolo Veneziano, Lorenzo Veneziano, Michele Giambono); the altarpieces that display the first influences of the Renaissance (Antonio Vivarini, Cima da Conegliano, Giovanni Bellini); the large scale narrative works so valuable as an insight to the cityscape of that era (Gentile Bellini, Vittore Carpaccio); some of the masterpieces that validate Venice's golden age (Giorgione, Titian, Tintoretto, Veronese); paintings from the succeeding Mannerist and baroque period (Lorenzo Lotto, Jacopo Bassano, Sebastiano Ricci, Gian Battista Piazzetta, Gian Battista Tiepolo); and finally, the last of the Venetian school, the *vedutisti,* or view-painters, (Francesco Guardi and Antonio Canaletto).

Ca' Rezzonico and Palace Architecture

With these last two artists in mind, it is appropriate to move on to the next museum, the Ca' Rezzonico,[1] which once was the palatial home of a typical 18th-century aristocrat. With its architecture and rich collections, Ca' Rezzonico is a good example of the culminating phase of Venetian civilization. While the floor plan of the building reflects the long continuity of the traditional Venetian house, the design of the elevations and the decoration of the surfaces illustrate the final phase of the classically-motivated Renaissance style as redefined and elaborated during the baroque period.

The Buon (or Bon) family started building this palace in the 17th century, but they were financially unable to carry on the construction. The house remained half-finished until the mid 1700s[2] when the Rezzonico family acquired it and completed the work, which included adding the upper part of the façade, the grand ballroom and ceremonial staircase at the rear

---

[1] Until the end of the Republic, ca', the Venetian shortening of casa, was generally used to describe a large patrician house. Only after the Austrian takeover and the use of titles increased in the 19th century did many families substitute the more aristocratic word *palazzo.*

[2] There are several drawings by Canaletto showing the palace in its unfinished state.

and the interior frescoes and decorations. The Rezzonicos, having come from Lombardy in the 16th century, were not an old family in Venetian terms, but they were rich and powerful. Their Charter of Nobility, still in its original Morocco and gold binding and displayed in the library room, dates from 1687 and cost them 100,000 ducats. One of their number, Carlo, became Pope Clement XIII in 1758. Under the Rezzonico tenure the palace gained its name and reputation and was the scene of many splendid balls, receptions and other sumptuous entertainments during the last years of the Republic. After 1810 the palace changed hands a number of times (it was owned for a while by poet Robert Browning) until 1935, when it was purchased by the city to house the 18th century collections of the Correr.

Even as early as the turbulent 12th century, the Venetian townhouse was unfortified, clear evidence of the absence of internal strife or fear of outside attack, in contrast to the situation elsewhere in Medieval Europe. Moreover, those houses located on a canal always included easily accessible and unprotected entrances from both land and water. All had their main foundations resting on hundreds of oak or larch pilings driven deep into the mud and fully submerged, many of which remain amazingly solid over the centuries. The pilings were then covered by a layer of planking, upon which several courses of cut Istrian stone were placed. These served as a base for the walls above, constructed mostly of brick, not stone, to minimize the weight.

The earliest major domestic buildings extant in Venice (e.g. the Palazzo Loredan and the Palazzo Farsetti[3]) exhibit what became the accepted Venetian architectural formula for the façade: a generous arcade across the lower floor, loggia with balconies on the one above, and then one or two additional floors with similar fenestration. As styles changed the architectural particulars changed: Byzantine windows, with their stilted or horseshoe arches gave way to the Gothic—at first with simplified, then progressively more complicated, pointed arches, and later, to those distinctive stone circles inscribing a quatrefoil above the slender columns. The Ca' d'Oro shows the evolution beautifully.

Later, as Renaissance ideas swept over Europe, new motifs were adopted in Venice, but usually with reserve and with local modification, and always

---

[3] These and the other palaces mentioned immediately hereafter are all facing the Grand Canal.

with the continued emphasis on color and surface decoration (see the Palazzo Dario). Again the fenestration was restyled, using concepts developed by Alberti and the Florentines, such as the double-headed windows under a larger, rounded arch above (Palazzo Corner-Spinelli and Palazzo Vendramin-Calergi). Cornices and roof lines, relatively modest and simple in the Byzantine and Gothic eras, assumed more importance, projecting out over classical friezes. New elements appeared: rusticated walls, coupled columns, oval attic windows. These were to be repeated and elaborated in the baroque age that followed (Palazzo Corner della Ca' Grande). Finally, overdoing a good thing, palaces of outsize scale and imperious bearing were built, often with the overuse of classical columns and pilasters, which culminated in their exaggerated importance on the façade of the Palazzo Grimani. Thereafter, a sense of proportion returned, but the process of stylistic borrowing and adaptation continued, blending ever more sophisticated combinations of Roman, Florentine and Venetian tradition to produce a series of magnificent late Renaissance and baroque façades in the Palazzi Balbi, Pesaro and Rezzonico.

The monumental architectural treatment of the Ca' Rezzonico exterior, though a far cry from the subtleties of the Gothic era, maintains the same traditional Venetian system of domestic construction. As in many earlier palaces, the main façade on the canal is divided into three horizontal sections with a fourth narrow floor or attic added at the top. The lower story has heavy, rusticated pilasters, while the floors above are of lighter masonry with larger windows behind balustrades. To this armature were added all the classical features that developed out of the Renaissance—the columns and round arches, the classical order of the capitals as they ascend (Tuscan, Ionic, Corinthian), the jutting cornices, the elegant carvings in high relief.

The interior arrangement of the Rezzonico also follows the traditional Venetian floor plan. Each story is divided into three rows of rooms going back to the rear. On the level above the ground floor, which the Italians call the *piano nobile* (the owner's quarters), we find the customary *portego*, or deep central hall running back from the front, and off of which the other rooms open. In the Ca' Rezzonico, the middle three windows above the main entrance on the canal light the *portego;* the two windows on either side belong to the corner rooms. Below the *portego* on the ground floor is another conventional long passage (the *androne*), leading back from the main door on the water to the light and air of the *cortile* (courtyard), which is open to the sky at the rear.

The evolution of palace façades from the Loredan (upper left: Byzantine horse-shoe arches) and the Dario (upper right: early Renaissance), both emphasizing height, to the Corner-Spinelli (lower left: Tuscan rusticated lower story) and the Vendramin-Calergi (lower right: pronounced cornices and paired columns), both introducing Florentine double windows and emphasizing the horizontal.

The boldly sculptured baroque façade of the Ca'Rezzonico reflects the culminating phase of Venetian palace architecture.

By the 18th century the *piano nobile* had come to be used less for daily living and more for receptions and formal entertaining, supplemented, in the case of the Ca' Rezzonico, by the grand ballroom and monumental staircase at the back. For everyday use the family normally occupied a mezzanine floor *(mezzanino)* squeezed between the ground level and the *piano nobile* on either side of the *androne*. The smaller proportions and lower ceilings of the rooms on the *mezzanino*—parlors, studies, bedrooms—made them cozier and easier to heat and this is where business and domestic life was carried on.

Above the *piano nobile* is another floor of similar scale and arrangement with its own *portego* and rooms opening off to the sides. These were originally drawing rooms and family or guest apartments. Still higher is an additional story in the attic space below the roof, where there were extra rooms and servants' quarters.

Today, throughout the palace, the sum of upper-class 18th-century life is once again spread out for inspection. Visitors enter from the rear where,

The ornate ballroom of the Ca'Rezzonico, where the royalty of Europe were often entertained.

following in the footsteps of the 18th-century party-goer in mask and *domino,* they climb the grand stairway to the ballroom. With its gilded chandeliers and marble architectural motifs—illusionistic as well as real—the ballroom was a place suitable for entertaining the royalty of Europe who regularly came there. Visitors then go on to the main part of the *piano nobile* with its sumptuous furnishings and famous ceiling frescoes, several of which are by the great Giovanni Battista Tiepolo. Noteworthy are the elaborately carved and gilded or lacquered tables and chairs, bureaus and desks, all products of Venetian craftsmanship. Among these, a most extraordinary throne is the ultimate in baroque fantasy.[4] Even more amazing is a gigantic carved and gilded picture frame, partly composed of statues in the round, that easily overpowers the portrait within. Another piece (in the Tiepolo room), a green

---

[4] This throne, which gives its name to one of the rooms, was used by Pope Pius VI on his visit to Venice in 1782.

The famous Ca'd'Oro, epitome of Venetian Gothic palace architecture.

baize–covered card table that no doubt catered to the addictive gambling needs of the time, is a remarkable feat of design and execution. On this floor, the Mannerist sculptors Alessandro Vittoria, Andrea Brustolon and Antonio Corradini are represented by a number of beautifully carved statues, tables, chairs and vase stands. One especially significant stand by Brustolon displays several Chinese porcelain pieces supported by a tableau of figures, all of which is held up by a powerful kneeling Hercules at the base.

On the floor below, in the more intimate and more modestly decorated chambers of the *mezzanino* and on the floors above are gathered the remainder of the collections. These rooms illustrate almost every aspect of the life of the settecento Venetian patricians, from lacquered chinoiserie, wall hangings and ceramics, to drawing room and boudoir furnishings. More important, however, are the paintings—frescoes, framed oils and pastels—by all the great artists of that period—Piazzetta, Longhi, G.D. Tiepolo, Francesco Guardi—and their followers. Altogether, a few hours in this building can take the visitor back to the days of the old order—before the French Revolution and Napoleon, before the democratization and industrialization of the modern world—back to an archaic era of decadence and vanity that was also clinging desperately to the last vestiges of elegance, privilege and grandeur.

Ca' d'Oro

Farther along the Grand Canal, past the Rialto Bridge, on opposite sides almost facing one another, are the last two state-owned museums, the Ca' Pesaro and the Ca' d'Oro. The Pesaro, on the left, is similar in many respects to the Rezzonico; it was built about the same time, on the same scale, and is also a masterpiece of baroque civic architecture. It presently houses the city's modern art collection, which is mostly comprised of 19th- and 20th-century Italian.

The Ca' d'Oro is in another category and of another age. World famous as the most beautiful palace in Venice, if not in all of Italy, it stands as the epitome of the synthesis between eastern and western artistic influences. Unfortunately its once brilliant gilding (from which it derived its name, House of Gold) has long since worn away and it has suffered innumerable other hardships during its many changes of ownership over the centuries. However, the building was partially restored inside and out by its last private owner, Baron Giorgio Franchetti, and, together with his collections, was bequeathed to the state in 1915. The original collections, which consisted of a cross-section of Renaissance and baroque art covering several hundred years, include some detached fresco fragments by Giorgione and Titian, marble sculptures by Alessandro Vittoria, Tullio Lombardo and Jacopo Sansovino and paintings by Vittore Carpaccio, Andrea Mantegna and Francesco Guardi, as well as works from artists further afield. The building itself, constructed in the 12th century and rebuilt in the early quattrocento for a wealthy private family, ingeniously fuses the Byzantine and Gothic traditions in an unsurpassed combination of form, line, proportion and color that could only have manifested itself in Venice. With the sun's angled rays bathing the façade and highlighting the beauty of the fenestration, and with the dappled waters of the canal reflecting back the shimmering light and color, here indeed the essence of this unique city is captured.

A Culture Appealing to the Senses

In such an environment, it is not surprising that it was the visual arts, in particular architecture and painting, that the Venetians determined as their medium of greatest inspiration and expression. Not that other modes of artistic or intellectual achievement were overlooked; the Venetians also made major contributions in theater, book printing and publishing, and especially music. But because visual art has made the widest impression, is tangible and relatively accessible to the visitor, that it must take precedence within these pages.

The sum total of this artistic inheritance, spread out for view in churches, palaces, *scuole,* museums, civic buildings, etc., forms a complex body of work from many traditions, eras and diverse sources. Unlike Florence, which mostly molded and trained local artists, Venice, particularly in the 15th century, drew heavily upon foreign talent that had already matured elsewhere. This was especially true of the sculptors and architects, many of whom were from Tuscany (Lamberti, della Quercia, Donatello, Verocchio, Sansovino) or from the North Italian lake area (Coducci, Buon, the Lombardi, Bregno). Others came from the nearby Veneto (Rizzo, Sanmicheli, Palladio). Though less true of the painters, most of whom were local and developed their techniques in Venetian workshops, some significant ones were outsiders (Gentile da Fabriano, Paolo Uccello, Andrea del Castagno, Antonella da Messina) or from the Veneto (Giorgione, Montegna, Cima). Even so, by the 16th century, all these various influences, especially in painting and architecture, co-mingled and blended in the Venetian environment to produce new and unique art forms within the city and ushered in its golden age. The Byzantine thread remained but was now interwoven with all the many strands of the Italian Renaissance. The result was a city and urban skyline of striking beauty rising above the waters of the lagoon. And sheltered within this architectural framework of brick and stone is an incredible display of painted canvas probably unequaled in scope and creativity anywhere before or since.

Display, Pageantry and Festivals

It can be argued that much of Venetian culture owes its origins to an inherent love of display and pageantry. Both have a long history and special meaning there, even within an Italian context. Nowhere existed a

Modern day Carnevale in the Piazza San Marco.

richer cultural continuity, religious and secular, that went all the way back to Byzantium, and which encouraged the arts and stimulated inspiration. The interior of San Marco alone speaks for that, but many other Venetian buildings, to say nothing of the decorative and pictorial arts, the rituals and processions and ceremonies of all kinds, were designed to impress and excite the senses. The clergy's vestments were beautiful to behold and even the costumes of the Patriciate became, in spite of the sumptuary laws, progressively more elaborate. Music, both sacred and profane, evolved and matured ever richer, embracing every form known to Europe, from church and convent choirs to chamber ensembles, orchestra concerts and grand opera. Theatricals, long part of the Venetian scene, developed along two main lines—morality plays directly associated with biblical stories and those based on folklore and local life. The latter progressed into the *commedia dell'arte,* which had started out ribald, slapstick and spontaneous, but later became more structured and civilized, ultimately leading to the sophisticated comedies and dramas of the 18th century. Punctuating every season was an unending series of colorful processions, regattas, pageants and street shows. Carnival itself, emanating from both sacred and pagan roots, continually lengthened its stay—by the end of the Republic, it lasted all but half the year.

Gondoliers competing on the Grand Canal in a Regata Storica.

In fact by then, Venice had become addicted to extravagance and display, to art for art's sake alone, to every form of entertainment, and to pleasure morning, noon and night.

To a degree all this has resumed in the present, since the city has once again become a center for amusement and recreation. Music (opera, symphonies, church concerts), theatre, cinema with its annual Film Festival, year-round gambling, antiques and art exhibitions, including the Biennale, are important, and tourism itself is vital, the *sine qua non*. Off-season there is a welcome hiatus, a moment of calm when Venice is left to itself, but even in winter the quiet is now interrupted by Christmas and New Years festivities and especially by Carnival in February, which has been revived after a century of quiescence.

As for the rest of the year, there are frequent festivals, pageants and celebrations. The Festa di San Marco (gondola races) on April 25, La Sensa (marriage to the Adriatic) the Sunday following Ascension day, Vogalonga (the 20-mile-long row) the Sunday next, the Festa del Redentore (bridge of boats to the Giudecca) the third Sunday in July, the Regata Storica (pageant on the Grand Canal) the first Sunday in September, the Festa della Salute (bridge of boats to the Salute church) November 21—these are only the

The *mercato del pesce* (fish market) at Rialto.

main ones. Most are accompanied by a good deal of eating, drinking and general merrymaking, though not to the frenzied levels attained in the 18th century.

Venetian Specialties

Food is a large part of the adventure and Venice will not disappoint. Almost everything that swims is plentiful—tuna, sole, mullet, sardines, mackerel, salt cod *(baccala'),* various types of local Adriatic fish (Coda di Rospo, Sampiero), as well as eel (either cooked in lemon or a light tomato sauce), squid and octopus. Equally available are shellfish—lobster, crab, shrimp, prawns, clams, mussels. The latter two are often served with pasta *(spaghetti alla vongole)* or rice *(risotto con cozze).* Rice is served in many delicious ways—with ink from the cuttlefish *(risotto alle seppie),* with clams *(risotto alla marinara),* or simply with peas in an oil and celery sauce *(risi e bisi).* Besides rice and pasta, polenta, a yellowish cornmeal, is a local staple, often served with fish or calf's liver. For example, *fegato alla Veneziana,* one of the most popular local dishes, is simply liver with onions cooked in olive oil. Generally speaking the balance of the menu—antipasti, *minestre,* meat dishes (the latter

Negozio di maschere or shop of masks and costumes.

not really a Venetian specialty)—is not unlike other northern Italian meals, though there are numerous local ways to prepare poultry, game birds and especially vegetables from the many market gardens on the neighboring islands. Also, there are some special local wines produced in the Veneto —Soave, Valpolicela, Bardolino, Prosecco (sparkling) and Grappa (a strong distilled drink from the dregs of the grape fermentation process).

But the tempting displays of fruit and produce and the wafting smells of cooking around midday are only part of the allure. In the many shops, there is also a lavish array of merchandise, from world-famous Venetian glass to jewelry to fabrics to the thousands of carnival masks. All are intricate parts of this unique city with its dark canals, arching bridges, towering campanili and splendid church and palace façades. But, while not discounting the sensual pleasures the city has to offer, there still remain the intriguing questions: how did it all get here, how did it evolve?

There are few, if any, cities with as long, as continuous, as interesting a past as Venice. Accordingly, the remainder of this book will review the high points of its history, the nature of its government, the rise and decline of its commerce and empire, the evolution of its art and architecture and, occasionally, its chief personalities. In the process we can better appreciate this singular place and encourage the preservation of that which miraculously survives, of that which arrests the eye and has fascinated countless generations.

PART II

The City of Venice as History

5 THE EARLY YEARS TO A.D. 1000

In the beginning was the lagoon—a long shallow bay at the head of the Adriatic Sea—formed by the sheltering arms of a chain of narrow sand spits. These so-called *lidi* both separated and protected this bay from the open sea while at the same time permitting the ebb and flow of the tides to funnel through a number of openings or channels. To the west several rivers—the Brenta, the Sile, the Piave—entered the lagoon to release their fresh water gathered from the Veneto and the Dolomites to mix with the salty tidal flows from the Adriatic. It was, in fact, the interaction of these rivers, intermingling with the sea, that first created the *lidi* and the lagoon, as well as the multitude of low, marshy islands and mudflats within. Melancholy and desolate, only the screeching of the gulls would have disturbed the tranquillity of that primeval scene.

During the centuries of the Roman conquest and empire, this watery region was inhabited by only a few primitive fisherfolk living here and there in reed huts on the marshy islets. The Romans called the surrounding country on the mainland Venetiae and later established there a number of towns, several of which prospered and still survive today—Padua (the Roman Patavium) and Treviso (Roman Tarvisium). Others, subsequently destroyed in the barbarian wars or bypassed by history, exist now as tiny villages or in name only: Concordia, Aquileia, Altinium. The last, for example, developed not far from the lagoon proper at the junction of several important Roman roads coming from the Dolomites and from the head of the Adriatic to join the one running south to Rome. Today Altinium is only a memory.

Farther away to the northeast is the small village of Aquileia, which, during the period of the Empire, was one of the most important trading places in the Venetiae and, after the triumph of Christianity, the seat of a patriarchate. Here, extensive Roman ruins, including a forum and a port, as well as some early remnants of Christian art—mosaic pavements dating from the 4th century combining Old Testament themes (the Good Shepherd, Jonah, etc.) with pagan motifs—have been unearthed.

Barbarian Invasions and the First Settlements in the Lagoon

Driven from their homes by the barbarian invaders, the populations of these Roman provincial towns became the earliest permanent settlers of the lagoon communities. The Visigoths were the first of the hordes to sweep over the Alps and begin the breakup of the Roman Empire. They attacked the cities of the Venetiae on their way to the capture of Rome in 410. The Visigoths were followed by the more destructive invasion of the Huns from beyond the Danube. Under their leader Attila, they ravaged the Po Valley, including the towns of Padua, Altinium and Aquileia, in 452. Many of the inhabitants were annihilated, though some managed to escape and sought refuge on the marshy land along the extreme edge of the coastal shore. Their first settlements were remote and uninviting. Built on sand bars delineated by the channels through which the tides ebbed and flowed, they were apparently difficult to attack in their watery surroundings. Many of these communities still survive under the same names: Chioggia, Malamocco, Jesolo, Heraclea, Caorle, Bibione, Grado. Other refugees settled on the even more inaccessible islets of Murano, Burano or Torcello as army after army of invaders swept down from the north. Daily existence for the indigenous population became progressively less secure until 493, when Theodoric the Ostrogoth put a final end to the Western Empire and established a degree of control over not only the Venetiae, but over most of the Italian peninsula, as well as present day Provence, Bavaria and Dalmatia.

The eastern empire, centered at Constantinople, however, survived and when Justinian became emperor in 527, he dedicated himself to the reconquest of the west. In this he succeeded to a remarkable degree; by mid-century he had extended his effective jurisdiction all the way across the

Mediterranean to Spain, and reconquered all of Italy and Dalmatia after a long struggle with the Ostrogoths. At the same time, Ravenna, just south of the lagoon area and the then-principal port on the Adriatic, was established as his headquarters for administering the western territories through a governor called the exarch. This was an important development in the future history of Venice for it established the contact with Constantinople that was to be of vital consequence for both cities over many centuries.

The new arrivals on the *lidi* and the islands were town people, and though they had been forced to adopt a seafaring life—building boats, fishing, and gathering salt—they were also determined to recreate an urban environment. Fortunately, the areas they selected to inhabit, though appearing to be unstable swampland on the surface, possessed a hard clay base capable of sustaining the pilings of larch and oak, which they learned to drive deep into the earth to support their buildings. Even at that time, attempts were made to regulate the flow of the tidal waters by constructing dikes and embankments, called *fondamente* by the Venetians, along the natural channels, thus defining and forming the first canals. And there is evidence that by the 6th century, several communities had taken steps toward a common government. Each sent a representative they called a maritime tribune to confer on defense and other common concerns meeting together at Heraclea. Apparently, their organization was effective because it managed to survive as an independent entity throughout the long period of Lombard domination that followed.

The Lombards, who commenced their incursions across the Alps in 568, made up the last great wave of barbarian invaders. Their kingdom, which lasted for almost two full centuries, included most of northern and central Italy, with the exception of Ravenna and the papal state around Rome. Neither did they manage to overrun or subdue the Venetian communities. This was due partly to the natural difficulty of penetrating the lagoon defenses and partly to the military aid and support supplied by Ravenna, which remained in Byzantine hands.[1] In return for this and for special trading privileges within the empire, the Venetian tribunes were called upon, beginning in 584, to make a formal act of submission to the Byzantine Emperor through the exarch of Ravenna. It is interesting to note, however, that this act of fealty

---

[1] From about this time, historians generally refer to the Eastern Roman Empire as Byzantine (from Byzantium, the old name for Constantinople) due to its increasingly Greek character and language.

was specifically not required to be made under oath, which was customary for other cities owing allegiance—an apparent concession to the semi-independent status the lagoon communities had managed to attain.

Venice's Earliest Christian Constructions

Most of the buildings constructed by the Venetians during these centuries were of timber, but a few were of brick or stone. One of these, the cathedral at Torcello known as Santa Maria Assunta, dates from about 639 and still stands today as the oldest structure in the lagoon area to survive a continuous existence.[2] Though modified several times in later centuries, the building retains its early Christian character in all its essentials, and is similar to two even older churches at Ravenna that provided the inspiration.[3] All share a common structural ancestry: the rectangular ground plan of a Roman basilica or civil meeting hall with an apse (semi-circular projection) located at one end. They all have aisled colonnades (which early Christian builders placed inside the walls and not outside, as was often the case in pagan buildings) that lend a directional thrust and focus attention on the apse with its altar at the far end. In the earliest church basilicas, the columns usually supported an architrave, which in turn supported the clerestory wall above. This soon gave way to a series of arches springing from the capitals of the columns, as can be seen at Torcello, since this method permitted a higher and more open nave without increasing the length of the column shafts themselves—Greek marble in this case—which would have been an expensive consideration. The roof was constructed either of timber beams or brick vaulting, and outside a porch or narthex, similar to those in Roman houses, was often included in front as a means of sheltering the entrance.

Variations on this theme were, of course, many. The cathedral at Torcello, for example, has two smaller apses on either side of the central one, each with a special liturgical purpose in the celebration of the Eucharist. In the one on the right is a small tabernacle for the holy vessels, an original component of the early building and in the vault above is the

---

[2] The original foundation stone exists with a Latin inscription reading, "In the reign of Heraclius Augustus, by order of Isacius, exarch and patrician" the oldest written record in Venetian history.

[3] San Apollinare Nuovo (c.490) and San Apollinare in Classe (549).

oldest mosaic[4] in the lagoon area. Inspired by a similar mosaic at San Vitale in Ravenna, this one depicts the mystic lamb of God supported by four angels and surrounded by iconographic symbols, including wheat grains and grape bunches, a reference to the bread and wine of the last supper. There are also some other remnants from that era: the Greek marble altar table, several of the capitals in the nave (second and third on the left), the pulpit and lectern, made up out of fragments from the original church.

The First Doges and the Establishment of the Capital at Rialto

The office of the doge[5] was created in the late 7th century to unify the scattered, divergent and often quarreling lagoon communities. According to tradition, the tribunes elected the first doge, one Paolo Anafesto, in 697. More probably, modern authorities claim, Paolo was not elected but appointed by the Byzantines and installed at Heraclea in an attempt to exercise some degree of control. If so, it was only temporarily successful, for within a few years a major religious crisis shook the foundation of the empire and weakened its authority abroad. This was the famous iconoclastic controversy that split the Orthodox world between those led by the emperor who believed the worship of idols and icons to be heretical and demanded their destruction and those who wanted to continue the ancient practice.[6] The Italians, including the Venetians, supported the latter position, resisted compliance and finally rose in revolt. In 726 the exarch was assassinated and his administration overthrown. Concurrently, a new doge, Orso Ipato, this time unquestionably elected by the maritime tribunes, took office. At least for the lagoon communities, the argument with the Byzantines was quickly resolved and their authority under a new exarch at Ravenna was firmly reinstated. At the same time, with renewed pledges of fealty, Orso's appointment received imperial recognition. However, he and his successors were only partially successful in persuading the inhabitants to act in concert, as rivalries continued and the center of government and the residence of the doge was moved from Heraclea to Jesolo to Malamacco and then back

---

[4] Restored, however, in the 12th century when other mosaics in the church were composed.

[5] The title doge derives from the Latin dux (leader), as do the words duce and duke.

[6] It has been suggested that the imperial court, always in need of money, was also motivated to melt down the church's vast accumulations of sacred objects for their precious metals.

and forth several times. A measure of unity, however, was precariously maintained, not so much from internal compromise, but, as is often the case, from outside dangers, for following the Lombards, the Frankish Kingdom was next to threaten the Italian peninsula.

Throughout the first half of the 8th century, continued pressure by the Lombards against Rome and the surrounding papal territories had prompted the pope to seek assistance from the Franks. Their king Pepin was finally persuaded to cross into Italy and, with his son Charlemagne, overthrew the Lombard Kingdom in the 760s and 770s. At the same time, all remaining Byzantine control over Ravenna and its surrounding area (with the notable exception of Venice) was swept away and its territory and sovereignty was linked to the pope's lands to the south, thereby creating in rough outline the Roman Papal State, which was to survive until modern times.

Charlemagne's Frankish Empire, however, was not long-lived, hardly outlasting the great man himself. But out of it evolved the Kingdom of France and the German or Holy Roman Empire of the Middle Ages, the latter of which was to include under one suzerainty—at least in theory—all of what is now the Low Countries, Germany, Austria, Switzerland and most of Italy as far south as Naples. But as with the Lombard Kingdom before, this did not include the Venetian community. A Frankish naval force had tried to invade from the sea in 809, but, unable to navigate in the shallow and deceptive waters, was outmaneuvered and defeated by the islanders. As a result, Charlemagne and his successors agreed to concede to Venice an independent status and to confirm its Byzantine alliance (811). Chioggia, Malamocco and other settlements on the *lidi*, however, had been threatened in the first Frankish assaults, so the Venetians deemed it advisable to move the government and doge's residence to a more secure place. The site chosen was an island cluster in the very center of the lagoon known as Rivo Alto (later contracted to Rialto), meaning either "high bank," taken from its relatively elevated topography, or, more likely, "deep channel," from the one major waterway that divides it (the present Grand Canal). Equally removed and immune from attack from land or sea, this remained the permanent capital from that time on.

Angelo Participazio was the first doge to rule from Rialto (811–827) and the first of seven doges of that family name. In those early years, there was a strong possibility that the dogeship would become hereditary. Although this never happened, the office was dominated throughout the 9th and 10th centuries by only three families: the Participazio, the Candiano, and the Orseolo.

During his term of office, the records indicate that Angelo appointed three commissioners to plan and supervise improvements on a grand scale for the future city at Rialto: one to build the canal embankments and drain marshy ground, another to strengthen the sea walls along the *lidi*, so vital for the lagoon's protection, and the last to be responsible for the new buildings that were needed. One of the most important of these buildings was a fortified structure to house the doge, probably constructed mostly of wood and located on the west side of the present Rio di Palazzo where the east wing of the Ducal Palace stands today.

St. Mark and His Legend

Within a few years of taking office in 827, the second Participazio doge, Giustiniano, son of Angelo, initiated the plans for the earliest church to serve the ducal household. It was built where San Marco stands today, and was not a bishop's seat, but instead the doge's private chapel. The church was dedicated to the Evangelist Mark, whose relics—in this case his actual bodily remains—had been purloined from a crypt in Alexandria by Venetian merchants in 829 and brought to Rialto to fulfill an ancient prophecy.

Tradition had it that Mark had been the apostolic missionary to the Adriatic ports and that an angel had appeared to him while he was visiting the lagoon area saying, *"Pax tibi, Marce Evangelista meus. Hic requiescet corpus tuum"* (Peace be to thee, Mark, my evangelist. Here will rest your mortal remains). This was the popular justification for the theft of his body and its transference to Venice.

The significance of relics in an age when the promise of Christian redemption and the heavenly hereafter were of far greater importance than earthly concerns cannot be exaggerated. These were tangible, visible pieces of evidence connecting the worshipper to the church's very foundations. Accordingly, they served not only to satisfy the religious needs of the local population, but also as a magnet of veneration for pilgrims the world over. And when one considers the great esteem that was attached to mere fragments—a saint's finger, locks of hair, swatches of clothing, bits of the true cross, etc.—the value of the entire remains of one of the Apostles was incalculable.[7]

Thus, while the possession of the saint's relics was of great religious importance, there was also a political purpose. Until that time the protector and patron of the lagoon communities had been St. Theodore, a Greek martyr venerated by the Byzantine world. His effective replacement by St. Mark served to proclaim that the doge at Rialto intended to reserve a semi-independent status under the Greek emperor. The fact, too, that the saint's body was to be interred at the church adjacent to and directly under the control of the doge's government, not at the Patriarchal seats of either Aquileia or Grado, nor even at the Bishop of Venice's church, San Pietro di Castello,[8] also emphasized St. Mark's role as patron primarily of the civil authorities rather than of the religious establishment, and so it remained throughout the long history of the Republic.

The City Takes Shape

Nothing of these early buildings remains, though it is thought that remnants of the brick foundations for the defensive walls that surrounded both the church and the doge's house can be identified here and there. However, it is certain that the shape of Venice as we now know it began to take form at this time. In particular, the canals and the land areas were defined once and for all, the waterways dredged and the mud confined behind the *fondamente*. At the same time, the *campi*, or market squares, were laid out to become local centers of urban life. These squares usually contained a wellhead or two to supply fresh water to the neighborhood and were ringed with shops and houses.[9] Close by or adjacent to the *campi*, parish churches were built, now of stone, and supported on dense pilings driven down into the reclaimed land, and

---

[7] It is interesting to note the many precious items the English diarist John Evelyn was shown when he was admitted to St. Mark's treasury by special permission in 1645: "a small ampulla with our Savior's blood, a great morsel of the real cross, one of the nails therefrom, a thorn, a fragment of the column to which our Lord was bound when scourged, a piece of St. Luke's arm, a rib of St. Stephen, a finger of Mary Magdalena . . ."

[8] San Pietro (called "of the castle" because of an early fortress there at the extreme eastern part of the city) was from its origin in the 8th century the cathedral church and bishop's seat of Venice, until 1807 when Napoleon transferred the title to San Marco.

[9] From the earliest times, the main sources of drinking water for the island communities have been the subterranean cisterns located under the *campi*. Rainwater was channeled through openings in the paving stones, down through sand to filter out impurities and into the reservoirs at the base of the wells.

always accompanied by their indispensable campanili. These towers were primarily built to house the church bells that called the faithful to prayer, marked the work day or assembled the populace for matters of great concern (the name in Italian comes from *campana* meaning bell). But they were also important for a seafaring people since they served as watchtowers, lighthouses and maritime landmarks—at one time there were more than 200 campanili in Venice. One of the earliest, and by far the most prominent, was the campanile in front of St. Marks—the one that collapsed in 1902—which was originally constructed around the year 912 and modified in later times with the reconstruction of the bell chamber and spire at the top. As the critic John Ruskin wrote, ". . .it owes none of its effect to ornament. It is built as simply as it can be to answer its purpose . . . one bold square mass of brickwork."

Byzantine Trade Brings Art Treasures to Venice

During the 9th and 10th centuries, while the rest of Europe remained backward and feudal, the island communities of the lagoon, now collectively known in the lingua franca of the time (i.e. Latin) as Civitas Venetiarum (or City of Venice), began to enlarge the scope of their trading activities and lay the basis of their wealth and prestige. While not strictly an integral part of the Byzantine Empire, the city remained the eastern empire's only considerable foothold in the west and hence was of vital importance to Byzantine trade. Not only was Venice the most convenient and secure port through which eastern goods could enter Europe, its merchants proved early that they were effective in negotiating exclusive trading privileges with the towns of the Po Valley and others beyond the Alps for cargoes going in either direction.[10] The Venetians were therefore often able to control not only the distribution of Byzantine products and luxury goods going west, but also the return commerce in timber, grain, iron and other metals, as well as slaves (mainly Germanic and Slavic heretics or non-Christians), which were transported down the mountain passes and rivers of northern Italy, heading east.

A few precious objects left over from this early trade may still be seen in the churches and museums of Venice. In St. Mark's church itself, especially

---

[10] A treaty with the Western emperor, dating from 840, set forth trading areas and rights and specifically acknowledged Venice's primacy in the Adriatic; this is the earliest such written record of Venetian diplomacy to come down to us.

in the Treasury (the two rooms on the south side), are preserved a number of the rarest and most beautiful examples from Constantinople—icons, reliquaries, patens, chalices, crowns, etc.—many dating from before 1000, when that imperial city produced and exported a vast stream of gold, silver and enamel work, carvings in ivory, illuminated texts, etc. Perhaps nowhere in the West is there as fine a collection of early medieval objets d'art as here in Venice. At that time only the workshops of Byzantium could produce the quality of craftsmanship that alone preserved the art traditions of classical antiquity. Some pieces were gifts to the city by Byzantine emperors or religious leaders, others were purchased by Venetian doges or rich merchants, still others were stolen before or during the Crusading era by Venetian citizens eager to acquire holy and devotional objects and precious works of art.

San Marco's Early and Middle Byzantine Objets d'Art and Religious Icons

In St. Mark's treasury there are more than 100 reliquaries (gold and silver-gilt caskets, cross-shaped boxes, columnar configured receptacles, flat book-like cases, etc.) containing Christian relics from all over the eastern Mediterranean. One of these, of a uniquely different character, is a reliquary in the form of an alabaster marble chair from Byzantium carved from a single block. The holy relics were kept at the base and were accessible through an opening in the side. Known as the Sedia di San Marco, it is one of the oldest items in the collection, dating from the 6th century, and is covered with carved reliefs depicting the Mystic Lamb in the Garden of Paradise with the four rivers flowing from the Tree of Life, the Evangelists and their symbols, and angels blowing trumpets for the Second Coming. It may have come to Venice from Alexandria with St. Mark's remains, or even earlier as a gift from the Byzantine Emperor Heraclius.

Then there are a large number of vases and amphorae made of glass or rock crystal. Some of the most impressive are a 7th-century cut-glass *secchio* (bucket) with scenes from the hunt, and two ewers, one of sardonyx from 4th-century Persia and the other of agate from 7th-century Byzantium, both with handles in the form of leaping panthers. Most beautiful are the chalices, works from the 9th and 10th centuries of the highest refinement and of rare and costly materials. Sometimes both cup and stem are of stone—sardonyx, agate, serpentine or malachite—sometimes only the cup, with the stem made

One of two Byzantine enameled icons of the Archangel Michael in gilded relief and surrounded by precious stones, displayed in San Marco's treasury.

of silver gilding. Many are studded with pearls and cabochons and decorated with cloisonné enamel images, examples of the superior craftsmanship that only existed in Byzantium during that era.

The cloisonné technique perfected by the Greeks involves the fixing of thin strips or partitions of gold (cloisons) to a metal backing, creating compartments for the colored enamel pastes that constitute the picture surface, while at the same time forming a network of lines (the exposed edge) to indicate contours and patterns. The art of the enamelist consists of heating the pastes and gold to just the right temperatures to fuse them together at just the right level. Nowhere else did artists in enamel achieve the lustrous colors, the translucent tones, the finesse in manipulating the gold and the pastes. Works in enamel, like mosaics, were especially valued for their permanence. No other mediums stand up so well against time and the elements and retain their original brilliance and colors.

Two agate chalices believed to have been gifts of the Emperor Romanus II (around 950) are outstanding. Their rings of enameled plaques—half-length images of Christ, the Virgin and the Apostles—are good examples of the emphasis on two-dimensional frontal portraits of oriental caste that mark the Middle Byzantine period and would influence mosaic and icon painting in later periods.

A similar portrait of Christ can be seen in a medallion on an alabaster paten, also from the 10th century, ringed with precious stones set in silver gilt. One of the most remarkable pieces is a composite work called *The Grotto of the Virgin,* which is made up of several objects from different eras. The grotto itself is really a 5th-century rock crystal vase of singular purity, purposely modified to shelter the figure of the Virgin, which is a much later work. This vase is set upon a votive crown (dating from about 900) belonging to the Byzantine Emperor Leo VI, whose portrait can be seen in one of the medallions on the base. There had originally been 14 such medallions, in cloisonné enamel of exceptional color and design, each surrounded by pearls, depicting Christ, the 12 Apostles, and the emperor. Six have subsequently been lost.

Also in the treasury are two extraordinary Byzantine icons from around the year 1000. These fabulous pieces, which are sometimes mistaken for Gospel book covers, both bear silver-gilt images of the Archangel Michael in relief, surrounded by enamels of the finest work in minute detail. One shows a half-figure of the saint holding a scepter, and the other, a full-length figure holding an orb and a sword. Both are presumed to have been looted from Constantinople during the Fourth Crusade.

Icons were most often paintings on wood, but were also composed in mosaic or carved in stone or some other medium. The art of icon painting, originating in Byzantium, was pursued in Venice by Greek émigrés or their Italian disciples until well into the Renaissance period. Many now found in Venice were from the Greek mainland and the Aegean area, while others are local productions. Some may have formed part of an iconostasis; others were hung on the walls of private homes as devotional images in the eastern tradition. All had a direct influence on the succeeding school of Venetian painters.

One of the most venerated of all sacred objects at San Marco is the so-called Nicopeia Madonna (Giver of Victory). Probably dating from the 10th century, this Byzantine icon painting is surrounded by gold and jewels and can be seen not in the Treasury but over an altar in the north transept. Again, the Venetians are supposed to have acquired it in the sack of Constantinople, hence the association with victory.

Even more famous is the Pala d'Oro (Golden Screen), located behind the main altar and one of the most impressive medieval works of art extant. Within the upper frame are some 38 round cloisonne enameled medallions originally brought from Constantinople in the 10th century. These well illustrate the Middle Byzantine style—the elongated frontal aspect of the figures, the large staring eyes and flat abstract designs—and have a purity and harmony of color and a finesse in execution that are not found in the work of later centuries. It was from religious objects like these that Venetian craftsmen derived their own artistic method.

Naval Successes in the Adriatic

From the earliest times the principal source of wealth for Venice had been the sea. Fresh fish, salt fish and salt itself were traded along the Adriatic coasts and up the numerous rivers on the mainland. By necessity, the inhabitants became boat builders and mariners. Before the year 800, most long range maritime activity in the Mediterranean was carried on by Greeks, Syrians and other easterners, but by the 10th century, Venetian ships were competing successfully, not only in the lower Adriatic, but beyond to the Levant, which they called Oltremare (across the sea). Easy access to timber and iron, so essential for shipbuilding, and the foundries that were springing up, gave them an advantage. A Venetian trading network began to replace the older Byzantine one, whose merchants, weighed down by taxes to support the overhead of an empire and pressed on all sides by Slavs, Magyars and Arabs, were competitively handicapped. The Venetian merchants, on the other hand, were not impeded but supported by their government, which existed primarily for their benefit. And unlike other Italian communities of the time, Venice was not burdened by a land-owning aristocracy or a feudal caste. Its leaders were drawn from among the merchants and ship owners. As a result, commercial policy and state policy were synonymous.

This is illustrated by Venetian efforts in the Adriatic and Ionian Seas during the 10th century. These waters had always been infested with pirates who operated from the maze of islands and inlets along the Dalmatian coast. Especially predatory were the Narentines, who preyed on the city's trading vessels from their bases up the Narenta River. With the weakening of Byzantine power, more and more of the responsibility for protecting vital maritime commerce fell upon Venice. Particularly under the leadership of the Candiano dynasty, which supplied four doges during this period, fleet after fleet was organized and dispatched in an attempt to destroy or disperse these marauders. But it was not until 997, under the dogeship of Pietro Orseolo II (991–1008), one of the ablest to hold the office, that a decisive victory was finally achieved. Most of the coastal settlements were brought under Venetian control with the enforcement of an annual tribute and oaths of loyalty. This in turn led to the establishment of trading stations up and down the eastern coast, new sources of timber and food products, and most importantly, security for shipping from piratical attacks. The doge's ancillary title, Duke of Dalmatia and Croatia, originated at this time.

Doge Orseolo's effective command of the Adriatic apparently did not displease either the German or Byzantine Emperor. Pietro was able not only to secure favorable commercial treaties with each of them, but also to marry one of his sons to the German Emperor's sister-in-law and another son to the Byzantine Emperor's niece. Thus, the Republic of Venice had not only cemented alliances—the sons of merchants and sea captains were now the equals of dynasties ruling the two great empires of the east and west—but had also won clear acceptance of its unquestioned independence from each.

6 THE FOUNDATIONS OF EMPIRE: YEARS 1000–1200

The year 1000, so dreaded by medieval chroniclers, came and went, and instead of impending doom, at least for Venice, the second millennium opened with prosperity, confidence and a royal visit. The German Holy Roman Emperor paid a formal state call to confirm the city's independence, grant further trading privileges within his territories and recognize Venice's newly won jurisdiction over the Adriatic and its coasts.

The city by this time had achieved its basic topography: the main canals we see today were delineated, the location of parish churches and belltowers had been fixed (even if the original structures have been replaced), the Piazza San Marco had become the center of political and religious life, just as the Rialto area had become the economic hub. Venetian fleets were ranging ever wider, carrying their commerce well beyond the Adriatic where they already enjoyed a virtual trading monopoly in many commodities, including salt, which was one of the most valuable of medieval staples.

Continuing Byzantine Influence

Gradually, as the city prospered, wealth and power filtered down among a larger class of merchants until these men were no longer content to permit the dogeship to remain the exclusive property of a few old families.[1] For the first time in centuries, a man representing this broader constituency, a merchant named Domenico Flabianco, was elected doge in the year 1032. At the same time, to lessen the risk of tyranny, certain restrictions were imposed upon the powers of the office. No change occurred, however, in the basic thrust of Venetian policy—namely, strength at sea and cooperation with the Byzantines to insure commercial prosperity. In return the superior cultural and artistic influences of the eastern empire continued to flow into Venice.

The best extant examples of this are not in Venice proper, but in the decoration of Torcello's cathedral of Santa Maria Assunta: the beautiful

---

[1] Pietro Orseolo II had been succeeded by his son Otto as doge and other members of his family had been appointed to important offices (e.g. Patriarch of Grado), but the high-handed manner in which they exercised their powers alienated the other patricians and ended the Orseolo's influence on Venetian affairs.

colored marble mosaic floor laid down in 1008 when the building was heavily restored; many of the column capitals (considered by Ruskin as exceptional), probably added when the roof of the central nave was raised higher; the carved marble panels *(plutei)* of the iconostasis;[2] the holy water basin. All of these were either imported from Constantinople or executed by craftsmen from that city.

Byzantine Church Architecture

Later in the century, construction began on two buildings with a common Byzantine architectural heritage: one, small and little known, is the church of Santa Fosca adjoining the cathedral at Torcello; the other, large and world famous, is Venice's own San Marco. Both are based on the centralized, or Greek-cross, plan much used in the eastern Mediterranean. The type traces its origins back through the circular or octagonal *martyria* (early Christian shrines or burial places of a saint or martyr) to the imperial Roman mausoleums. They were round or centralized for one simple reason: to permit pilgrims to approach and view at the closest proximity the object to be revered, the emperor's tomb or a martyr's holy relics, at the exact center of the building. Their floor plans thus have a continuous historical development, as does the basilican, or rectangular, church plan, adopted from Roman civil architecture. Both types were used, often complementing one another, almost from the time Constantine recognized and legalized Christianity by the Edict of Milan in 313, and Torcello provides examples of each. Here, near the older basilica-type cathedral of Santa Maria Assunta, a *martyrion* was built in honor of Santa Fosca.[3]

The early centralized buildings were relatively small in size in order to simplify the construction of the roof, which was usually made of timber. Some were roofed with brick vaultings on interior columns and later, a

---

[2] The critic John Ruskin commented in his famous book The Stones of Venice:
  The capitals are all of white marble and are among the best I have ever seen as examples of perfectly calculated effect from every touch of the chisel . . . The bas-reliefs on this low screen are groups of peacocks and lions, two face to face on each panel, rich and fantastic beyond description, though not expressive of very accurate knowledge either of leonine or pavonine forms.

[3] There was also a third structure, a baptistry, of which only a few ruins remain. The three buildings—baptistry, church and martyrion—thus completed an architectural trilogy, perhaps symbolizing birth, life and death.

few even with masonry domes in the ancient Roman manner. As long as the buildings were small and round or octagonal in shape, this presented few problems. But sometime in the 6th century, Byzantine church design underwent a change. The two types—the basilican parish church and the centralized *martyrion*—were on occasion merged, the result of a change in religious practice. The cults of the martyrs, along with their relics, were being moved into the parish churches, and even into the cathedrals, so that the same building now had to serve both pilgrimage and liturgical purposes.

As it happened, this innovation coincided with the idea that the ground plan of Christ's holy house should assume a cruciform shape in remembrance, or as the symbol, of His sacrifice. The Byzantine solution was a Greek-cross of four equal arms—a nave and transepts for the congregation and a chancel for the clergy. This provided sufficient room for daily services, while keeping the focus of attention on the holy relics in the center of the building, surmounted now, if practical, by a masonry dome. The problem, however, was in implementing this. Where the four arms of the cross met, there resulted a large, square area—the crossing. Never in Western Europe had a round dome been placed on a square of walls, but the Byzantines had earlier found a solution to this with two architectural inventions: the squinch and the pendentive.

Santa Fosca is an example of the former device. Here, a cube of supporting walls is gradually transformed into a circular drum above by means of small concave vaultings, or squinches, in the corners. Originally a brick cupola probably spanned the opening, but this unfortunately has since been replaced by a timber roof. The walls are relatively heavy and thick to support the outward thrust from the weight of the original or intended dome, which was to have been further buttressed by the structure of the four arms with their barrel vaults. The squinch was the simpler, more primitive solution. The more impressive solution, the use of the pendentive, was employed about the same time across the lagoon at San Marco.

The Construction of the Church of San Marco

Around 1063 the old church dedicated to St. Mark was pulled down and a new building commenced. Now entirely composed of brick and stone, the basic core and framework as we know it today was largely completed before the end of the century. It, too, was laid out on a Greek-cross plan similar to churches in Constantinople, but differs from Santa Fosca in one major structural feature. Instead of four massive walls at each angle enclosing the crossing, San Marco was to have four giant arches that would stretch across the full square to each of the corner piers and reach up to the great cupola itself. To provide a base for the latter, the pendentive was used. This Byzantine invention is simply an upside-down spherical triangle whose apex springs from the junction where the two arches meet in the corner. One pendentive at each of the four corners produces a circle at the top. On this the dome rests, distributing its weight to the arches. However, the cupola, being constructed of masonry—the traditional Byzantine building material—exerts a tremendous outward thrust that must be balanced by buttressing. At San Marco the four arms of the church—of necessity much larger in dimension than at Santa Fosca and each having its own cupola— provide this lateral counter-force and serve to support the central dome. They in turn are buttressed by the exceptionally massive walls of each arm.[4]

The resulting effect of the use of pendentives and cupola resting on wide-reaching arches, is to give a visual sensation of weightlessness and spaciousness. Interior openness had never been a major consideration in Greek or Roman temples, but, after its early articulation in the first Christian churches, it became a guiding Byzantine principle. Just as the Christian religion sought to relate the earthly mortal with the risen Christ, so church architecture strove to relate sacred interior spaces, as defined by the great masonry arches and domes hovering in midair, with the greater heavenly sphere above.

But in addition to the centralized floor plan and the use of pendentives and domes, the link with Byzantine tradition is even more strongly emphasized at San Marco by the integrated decorative elements—the wonderfully carved capitals of the columns, the iconostasis (choir or chancel screen), some of the façade reliefs, and especially the early mosaics from the 11th and 12th centuries. Later on, architectural and decorative additions were made in other styles, so that the whole scheme became exceedingly complex, but it is interesting to identify the original elements that connect

---

[4] The famous church of Hagia Sophia (constructed 532–537) in Constantinople, the greatest surviving masterpiece of Byzantine architecture, built on a similar centralized plan with a dome on pendentives, proved to be inadequately buttressed as the dome collapsed and had to be rebuilt. Subsequently the buttresses supporting the main arches of the crossing have had to be reinforced several times.

the building to Byzantium when Venetian relations with its suzerain were still friendly and cooperative.

Mosaic Decoration and the Eastern Tradition

The origin of mosaic—the art of imbedding tiny colored stones and pieces of glass (tesserae) on plaster to form a design or picture, at first on floors and later on walls—goes back to the classical age. With the growth of Christianity, the technique became useful to spread the new religion to the many who were unable to read. In the west, mosaic was sometimes employed in basilican-type churches to decorate the walls above the columns of the nave and in the apse beyond the altar, but it remained of secondary importance to the architecture itself, a decorative adjunct subordinate to the structural elements of the building. In the east, however, the centralized plan led to an emphasis on spatial concepts and unity and away from the classical emphasis on clearly defined structural forms. It especially encouraged the use of mosaic, not only to decorate and to teach, but also to draw together all the interior surfaces into one harmonious synthesis. Contemporary architectural elements—arcades of massive pillars, engaged half columns, fluted pilasters, cornices, string courses, compound piers and arches—are deemphasized and merged into the wall surfaces, the better to receive the vital element—the mosaic lining. Edges, corners and junctures are blunted or rounded and made to flow into one another. The building itself becomes subordinate, like an armature or frame to support the spatial surfaces of mosaic and the sacred Christian message they impart. This aspect of the Byzantine aesthetic is evident in San Marco, as is another quality, its abstract and symbolic character.

The very nature of the mosaic art tends away from naturalism toward formalism, away from earthly realism toward the abstract and mysterious. Unlike the mediums of fresco and oil paint, which can produce the illusion of reality on a flat surface, the tesserae of mosaic, especially on concave or convex surfaces, are subject to some inherent limitations. In general it is more difficult to express subtle gradations of shading, texture and perspective in this medium. (This was attempted much later during the Renaissance, with debatable results.) But the overriding purpose of the early mosaicists was to instruct, to decorate and to glorify, rather than to duplicate earthly reality. Episodes from Biblical history, the saints, martyrs and apostles had to be recognizable from a distance, simplified and clear. Individualized facial characteristics counted for little. Instead personalities were identified by some attribute, symbol, pose, or color arrangement.[5] Backgrounds were normally ignored in order to concentrate attention on the main theme. The apparent simplicity of these mosaics is the result not of primitive craftsmanship, but of highly sophisticated artists pursuing special objectives.[6] Unambiguous storytelling and reminders of faith were foremost, but formalized design, sumptuous colors and an other-worldly spirit of mystery were also employed to inspire the worshiper.

Santa Maria Assunta's Byzantine-Influenced Mosaics

The earliest mosaics at San Marco, found over the main entrance door within the porch and probably dating from the building's dedication in the late 11th century, seem to reveal these eastern tendencies—in particular several small niche mosaics portraying the Virgin, six saints and the four Evangelists, which are all in the Middle Byzantine style.

An even better example, however, is not at San Marco, but at Santa Maria Assunta on Torcello where similar Biblical effigies are dramatically depicted in the mosaic in the great apse. Completed when the church was restored in the 11th century, the regal figure of the Virgin in a dark blue gown against a glorious gold background, and surrounded by the twelve Apostles, serenely gazes down from above, and is a striking example of Byzantine art and religious tradition.[7]

Equally monumental, though somewhat later (12th century), is another mosaic wall in Santa Maria Assunta. This work, of Byzantine inspiration but composed by Venetian artists, depicts the Last Judgment and epitomizes medieval Christian belief. At the top of the mosaic is the crucifixion, which is followed below by the descent into hell. The lower sections present the

---

[5] For example, St. Peter's round white beard or his keys; the Virgin's blue mantle; St. John the Evangelist with his book or his eagle; St. Mark with the winged lion.

[6] The uneven setting of the tesserae, for example, was often done on purpose to avoid surface glare and lend a textural effect.

[7] According to Greek orthodoxy, the Virgin is shown gently descending from Heaven with the Christ child to free man from original sin. The description below this mosaic, literally translated from the original Latin, reads, "Mary, formula of virtue, star of the sea, door of salvation, liberates those whom Eve has reduced to sin."

Byzantine mosaic of the Virgin and Apostles in the apse of S. Maria Assunta on Torcello.

main message with Christ in the center mandorla between the Virgin and John the Baptist. On both sides the Apostles are gathered to witness. Below in the center are the two archangels, Michael and Gabriel, who stand over a kneeling Adam and Eve praying at an altar adorned with symbols of the crucifixion. To the right runs a stream of fire that forever consumes and torments the damned, while on the other side the blessed stand in reverent attitudes. This is the Orthodox concept of Christ Pantocrator, the stern judge proclaiming to the world that there shall be no uncertainty, no equivocation, and that man's fate is forever sealed.

The Mosaics of San Marco and the Pala d'Oro

The next mosaics in point of time are at San Marco and date from the completion of the vaulting and domes in the 12th century. These illustrate a gradual evolution in style away from the strict formulas of the Middle Byzantine period. Some classical manifestations—modeled figures, the three-quarter view of the head, Hellenistic architecture—have reappeared, though still within the context of the eastern tradition of color, symmetry, rhythm and two-dimensional space. Also, the arrangement of the iconography or sacred subject matter throughout the building follows the Byzantine custom. The Old Testament stories are illustrated in the atrium mosaics (e.g., Genesis, Noah and the flood, the stories of Abraham, Joseph, Moses), while the interior is reserved for the life of Jesus and the triumph of the Christian church. Each personage or scene is placed according to its relative importance in the doctrinal hierarchy.

The most markedly Byzantine mosaics are those in the Pentecost cupola, which is the first one encountered past the main entrance in the nave. At the center is the throne for the God-Judge, where rests the Holy Spirit, symbolized by a white dove whose radiance animates the twelve Apostles below. Figures representing the nations summoned to hear the sacred message at the Pentecostal feast are gathered between the windows, and below this are the four archangels on the pendentives.

The larger cupola over the central crossing contains the great Ascension mosaic with Christ Pantocrator (again the Byzantine concept of Christ as austere judge and ruler) against a blue, star-studded sky and surrounded by the 12 Apostles, the Virgin and two angels. Between the windows are the sixteen Christian virtues, on the pendentives are the four Evangelists writing their gospels, and on the four connecting arches are scenes from Jesus' childhood, Passion, Crucifixion, and Resurrection.

Over the high altar within the eastern cupola is the so-called Emmanuel mosaic. Christ is at the center, this time surrounded by the prophets of the Old Testament, and again on the pendentives, the four Evangelists, here represented by their winged symbols: the lion of St. Mark, the ox of St. Luke, the man of St. Matthew and the eagle of St. John. Finally, just below the half-dome of the apse and between the windows are some of the oldest and most impressive mosaics at San Marco—the four patron saints of Venice.

It is behind the high altar beneath the eastern cupola that the Pala d'Oro, the Cathedral's greatest treasure, is located. Most of its plaques and

In the middle panel of the upper tier of the Pala d'Oro is the figure of the Archangel Michael surrounded by some of the oldest cloisonné enamels.

panels were made in the 12th century, either in Constantinople or in Venice, by Greek artists and their Venetian followers.[8] These include the six large Gospel scenes[9] at the top on either side of the Archangel Michael; the central figure of Christ the Judge, surrounded by the four Evangelists in rounds; the three rows of angels, Apostles and prophets; the smaller scenes from the Gospels and the life of St. Mark which appear in squares (27 total) that surround all the others on three sides. One should note the intricacies and detailing of the cloisonné work of the robes. All these enamel pieces reflect the Late Byzantine style and are more sophisticated and complex than the small round medallions, mentioned earlier, from two centuries before.[10]

---

[8] The inscriptions, which are either in Greek or Latin, do not necessarily hold the key to their origins.

[9] The six great feasts of the church: the Entry into Jerusalem, the Crucifixion, the Harrowing of Hell, the Ascension, the Pentecost, the Death of the Virgin.

[10] The Pala d'Oro, as we see it today, glowing with gold and precious stones, is the result of several rearrangements and enlargements from the 11th to 14th centuries. Its overall Gothic appearance stems from the final version of 1345.

The central figure of the Pala d'Oro, Christ Pantocrator (or judge), a 12th-century Byzantine work, with later Venetian enamels of the four Evangelists on either side.

In retrospect it is indeed remarkable that by the 11th century, the Venetians, having established themselves under the most difficult circumstances and with few material resources, had acquired sufficient wealth, perseverance and discernment to not only raise up such a magnificent building, without peer in western Europe, but also to adorn it with treasures and artworks that were the envy of Christendom.

The Weakening Byzantine Empire and the Venetian Navy

However, while life and trade were prospering in Venice, all was not well within the Byzantine Empire. Throughout the 11th century, continuing pressures were exerted against all its far-flung borders, particularly in the east by the expanding dominion of the Seljuk Turks. At the same time, the Normans, from their base in Sicily, were overrunning the last remaining Byzantine provinces in southern Italy, and threatened to cross the lower Adriatic, cut the vital trade routes, and establish themselves in Macedonia, the heart of the Empire. In this emergency, the emperor, caught between aggressive armies on both sides, appealed for naval assistance to the Venetians and in particular to the doge, Domenico Selvo (1071–1084) who was married to the emperor's sister.[11] This assistance, being in Venice's interest, was readily extended in return for further trading privileges, the right to own land and maintain depots in key Byzantine ports and exemption from tariffs throughout the Levant.[12] In the ensuing series of sea battles off the Albanian coast (1081–1084) the Normans were stopped and the east-west commercial routes were, for the time, safe-guarded.

Naval battles between fleets at that time had come to demand a high degree of professionalism. Not only were such encounters violent and without mercy, but they had become tactically complicated. The Venetian navy, like others, consisted principally of light galleys. These were fast, low-profile "long" ships—their length some eight times their width—with ramming prows and banks of 20 to 30 oars to a side. The remaining force was made up of slower, heavier "round" ships—broad of beam as their name implies (their width was about one-third their length)—that had raised fortified platforms, fore and aft, and were armed with missile launchers. All these ships carried masts and sails, but the round ships were completely dependent on them. The tactical objective was usually to try to get the enemy to engage the round ships, which, though less maneuverable, were defensively strong and often able to disrupt and scatter their attackers, which gave time for the main force of long ships to get to windward and into an advantageous position to counterattack.

Battles usually began with an exchange of missiles and arrows, followed by the galleys attempting to ram the enemy and, finally, the crew boarding and overpowering the opposing forces in hand-to-hand combat. Aside from the skill of the officers in charge, everything depended on the fighting spirit of the men. In the case of Venice and the other developing maritime republics, such as Pisa and Genoa, these crews were made up of free citizens—not slaves—either working for wages or serving their military obligation. When a war fleet was to be armed in 11th- and 12th-century Venice, each parish drew

---

[11] She was the Dogaresssa Theodora, who was criticized by the Venetians for her sybaritic life and idle luxury. Her rooms were always heavily laden with perfumes. She was said to bathe only in fresh rain rainwater collected by her servants, and disdaining from soiling her hands, to take her food only by the then novel means of a fork—and a golden one at that.

[12] As set forth in the Golden Bull of 1082.

up lists of able-bodied men, from which one name of every 12 was drawn by lot for service. The only galley slaves in the Mediterranean during the Middle Ages were found in the Turkish, Arab and pirate crews. The many references to them in the west belong much later to the 17th century.

A Venetian light galley that was ready for combat had between 140 to 180 men aboard, and there was little distinction between oarsmen, sailors or soldiers. All were equal and all were required not only to possess arms and armor, but to know how to use them at sea. In practice there was often very little difference between the sailing of a war fleet and that of an escorted merchant convoy. Both were armed, but the merchant fleet would include many more large round ships that were heavily loaded. In a Venetian convoy, these merchant ships, some privately built and owned, others state-owned and leased out, were subject to detailed government specifications and rules. The government dictated how the ships were to be rigged and armed, the number of crew members and their rights, the weight of cargo and amount of freeboard, and, at least on the main trade routes, convoy requirements, sailing schedules and ports of obligatory call.

The shipmaster or captain of each vessel represented the owner or entrepreneur, but he also was a kind of public official representing the state as well and was obliged to adhere to all government regulations. Contrary to the old Roman-Byzantine custom, he was far from being an absolute dictator on board and was required to consult with his crew and his merchant shippers, who usually traveled with their cargoes, on important questions affecting the outcome of the voyage. And with the primitive navigational aids available, the hazards were many—storm and shipwreck—in addition to enemy action. Accordingly most commercial undertakings were divided among many participants in order to split up the investment in any one ship or cargo and spread the risk. A popular Venetian form of this was the *colleganza*, a type of partnership whereby a traveling merchant agreed to return not a fixed rate of interest on the investment of each participant, but, say, 75 percent of any profit finally realized at the end of the voyage. On outright loans, interest rates ran high—at least 20 percent, depending on the risk.

The First Crusade

Venetian successes at sea had made it clear to the Byzantines that the security of their trade, at least west of the Greek isles, depended on Venetian naval power. But while the Normans had been halted at the Adriatic, the rampaging Seljuk Turks seemed invincible in the east. Between 1071, when a Byzantine army was all but destroyed at the Battle of Manzikert, and 1092, most of Anatolia (modern Turkey) as well as the Holy Land had been overrun by the Turks and only the strait of the Bosporus saved Constantinople. By then, the Byzantine Empire had been whittled down to a third of its former size.

Again the emperor appealed to the west for help, and Europe responded with the First Crusade in 1095. However, this, the fore-runner of that series of remarkable expeditions that pitted the Christian West against the Muslim East, was undertaken not so much to preserve the Byzantine status quo, as to recover the Holy Land and to carve out new principalities in Palestine and Syria,[13] over which the Crusaders could exercise sovereignty. The Venetians took only a secondary role in the First Crusade, but they did send out their war fleets in 1099, and again in 1110, in return for commercial concessions in places like Jaffa, Haifa, Acre and Sidon in the Levant. In 1123 a Venetian fleet successfully defeated a Muslim force off the coast near Jaffa, and the following year helped to take Tyre, the last Muslim coastal stronghold within the Crusaders' new territories. But it was the Adriatic and the Aegean, with their ports and bases protecting the trade with the east, that remained the Venetians' principal concern and they left to others the establishment of the petty states in Oltremare.

It was also in the early 1100s that the Rialto city suffered two separate and devastating conflagrations that wiped out large sections of the town, which at that time was still built largely of wood. Unusually strong winds fanned both fires and spread the flames from house to house—even jumping across the Grand Canal. In general, the buildings that survived were those of masonry construction, in most cases the parish churches.[14] The lesson was clear, and thereafter the government did all it could to encourage the use of local brick and Istrian stone for all buildings of any consequence.

---

[13] Known under such names as the Kingdom of Jerusalem, the Principality of Antioch, the Principality of Tripoli, etc.

[14] For example, the little church of S. Giacomo di Rialto, completed shortly before, survived the flames. It, or rather its predecessor on the same site, is said to be the oldest parish church in Venice proper.

The Establishment of Venice's Famous Arsenale

Partly because of these disastrous fires and partly to improve efficiency, these same years (c. 1110–1118) saw the consolidation of Venice's shipbuilding yards, which had previously been scattered all over the lagoon, in one relatively secure place behind protective masonry walls in the eastern section of the city. Soon to be known as the Arsenale,[15] here were concentrated, under government supervision, the foundries, docks, work shops and warehouses necessary to undertake a shipbuilding and maintenance program on an unprecedented scale and of a unique character. For the first time, an industry was created that utilized long-range planning, standardized design, modular construction and the specialization of labor. Ultimately many thousands of carpenters, armorers, riggers, etc. were employed at the Arsenale shipyards to fit out, repair and store galleys of all types for war and commerce. No other maritime nation in the Mediterranean or elsewhere ever developed anything comparable and it remained a factor for several centuries in Venice's ability to compete on the high seas with other larger and more populous states.

To be sure, there was no scarcity of adversaries. In addition to their more remote enemies—the Saracens[16] to the east and the Normans of Sicily to the south—tensions were developing closer to home on the *terrafirma* to the west. These grew out of the long quarrel for supremacy between the German Empire and the papacy and came to a head mid-century when the ambitious Frederick Barbarossa ascended to the imperial throne and was opposed by the equally strong personality of Pope Alexander III. The cities of the Po Valley, growing in prosperity and independence, had generally sided with the papacy, resisting Barbarossa's feudal claims, and had formed the so-called Lombard League to oppose him. Venice was pressured to join, but it was not in its long-term interest to alienate the western empire and upset commercial relations. Accordingly, the government compromised, offering vague assistance to the League but no forces; this proved a wise course as the Serenissima again managed to avoid expensive entanglements on the mainland.

---

[15] The word, which has also been adopted into many other languages, comes from the Arabic meaning a place of construction. Several centuries later Dante refers to the Arsenale in Canto XXI of the Inferno.

[16] A term loosely applied to all Muslims, especially the Arabs and Turks.

Conflict with Byzantium and Formation of the Great Council

The old alliance with Byzantium was, however, neither a static nor trouble-free arrangement, and there were many occasions when the two powers were at odds or even actively fighting. For example, the eastern emperor repeatedly attempted to modify or discontinue the special tariff and trading concessions that the Venetians enjoyed throughout the empire, but retaliatory raids against his shipping and ports always induced him to reconsider. Sometimes these attacks were explicit government policy, but more often they were simply piratical actions by individual Venetian captains. These incidents had become commonplace in the eastern Mediterranean due to the increased maritime activity brought on by the Crusades. Mutual rivalries between the participants—Genoese, Pisans, Greeks, Normans, French, as well as the Arabs and Turks—led to attacks and reprisals, one against the other, until it was difficult to know who the true enemy was. The Genoese in particular became serious competitors, often favored by the Byzantines when commercial advantages were being sought.

All these tensions and confused alliances came to a head in 1171 when the Byzantine emperor, finally fed up with Venice's commercial aggressiveness and ascendancy, arrested the many thousands of Venetians living in his capital of Constantinople and confiscated their goods, warehouses and ships. The immediate excuse for this was an attack on the local Genoese commercial settlement for which the Venetians were unjustly blamed. The government in Venice, ignoring the advice of cooler heads, reacted by immediately sending out a war fleet under the personal command of the doge, Vitale Michiel II (1156–1172), to compel the emperor to reinstate the colony and make reparations, by force if necessary. After being outmaneuvered by the Byzantines, the mission, an expensive failure, returned the following year with little accomplished and the plague on board. Tempers flared, the doge and his followers were held to blame, and a tumult erupted, ending in the assassination of Doge Michiel. This in turn prompted a constitutional crisis of great importance, as it provided an excuse to end the system that had based the doge's election and ultimate authority on general popular opinion and consent. It was decided that, henceforth, the election of the doge would no longer result from the private arrangements of a few insiders and then imposed on the general citizenry, but would issue from the decision of a formal new body to be known as the Maggior Consiglio (Great Council).

The Maggior Consiglio was to be made up of 480 adult male citizens (80 from each *sestiere*), representing the most venerable and wealthy merchant families, as well as all those men who had held high office (judges, admirals, ambassadors, etc.). At the same time, it was agreed that no future doge could act without the concurrence of his immediate advisors, soon known as Ducal Councilors, who also were to be elected by and responsible to the Great Council.

With this change, future doges were no longer able to act arbitrarily nor treat their office as a personal possession. The doge was now only the formal head of the commune and was subject to a continually increasing set of restraints laid down by the Great Council. While a number of subsequent occupants of the office were strong and effective leaders, the doge's power was now hedged by many constitutional limitations. Within a few years the number of Ducal Councilors became fixed at six, one from each *sestiere*. They were named for a term of one year and were not eligible for re-election for another two years. Sanction from the Ducal Councilors was required for all official acts of the doge.

The German Emperor, the Pope and the Diplomacy of Doge Ziani

The first man to be elected to the ducal throne following these reforms was Sebastiano Ziani (doge from 1172 to 1178), one of the city's richest merchants. Ziani had built a fortune in the eastern trade and excelled at diplomatic negotiations. At the beginning of his term he and his government were faced with many serious problems, not only the plague and the break with the Byzantines, but also a worsening situation on the Italian mainland.

German Emperor Frederick Barbarossa had spent more than two decades trying to impose order on his fractured empire and especially to bring the newly thriving communes of northern Italy to heel. In the course of the struggle, he had tangled with Pope Alexander, whom he refused to recognize as the legitimate occupant of St. Peter's chair. The pope, in turn, had pronounced a sentence of excommunication against him. This action, together with the resistance of his rebellious subjects, ultimately proved too formidable an obstacle, despite all his efforts, campaigns and sieges. He was finally defeated decisively by the Lombard League at the Battle of Legnano in 1176. After this, Barbarossa had no choice but to agree to a compromise and to a meeting with his adversaries, which Doge Ziani arranged to take place at the neutral and independent city of Venice the following year. From this meeting the historic reconciliation between pope and emperor came about. The Italian communes were henceforth to be self-governing, while recognizing the formal suzerainty of the German empire, and the city of Rome was confirmed to remain under the temporal sovereignty of the papacy.

Against this backdrop, a summer's day in 1177 witnessed the Emperor Frederick kneeling before Pope Alexander III at the entrance of San Marco to receive absolution and acknowledge the authenticity of his election. (A white stone set within a slab of red Verona marble still marks the spot where Frederick knelt.) All Europe was aware that this dramatic episode not only took place in Venice, but had largely been engineered by the doge's diplomacy, and the event ushered in a welcome period of peace. It also aided Venice politically and economically. Within the general context of reconciliation with the various cities of Northern Italy, the emperor enlarged the Republic's trading rights throughout his territories and granted exemption from imperial taxes. On the other side, Pope Alexander confirmed the spiritual jurisdiction of the Patriarch of Venice[17] (now permanently established at Castello) and by implication, validated the authority of the Serenissima over its colonies in Istria and Dalmatia. And, as an added bonus, the city played host during the negotiations to scores of Europe's nobility, lay and ecclesiastical, together with their thousands of retainers, all of whom left a great deal of foreign exchange behind them. For a few months Venice was literally the center of attention for the entire continent and its reputation was further enhanced.

Marriage with the Sea

Tradition ascribes to Alexander's visit the origin of Venice's major state ceremony, the Sposalizio del Mar (Marriage to the Sea). Even before that, however, a religious service of supplication and atonement had been celebrated annually on Ascension Day, usually when one of the city's great merchant fleets was set to leave, in hope of placating and calming Neptune's waters and assuring a successful voyage. As part of the ritual it became the custom for the doge, in full regalia and with his bishops and councilors, to

---

[17] Originally the Patriarch of Grado, whose jurisdiction extended from Istria along the coast to the lagoon, he was hereafter referred to as the Patriarch of Venice when the seat was transferred there.

sail out into the Adriatic in his gilded galley to cast a golden ring into the waves as a symbol of the Serenissima's perpetual lordship over that body of water. The original ring, symbolizing marriage, was supposed to have been a gift from Pope Alexander in recognition of Venice's claim, but though the story is apocryphal, the situation it describes was very real. Jurisdiction over the Adriatic was vital to Venice, especially with respect to the trade in salt, the distribution of which throughout the Po Valley had long been a Venetian monopoly. This commodity, difficult to come by inland, was essential for the flavoring and preservation of food. By the 12th century, the salt pans around the lagoon could no longer supply the demand, which had to be satisfied by imports from other areas. Having control of the north Italian market, Venice also insisted on control of the supply and required all shipments to pass through the government salt office to be taxed.

Civic Improvements

It was during Doge Ziani's regime that the magnificent piazza facing San Marco came into being. The old walls surrounding the area were torn down, along with a cluster of structures in front of the church that the doge owned personally and which he gave up to the city. Additional space—an orchard area surrendered by a religious order—was also acquired to the west and for the first time, the whole vast piazza was paved over. Concurrently, surviving documents indicate Ziani was also responsible for creating the open space adjacent to where the Ducal Palace now stands, since known as the Piazzetta, and erecting the two massive granite columns (earlier brought to Venice from the Holy Land) we see today.[18]

In Ziani's time, the complex of government buildings there, apart from some minor structures, apparently consisted of four main components: the private residence of the doge (palatium ducis) to the east along the present Rio di Palazzo; a fortified tower (torresella) on the south-east corner by the Ponte della Paglia; a communal hall (palatium commune) adjoining the tower and facing south on the Molo that contained the government offices and where the Great Council had its meetings; and another building fronting the Piazzetta that housed the judicial courts.

---

[18] Later the statues symbolizing the city's two patron saints, Mark and Theodore, were placed on top of each column. It is believed that the bronze lion (Mark) was cast in Persia (4th century) and that the human figure (Theodore) is from Greece, probably originally representing Alexander the Great.

Exactly what these structures looked like must be left to the imagination. All have either been destroyed or mortised into the subsequent rebuilding and not much remains visible. Some scholars believe, however, that the architecture of the *palatium commune* can be approximated by viewing the lower half of the façades (i.e. the first two floors) of two Venetian houses from the 12th century, the Palazzi Loredan and Farsetti, already mentioned, which stand side by side on the Grand Canal near the Rialto Bridge. These are two of the oldest buildings in Venice and are good examples of the Veneto-Byzantine style. Fundamental to this type is a ground floor arcade along the canal and an open loggia or gallery characterized by narrow Byzantine arches on the next floor (the *piano nobile*). The arrangement of arches, gallery and windows might be symmetrical as in these two *palazzi*, or sometimes asymmetrical, but the openings always correspond to the functional use of the rooms inside.

Sebastiani Ziani's term of office lasted only six years, but his rule was decisive and salutary for Venice. Not only did he provide the leadership for solid achievements, both domestic and foreign, but more importantly, through his restraint and support of the new constitutional limitations on the doge's power, he firmly established the republican or oligarchic system and attracted to it the allegiance of the common people. Even his most imperious successors, men like Enrico Dandolo (doge from 1192 to 1205) adhered to his example.

7 EXPANSION TO THE EAST: THE 13TH CENTURY

The 13th century marks Venice's coming of age. By the year 1200, the resident population was pushing 100,000 and sizable enclaves of Venetians had been established in the cities of the Levant under Christian control, where many of the old overland caravan routes from the east had their termini. The early crusades had provided the city with new opportunities to enlarge its trade and wealth. In return for the use and cooperation of the Venetian fleet, which had grown in strength and organization, the Crusader states had conferred special advantages. In particular, Venetian citizens living abroad were exempt from local taxes and their goods in transit were free of customs duties.

All in all, much of the increase in Venice's prosperity was at the expense of Constantinople, whose merchants continued to suffer a decline. Feelings against the doge's subjects in the Byzantine capital had already exploded in the confiscations of 1171, which in turn had accelerated the occasional acts of piracy by the Venetians into full scale retaliatory naval actions and organized raids against port cities. Subsequently, Doge Ziani and his successors persuaded the Greek emperor to reinstate some of the privileges once enjoyed by their merchant colonies in return for the withdrawal of the Venetian war fleet from the Aegean. Despite this agreement the animosity and privateering activity continued sporadically through the last two decades of the century.

The Fourth Crusade and the Sack of Constantinople

This was the background when, in 1201, the French and German organizers of the Fourth Crusade approached the Venetian government, then headed by Doge Enrico Dandolo, with the most ambitious undertaking so far. They offered 85,000 marks of silver if Venice would supply, man and provision 200 ships to carry some 30,000 soldiers, their horses and equipment across the seas to recapture the holy places still held by the Muslims. Agreement was reached but only after a supplementary treaty was appended: in return for an additional 50 armed galleys to escort the fleet and protect the expedition for one full year, half of all spoils and conquests on land or sea would accrue to Venice.

As it turned out, only about 10,000 Crusaders showed up in the lagoon area the next year, and they were lacking some 34,000 marks of the agreed sum. To compensate for this shortfall the western barons, leaders of the Crusade, were forced to accept the Venetian demand that the fleet, under the personal command of Doge Dandolo,[1] proceed not directly to the Levant but first to the Dalmatian coast to reinforce Venetian rule there. This diversion consumed the winter of 1202–1203 and led to still another change of plans. Instead of immediately proceeding against the Saracens, the whole expedition was persuaded upon Venetian initiative to divert to Constantinople.

The purported reason for this was to convince (by force, if necessary) the recalcitrant regime there, which in the past had sometimes cooperated with the Muslims, to provide aid and support to the Crusaders. In addition there was a religious justification: the hope of bringing the eastern church back under the Roman pope's jurisdiction and authority, a right and privilege that Rome had claimed since the very beginnings of Christianity. And of course for the Venetians, there was the practical objective of once and for all putting an end to the confiscations of their ships and property and the mistreatment of their overseas merchants by the Byzantines.

Underlying all this was the unspoken but tempting possibility of dividing up some of the wealth of the city itself, the richest in Christendom. The primary tactic to accomplish all this was the Crusader's demand that the current occupant of the imperial throne, who had deposed his own brother, step down to be replaced by the legitimate heir, his nephew, who would be more cooperative with the west and who, conveniently, was traveling with the Crusaders. Of course, this was an impossible request and the Byzantine court refused. The Fourth Crusade therefore set sail from Dalmatia in 1203 not to attack the Muslims, but first to overcome and rob another Christian power, the center of the world's oldest and most prestigious empire.

Venice Gains "One Quarter and One Half" of the Byzantine Empire

It took most of a year and several sieges, but despite Constantinople's massive walls and defenses, which had never before been successfully assaulted, the city fell to the Crusaders in April 1204 and the Byzantine

---

[1] The documents indicate he was well into his eighties at the time and either partially or totally blind.

imperial court fled. Burning, looting, and destruction followed for several days until order was restored and an alternative government set up, in which Venice, and especially Doge Dandolo, played a vital role. Known as the Latin Empire of Constantinople, it was to be ruled by a new emperor—not the legitimate heir who had been killed in the siege but a western noble, Count Baldwin of Flanders—who was appointed by the expedition leaders, crowned in Santa Sophia and awarded one quarter of the Byzantine city and its loot and one quarter of its remaining territories. The balance was to be divided equally between Venice and the other western barons. These latter lands were then to be enfiefed in the feudal tradition to lesser nobles in return for military service.

Venice thus received three-eighths of the empire, and thereafter the phrase, "Lord of one quarter and one half [of a quarter] of the Eastern Empire" enhanced the doge's title. For the Venetians, the most important parts of these new acquisitions, aside from their share of the city itself,[2] were the various strategic naval bases and islands throughout the eastern Mediterranean, especially Negroponte and Naxos in the Aegean, Gallipoli, a number of areas in the Peloponnese, including Modon and Coron on the Ionian Sea, and the major island of Crete, which was divided up into some 200 knight's fiefs. At the same time, all of the advantageous trading privileges were reinstated, to the exclusion of the Genoese and the Pisans, and the Venetian colonies at Constantinople and elsewhere were enlarged and reinforced. In one blow, Venice was freed from all Byzantine dominion and control and became the pre-eminent Mediterranean maritime power.

Such was the perverted outcome of the Fourth Crusade, which to the Venetians of the time seemed like one of their greatest achievements and a masterstroke by their wily old doge. Time, however, would show instead that the deceitfulness and avarice that brought about the plunder of Europe's most cultured and richest city and the dispersal or destruction of its wealth and art treasures, permanently undermined Constantinople's prestige. The Latin Empire itself only survived until mid-century when the Byzantines took back the city and its adjacent territories. But the damage had been done, for once the city's allegedly invulnerable walls had been breached, they could

---

[2] Venice was awarded the district surrounding the Patriarchate and the supreme church of St. Sophia, where the old doge, Enrico Dandolo, who died the following year (1205), was laid to rest and where his tomb may still be seen. A Venetian, Tommaso Morosini, was named patriarch.

be breached again. It would be almost two centuries of protracted conflict before this would happen, but in the end, it led to the city's capitulation to the Ottoman Turks and their occupation of a considerable part of eastern Europe for more than 400 years. The so-called Crusaders for Christ, influenced and misguided by the Venetians, had turned their backs on their primary objective of pushing the Saracens out of the Holy Land and helped to bring about the final demise of the Eastern Christian empire, the ramifications of which are still with us today.

Venetian Prosperity

But for the moment, Venice's domination of the eastern Mediterranean, along with the growth of European town populations and their developing taste for exotic goods stimulated by the Crusades, provided the city with the chance to capitalize on the expansion of east-west trade throughout the 13th century. The merchants on the Rialto soon became the principal conduit through which passed silks, furs, alum and dyes, sugar, honey and spices in one direction, and textiles and metals in the other. Taxes were levied on all this commerce, so that in addition to the usual trading and shipping profits enjoyed by the people, the city government also filled its coffers. As a contemporary, Martino da Canal, wrote in the late 1200s, "merchandise rushes through this noble city like water cascading from a spring."

The geographic location of Venice was very important. Cargoes coming over the Brenner Pass from northern Europe could be loaded on barges on the Adige and other rivers and floated directly to the city for sale and transshipment. Agricultural produce from the vast Po Valley, particularly grain and wine (the latter transported in large casks and not suitable for overland shipment), also came down the many river networks or, in the case of that famous sweet wine known as Malmsey, up the Adriatic from the Morea to Venice, where the cargoes were loaded aboard large merchant ships bound for the North Atlantic ports and England. Harbor and warehouse facilities in the lagoon were second to none. Timber for shipbuilding was readily available from the Alpine passes and from Istria, and a great many foreigners were active in the city. The Germans, especially, were provided with one of the largest buildings in the city—the Fondaco dei Tedeschi, still standing next to the Rialto Bridge—for their accommodation and goods storage.[3]

The Venetians were careful during this period to keep on good terms with the western empire in order to maintain their trading privileges, which were reaffirmed several times, especially by Frederick II (1194–1250), the most enlightened and forceful occupant of the imperial throne since Charlemagne. The emperor paid an official state visit to Venice in 1233 in a vain attempt to persuade the island republic to modify its policy of neutrality, for Frederick, like his grandfather Barbarossa before him, had continued a lifelong effort to reimpose his authority over Italy. But Venice was a unique case and the emperor had no choice but to reconfirm its special relationship, not only as a link between east and west, but also as the only city-state on the Italian peninsula over which the imperial writ did not run, even in theory.

Commercial Rivalry and War with Genoa

There were, however, other commercial rivals, the most purposeful of which was Genoa. Before the middle of the century, this other maritime city-state had been largely occupied in a struggle with Pisa for preeminence in the western Mediterranean. The Pisans were of pro–Holy Roman Empire (Ghibbeline) sympathies, but were fatally weakened in the year 1250 by the death of Frederick II and the collapse of imperial pretensions in Italy. Thereafter, Pisa declined as a major sea power and Genoa was able to turn its main energies toward the east in an attempt to obtain a larger share of the growing international trade there. Tension rapidly developed with Venice and sporadic clashes occurred between individual ships or members of rival trading enclaves. The situation came to a head in 1258 off the port city of Acre in Palestine with a full-scale confrontation and battle between their respective fleets. Genoa, though commanding more vessels, was soundly defeated, losing half of some 50 galleys and with many men dead or captured. At the same time, ashore in Acre, the Venetians overran the Genoese quarter, drove out the occupants and confiscated their goods and property. Amongst the looted treasures were two large, square stone columns, beautifully carved by Syrian sculptors, and one short, round one made of porphyry. These three trophies of victory were shipped back to

---

[3] The original building was partially burned in the 16th century and then rebuilt as we see it today. It now houses the central post office.

Venice and erected in the Piazzetta next to San Marco where they still stand to commemorate the first great naval success over Genoa.

However, the reconquest of Constantinople by the Greeks in 1261 and their alliance with the Genoese upset the entire situation. Venice found itself on the defensive and its vital possessions in the Aegean threatened. A series of sea skirmishes and battles followed, but Venice managed to maintain the upper hand until 1268 when peace was finally agreed upon between the parties. The Venetians were confirmed in their trading rights as before, but henceforth only on equal terms with the Genoese. At the same time, the other principal trade routes—to Cyprus and Armenia, to Egypt, to Flanders and England through the western Mediterranean and Gibraltar—were to remain open equally to all the powers.

Shipping and Financial Innovations

It was during this century that the slow evolution of European maritime techniques and improvements at last came to fruition. Earlier the volume of seaborne trade had been limited by a number of factors, not the least of which was the primitive state of navigational aids and ship design. Most voyages had been confined to coastal routes where landmarks could be checked continually, and ships ventured into the open sea only in fair weather. This meant little long-range trading activity was carried on in the winter months, not so much for fear of storms, but of losing all sense of direction when the stars or sun were hidden by cloud cover. Two inventions changed all this: the mariner's magnetic compass and the so-called portolan charts, which together made possible the navigational art of dead reckoning. The charts, a collection of maps of the entire Mediterranean area, as well as the Atlantic coast, showing land contours and bearings, had been worked out by the 1250s and allowed mariners to sail with the aid of the compass in almost any weather by plotting their course on paper.

At the same time, oared galleys, which had never before exceeded 50 tons, were now built to 100 or 150 tons, while cargo carriers, or roundships, wide of beam, were built to sizes two and three times that with correspondingly higher freeboard and carrying capacity. Together, navigation in all seasons by dead reckoning, along with an increase in the size of ships, allowed more freight to be moved.

Beyond this, the roundships, coming to be known as "cogs" in English (*coche* in Italian), underwent several major improvements, which were first implemented by the Dutch and British for the North Sea and Atlantic trade. One was a change in hull design that provided for a straight rather than curved sternpost, thus making possible the use of a single, central rudder in place of the old, awkward and less effective side rudders previously employed. Another change was the increased use of square sails with reef points and shorter, less cumbersome yardarms instead of the ancient lateen rigs. Both changes permitted a reduction in manpower, increased efficiency and improved maneuverability, either when tacking into weather or free-sailing before a following wind.

In Venice, the government supervised every detail of the organization of the great galley fleets to which the most valuable cargoes were consigned. Having oars as well as sails (and a large complement of armed oarsmen) and being of shallower draft with a narrower profile, the galleys were faster, safer and open to more routing options than the cogs, though they of course could not carry as much cargo. Many of the larger Venetian galleys were owned by the Republic. These, when operating as an official fleet in convoy, were commanded overall by a *capitano* who was appointed, paid and controlled by the government, as were each of the ships' *patroni* or masters. At other times when international conditions were more tranquil, the government would charter these galleys at auction to private *patroni* who could then operate them independently, usually a year at a time. Most other vessels—cogs and light galleys—were privately owned and the great majority of voyages were privately initiated, but always subject to state regulation and, if escorted in convoy, always under an official *capitano*.

Even under the best circumstances, risks were high, and as ships and cargoes increased in size, values mounted. Earlier, a venture might be divided up among a group of investors to spread the risk. But this was not always practical and a means was needed to transfer the risk without diluting the control and ownership of the venture. To accomplish this, marine insurance was invented, under which a written agreement allowed a merchant or shipowner to safeguard his entire investment by paying a small percentage of the values at risk ahead of time to others who would indemnify him in case of loss. This was the forerunner of all modern insurance contracts.

Standardized Currency and the Advent of Banking

Of course, none of the increase in commercial activity would have been possible without some advance in the monetary system itself. In addition to barter arrangements, payments had long been made in bullion or in the numerous and diverse coins in use, many of Byzantine origin. But there existed no standardization or fixed rates of exchange and coinage was routinely clipped or otherwise debased, making monetary settlements cumbersome and complex. Early in the 1200s, during Enrico Dandolo's dogeship, Venice introduced its first standardized silver coin—the large silver penny or *grosso*, which the city mint kept at a uniform weight (2.18 grams) and purity (.965 parts silver). This coin became the basic Venetian standard of value to which the coins of other political entities were often related. A *lira di grossi*, the basic "money of account" used by traders of many nationalities, was equal to 240 *grossi*. Gold was scarce in Western Europe during the Middle Ages and, except for the Byzantine coins (Bizants), virtually disappeared from all European specie until the 13th century when it was found that coins of manageable size and larger value were needed. Though the Florentines were the first to supply this with their golden florin in 1252, the Venetians followed with the minting of their first gold coin, the *zecchino* (ducat) in 1284, each containing 3.5 grams of gold, 99.7% pure and exactly equal in value to the *fiorino d'oro* and so it remained until the fall of the Republic.

Concurrent with all this trading activity and better coinage, the banking fraternity came into its own. Originally a profession dealing primarily in the assaying of the world's rare metals and the exchange of coinage in order to facilitate business, it gradually became a depository for capital and a means to finance commercial enterprise through loans and the extension of credit.

At the same time other improvements were made in the means of conducting business. Double entry bookkeeping was devised, as were bills of lading and bills of exchange, whereby a merchant could receive goods from a distant place and pay for them to the account of the seller without having to send bullion or coin or other goods in trade. To accomplish this the Venetians evolved the so-called *banche del giro* (from *girare*—to rotate— literally bank transfers by rotation) whereby instead of the physical shipment of coinage from buyer to seller, their respective accounts were debited or credited. By this means bankers were also able for the first time to create money by making credits to one account in excess of the other party's real obligations or resources.

Interest and Investment

Fees and interest for these services had always been charged, but by the end of the Middle Ages, the Catholic church began to enforce more stringently its prohibition against collecting interest on debt, especially if the rates were high. Venice, like other cities, paid some lip service to the church's stand against usury, but in practice seldom enforced the rule. In any case there were many ways around it, even when the actual rates reached 20 percent or more. If the contract did not express a fixed rate of interest but only an allotment or "share customary at the moment," the lender was thought of as a participant in the enterprise rather than a creditor. In other instances, a bill of exchange could be drawn requiring payment back at the end of a certain number of days in a larger amount. The demand for investment capital continued to increase and the risks of loss were very real. Gradually, the church was forced to recognize that some reasonable return was not sinful usury, but legitimate.

Venetian bankers generally conducted their business at *banchi* or counting tables under the portico on the Ruga degli Orefici (Goldsmiths) near the Rialto Bridge where *giro* transactions were duly recorded in their ledgers. As mentioned, this area of the city had from the earliest times been the commercial center as many of the street names attest to this day: Ruga degli Speciale (Spices), Calle dell' Olio (Oil), Calle Beccarie (Butchers), Calle dei Botteri (Coopers), Riva del Vin (Wine Quay), Campo della Pescheria (fish market).

In addition to entrusting their money to the bankers, wealthy Venetians also invested in government obligations. Normal day-to-day expenses were usually recovered by the city through taxes on wholesale and retail transactions in the market places, but extraordinary costs, such as war, meant government borrowing—originally forced borrowing—and the gradual piling up of a public debt. This had resulted in a long series of bond issues.[4] In 1262 all these were consolidated into the so-called *monte vecchio,* which from that time onward for more than 100 years regularly returned a fixed 5 percent to the

---

[4] The first ever government bonds were issued in Venice in 1157.

bondholders and provided a conservative and safe investment for the middle and upper classes, the *scuole* and other institutions, and even many foreigners.

Venice Further Institutionalizes Its Government

Venice's reputation for economic and political stability was earned during this century at the same time that its constitution was being perfected and the powers of its governing bodies more precisely defined. No written constitutional document was ever attempted, but like its modern British counterpart, it consisted of the whole body of statutes, oaths of office, judicial precedents and long-held customs. At the top of the system was the doge, but throughout the 13th century the powers of his office were further limited. Each time a new doge was elected he was required to swear obedience to an ever growing list of prohibitions or *promissioni*. Ultimate power continued to reside in the Great Council, which was empowered to pass all laws and to elect all officers, judges, and members of the intermediate councils. These latter councils included the *Quarantia,* or Forty, a body that was responsible for coinage and finance and acted as a court of appeal; the *Consiglio dei Pregatti,* a body usually translated into English as the Senate, concerned with commerce, the fleet and embassies abroad; and above these, the six Ducal Councilors, chosen to advise and assist the doge in the daily administration of his duties, while making sure he complied with his oath of office, the statutes and the decisions of the Great Council. These councilors, together with the doge and the three senior members of the Forty, were known as the *Signoria.* Here was concentrated the executive authority for all government departments—the colonies, the fleet, the mint, the tax office, the Arsenale, the grain warehouses, the salt office, etc.—although subsidiary committees conducted the day to day business.

Besides the doge, the Procurator of the Church of San Marco was the only other office filled by the Great Council for a life term. At first with only one occupant, then four, and later nine, the office was charged with safekeeping the church's treasures and ever increasing endowments, as well as maintaining the building itself, the city's greatest pride.

Within Venice proper, the six *sestieri* were subdivided into about 65 *cantrade* (parishes), each with its priest and its *capo di contrada*, who was always a leading resident of the parish, appointed by the doge and responsible for law and order there. At the same time, each *sestiere* was under a continual obligation to have ready at a moment's notice at least 500 armed militiamen in case of riot or insurrection. Outside Venice in such communities as Chioggia or the Dalmatian cities, a *podesta,* selected by the doge, presided, although each community had its local councils as well. In the more remote commercial enclaves, the island outposts and the colonies, a Venetian patrician was always sent, usually for a term of two years, to enforce the dictates of the *Signoria.*

It has been estimated that about 300 men were needed at this time to fill the various offices of the state—councilors, judges, admirals, governors, administrators—and that most of them came from perhaps 200 families, each rotating from office to office since the terms were seldom more than a year or two. This was government by an aristocracy—albeit a merchant aristocracy—and on the whole the Venetians accepted it, unlike in many other Italian communities where conflict developed between the rulers and the ruled.

The Guilds

The existence of the *scuole,* with their institutionalized activity, helped satisfy the aspirations of many who were ineligible to sit in the Great Council, as did the various guild organizations, set up on such occupational lines as carpenters, coopers, sailmakers, jewelers, apothecaries, glass-makers, etc.. There were about 100 of these guilds and membership varied from a few score up to 1000. Each had the combined characteristics of our modern unions and our trade associations. These guilds regulated membership, initiation rites, dues and fines, as well as set rules of fair competition and product standards. All, like the *scuole,* provided aid and benefits to members in need and sustained some charitable and religious obligations.

Interestingly, the most important vocations—merchants, judges and lawyers—had no guilds, probably because most of these men were either part of the government or relied directly on the government to look out for their interests. The mariners, the largest occupational group, did not form a guild either, but these men often carried on some secondary line of work – as fishermen or ship's carpenters—and were members of those guilds. Nor did there develop in Venice anything comparable to the great mercantile guild of the Calimala in Florence, which controlled the sources of supply and the marketing of that city's principal product, woolen cloth.

Venice never cultivated the textile business, nor any other manufacturing, on a large scale, but rather encouraged many small workshops and artisans, such as the glassmakers[5] and the metalworkers, who individually owned and controlled their equipment and materials and produced mainly for export. There were, however, two major exceptions, both pertaining to shipping: the hemp cordage and rope makers, who were gradually concentrated into one large, central workshop called the Tana, and, as already mentioned, Venice's most important enterprise, the Arsenale, where the galley fleet was built and maintained. Both of these enterprises were totally owned and managed by the government.

It was probably inevitable, with the unprecedented business ventures and far-flung trading activity flowing in and out of Venice during these years, that it would be a Venetian who would become the first European world traveler. Various merchants and seamen had ranged beyond the customary Mediterranean routes, but no Christian had ever covered the distances that Marco Polo, his father and uncle traveled, nor spent so long a time abroad. On Marco's principal journey he penetrated far beyond Oltremare, across Persia, India and Mongolia into China, where he entered the service of the Great Khan and lived for 20 years (1272–1292). His descriptions of these oriental countries, and especially of their wealth—his accounts were sometimes told with a degree of exaggeration, "a million of this, a million of that," which earned him the nickname *il milione*—did nothing to lessen the desire of Europeans to trade with the east.

The Second Genoese War and the Locking of the Council

For almost two centuries, during which the West maintained the small Christian principalities in the Holy Land, trade went on with the Muslims in the eastern Mediterranean. But between 1263 and 1291, the Mamluks of Egypt surrounded Oltremare and laid siege to the principalities, one by one occupying the trading centers of Antioch, Tripoli and Acre, and finally putting an end to European control and to the merchant colonies there.

---

[5] The art of glass-making had been practiced in ancient Rome, had survived in Byzantium and returned to Venice before the year 1000. At first scattered throughout the city, the craftsmen were moved to the Island of Murano in 1278, partly to safeguard the city from the frequent fires that spread from their furnaces and partly to concentrate the industry to better control its secrets and techniques.

This resulted in an unequivocal papal prohibition on further commerce with that area, which shifted the emphasis northward through the Aegean to the Anatolian and Persian silk routes, where the Genoese were especially active. It was therefore only a matter of time before a renewed Genoese-Venetian conflict erupted, initially between rival merchant convoys, but later between the war fleets of the two powers. In 1294 they met at the Battle of Lajazzo near Cyprus and several years later again at the Battle of Curzola in the Adriatic, in which some 170 galleys were involved, making this the largest encounter at sea ever fought between the two navies. In each case the Genoese had the best of it, but, because of internal divisions at home, they agreed to a treaty in 1299. This treaty suspended hostilities for a time, but did not resolve the conflicting trading priorities that were the basic causes of the war.[6]

One major constitutional change, however, did occur in Venice from these years of tension and conflict. In 1297, the old system of periodically adding or dropping men from the Great Council by a series of votes was abandoned in favor of a new law that recognized all current and recent members as permanent—their names were henceforth inscribed in the Libro d'Oro—while at the same time outlining a method of selecting a limited number of additional deserving applicants. More importantly, the law also laid down a new provision that made the legitimate male heirs of all members automatically eligible. In one stroke this decision created a hereditary Great Council. This act became known as the *serrata*, or locking of the Council, as the families already on the inside were henceforth effectively and permanently locked in.

Late Byzantine and Romanesque Art at St. Mark's

Besides the commercial cargoes flowing into Venice, there was also the loot, which after the sack of Constantinople filtered continuously back to the city on the lagoon. Few ships returned home without a load of booty—marble columns, alabaster, thin sheets of jasper, carvings in many mediums, icons, reliquaries and their relics, gold and silver. Examples of these may be seen inside and outside St. Mark's, which began to assume its present

---

[6] Marco Polo had returned home just in time to be called to serve on one of the Venetian galleys, only to be captured and imprisoned by the Genoese. His famous book of travels was written at that time, before his release.

The three superimposed, carved arches of San Marco's imposing central portal.

appearance in those years. In a sense, the decoration of the church became a declaration of victory, a symbol of triumph. The four magnificent bronze horses, taken down from their high places of honor in Constantinople where they had stood for centuries, were placed conspicuously in the center of the façade above the main entrance. A forest of Byzantine pillars surrounded the doorways. The six reliefs in the spandrels of the frontal arches and the varied carvings that cover the exterior side walls, including the four curious figures in porphyry at the corner facing south, are all loot from the East.

However, not all of the embellishments for St. Mark's came from overseas—local craftsmen were also at work. While it is true that, as with the mosaics, the earliest reliefs and carvings by Venetian sculptors show an unmistakable debt to Byzantium, by the start of the 13th century, other influences, especially the Romanesque from the mainland, were beginning to prevail. The best examples of this development are the series of carvings begun in the early 1200s that band the three arches of the central portal. Here a remarkable program is laid out, but one difficult to interpret. According to one version, the innermost archivolt, made up of allegories of the earth, sea, animal kingdom, etc., may represent the primitive and natural phenomena of the world; the middle arch, with its virtues and seasonal or agricultural occupations, perhaps indicates man's relationship to the earth and to his fellows; and the large outer arch, carved with figures engaged in the various Venetian trades (masons, shipbuilders, bakers, shoemakers, coopers, barbers, carpenters, smiths, fishermen) together with the prophets and Christ, may portray man's higher civilized life and religious aspirations. In other words, the whole cycle could depict man's adjustment first to the natural world and the seasons, then to his brethren and life in society and finally to God. In any case, the carvings illustrate stylistic trends—the figures of the virtues are more Byzantine, the months and seasons are more Romanesque—while the crafts portrayed on the outer arch introduce us to the most original aspects of the work and are the most distinctively Venetian.

At the same time, within the church, a continual program of Biblical illustration went on in mosaic form to instruct the faithful. The Byzantine style still dominates, but here and there local or Romanesque influence can be detected, as in the Old Testament scenes in the ceiling of the main porch (narthex) or in the church's greatest mosaic masterpieces, such as the *Agony* (or *Prayer*) *in the Garden* (found high on the south aisle) and the *Arch of the Passion* (western arch of the central dome). In the former, the artist reintroduces

111

Carvings on the middle arch of San Marco's main entrance showing labors connected to the seasons and Romanesque influence.

Early 13th-century Byzantine mosaic of Christ praying in the garden of olives as modified by Western influences.

a sense of space and natural landscape and supplements Romanesque figurative arrangements with Hellenistic elements in the Byzantine tradition. In the *Arch of the Passion*, the intense, agitated configurations of the New Testament personalities depicted and their awareness of the dramatic events described[7] clearly indicate western influences transforming the more conservative eastern approach.

The carvings on the great arch of the central door and the mosaics of the Passion best illustrate the first tentative penetration of the mainland Romanesque style into the context of Venetian-Byzantine art at St. Marks. However, for almost a century thereafter, Venetian artists returned for the most part to repetitive imitations of Byzantine formulas of varying merit. The many low relief, mosaic and painted icons produced by the thousands during this period fall into this category. Not until the arrival of the Gothic style in Venice were there any fresh new artistic departures.

Domestic Architecture During the 13th Century

Altogether, the 13th century was a decisive one for the city as its influence and power, even after the collapse of the Latin Empire of

---

[7] The Crucifixion, the Descent into Limbo, the incredulity of St. Thomas, etc.

Constantinople, continued to grow throughout the eastern Mediterranean and an unprecedented volume of trade flowed through the Rialto port. Many of the merchant families waxed rich and commenced to design and build for themselves more elaborate *palazzi*. One of the largest to survive from this period, although it was badly restored in the 19th century, is the so-called Fondaco dei Turchi on the Grand Canal. Originally built as a private house, it changed hands many times until finally it was taken over in 1621 by Turkish merchants (hence its present name) for use as their headquarters and warehouse. (They stayed there through peace and war until 1838.) The basic architecture, with its typical stilted arcades along the water and loggia on the upper floor enclosed by towers at either end and surmounted by a parapeted wall, was in the Venetian-Byzantine tradition. But the scale of the building and its openness attest to the wealth of its first owners and the relative security the city must have enjoyed at a time when houses in other cities were most often heavily fortified.

It is also possible to see how the common people lived at the time by visiting the narrow street known as the Calle del Paradiso, near the Campo Santa Maria Formosa, still lined by 13th-century houses and shops with their overhanging upper stories, their stone columns and wooden architraves. The buildings are nicely preserved and are still being used for the same purposes—an example of Venice's long continuity.

So it was that from the activity of this period the city had become the greatest trading emporium in the known world and continued to be so for several more centuries. In retrospect, we should also note that the Venetians of that time must accept much of the responsibility for the ultimate demise of the Byzantine Empire, to say nothing of the plundering of its capital. The events of this century ultimately led to the occupation of a large part of Europe by the Turks and, ironically, Venice's loss of its own eastern colonies.

8 VENICE TURNS TENTATIVELY WESTWARD: THE 14TH CENTURY

By the year 1300, Venice was entering one of its most prosperous periods, which was to last almost without interruption to mid-century. Much of Europe also experienced an advance in its living standards and civilization with the final maturing of the Middle Ages. Populations increased, town life flourished, the universities consolidated themselves as repositories of learning and literature, and Thomas Aquinas and Dante Alighieri, among others, set their culminating stamp on the political, religious and moral issues of the times. Contributing to this prosperity were the steady improvements in economic conditions across the continent, the result of new techniques in the mining and textile industries, in agriculture, in river, canal and ocean transport and in the security of commerce generally.[1]

As the European system stabilized, the great movable trade fairs gradually gave way to more permanent, year-round markets in the growing cities, Bruges being an outstanding example. All this had an effect on Venice and its commercial practices. Merchants, who had earlier spent much of their lives traveling with their goods, now remained at home, sending off their cargoes in the care of a ship's master for delivery to a permanent resident agent abroad, who in turn was responsible for the safekeeping and final sale of the goods. Such sophisticated, long-distance operations enhanced the importance of the Rialto market as a clearing house, not only for the cargoes themselves and for international financial arrangements, but most vitally as a focal point for information—news of sailing dates and routes, insurance and exchange rates, foreign prices, etc.—upon which the merchant could base his decisions and instructions. When Shakespeare's merchant of Venice asks, "What news on the Rialto?" he was not just curious for gossip; he wanted solid facts from which he could make his plans. Merchants were especially interested in information from the larger cities of Europe, whose growing prosperity coincided with an increased concern for the steadily expanding regime of the Ottoman Turks and prompted the Venetians for the first time to view their western trading contacts as of equal if not primary importance for the future.

---

[1] These improvements included more efficient pumps, ore crushers, the wheeled plow, the increased use of water mills and windmills to turn machinery, stone-paved roads and new navigational aids, such as the magnetic compass, better charts and lighthouses, the extensive dredging of ports and canals.

Papal Conflict and the Creation of the Council of Ten

Venice had always exerted diplomatic efforts to safeguard its commercial interests in the Lombard plain and the Alpine passes, but had never attempted to acquire political suzerainty over large territories there. In the trecento, however, Venice made the first tentative moves to exercise power indirectly over the adjacent mainland.

The initial attempt, however, was unsuccessful. In 1308 the death of the head of the powerful Este family left a contested succession at his seat in nearby Ferrara and provoked a conflict between its titular sovereign, the pope, and its commercial overlord, Venice. The Venetians were not united on the matter, but the doge's supporters prevailed after a long and acrimonious debate in the Great Council and an expedition was sent to confront the papal army at Ferrara. The resulting clash between the two forces proved humiliating for Venice; not only were battles lost but the city was excommunicated and placed under interdict, to the great discomfiture of the pro-war faction.

Excommunication and papal interdict during medieval times meant not only the cessation of all religious life—masses suspended, marriages and burial services banned, the churches locked and priests unavailable—but the interruption of all business activity since the papal bull declared all oaths and financial obligations absolved and the offending party's commercial and political agreements null and void. Accordingly, its ships, goods and property were subject to confiscation by its enemies and/or trading rivals.

This untenable situation soon led to an armed uprising against the doge Pietro Gradenigo (1289–1311) and the government by opponents of the war within the city. A fortuitous series of events[2] quelled the rebellion, but more importantly, the situation prompted the creation of a new political body, a kind of public safety committee that was soon dubbed The Council of Ten.[3]

---

[2] Not only did a rebel defector provide the doge with a last minute warning, but on the night planned for the uprising (June 15, 1310), a wild and drenching storm prevented one contingent of rebels from crossing the lagoon and disrupted the planned rendezvous of the others. Also contributing to the conspirators' undoing was the legendary slaying of their leading standard bearer, who, as he was about to charge into the Piazza, was struck down by a heavy stone mortar dropped from a window by an old woman, a Signora Rossi, who apparently sided with the doge. To this day there is a plaque affixed to the house just by the clock tower depicting the incident and a white stone in the street where the mortar fell.

[3] Ten men elected by the Great Council for a term of six months, no two of whom could be from the same family.

Though it was intended at first for a brief existence, the council evolved into a permanent fixture for the remainder of the Republic's life. It quickly came to fulfill two purposes. First, it served as an intelligence gathering network of spies to abort future conspiracies or attacks, whether foreign or domestic. Secondly and more importantly, the Council of Ten was empowered to meet in secret session with the doge and his councilors whenever a major crisis required the regime to act without delay. The government had concluded that only through a smaller body could the city move promptly and decisively when vital decisions faced it. The controversial and disastrous handling of the Ferrara war and the following rebellion had left its permanent mark.

Eventually, a new doge, Giovanni Soranzo (1312–1328), persuaded the pope to lift the interdict in 1313, but he only succeeded after he accepted the insulting condition of paying to the papacy 90,000 gold florins—not Venetian ducats—which the government was required to force out of the Florentine bankers residing at Rialto at the best rate of exchange it could manage.

This settlement with the papacy helped usher in a better economic climate and treaties were soon renegotiated with the mainland cities, even Farrara. Long distance trade over the Alps and by ship through the Straits of Gibraltar to the English Channel and to the older markets in the eastern Mediterranean resumed and expanded rapidly during the next several decades.

The Battle Over Padua

This was the period in Northern Italian history when the increasingly prosperous communes fell one by one under the rule of one or another despotic family, each more ambitious than the next: the Visconti in Milan, the Este in Modena and Ferrara, the Gonzaga of Mantua, the Carrara of Padua, the Scaligeri of Verona. The last proved especially rapacious, systematically taking over the smaller towns of Vicenza and Belluno, then Padua (at the expense of the Carrara family) and finally Treviso (1328–1333). With this came unwelcome increases in taxes and tolls on goods moving to and from the lagoon city.

Under the circumstances, it became increasingly obvious that unless the Scaligeri were stopped, Venice would lose control of its *terrafirma* sources of supplies, especially grain, and its markets in the Po Valley. Accordingly, a coalition was formed with other threatened cities and mercenaries were hired. Within a few years and several battles, the Scaligeri were overthrown in 1339 and their key family members imprisoned or banished. For the first time the Venetians obtained effective, though indirect, control over Padua (where the Carrara, their allies for the moment, were reinstated), as well as over Treviso and the neighboring areas.

Gothic Influence on Architecture and the Rebuilding of Venice's Government Center

Within the city itself peace brought the possibility of civic improvements, not only the paving of streets and additions to the Arsenale, but also the commencement of what were to be some of the city's most important buildings. Not surprisingly, this closer association with the Italian mainland coincided with the introduction of the Gothic style into Venice, which soon manifested itself in a number of new churches, as well as in the building that was to become the present Doge's Palace.

Throughout the early trecento, after decades of alterations and piecemeal remodeling, numerous proposals for completely rebuilding the complex of structures that then made up the center of Venetian government were considered. At last, in 1340, agreement was reached to allocate the money for substantial new construction. A committee was charged with the responsibility and architectural drawings were ordered. Surviving documents attest to the fact that the proposed new building—that is, the part running along the Molo to the south—was fully conceived and constructed as we see it today in one undertaking. Even so, the ancient *torresella* and adjoining parts of the old structure, constituting about a third of the total, were incorporated into the new building behind the present façade. This resulted in a noticeable irregularity: the two large windows at the eastern end are set lower than the other four due to the differing floor levels in the older and newer parts. The new building, which stretched down to the corner on the Piazzetta and back to the north as far, at that time, as the seventh and larger column, was entirely given over on the upper level to a gigantic new meeting hall for the Great Council.[4] For a time the part of the *torresella* tower that rose above the present

---

[4] The generous dimensions—80 feet wide by 175 feet long by 50 feet high—were necessary because the membership had increased to over 1,000 during the process of the "locking" of the Council.

View of the 14th-century Doges' Palace across the Basin of St. Mark by Canaletto. Later constructions are the Libreria on the left and the prisons on the right.

roofline remained intact, as an old print shows, but it was subsequently demolished to unify the appearance of the southern façade.

Perhaps no other governmental center anywhere achieved such a striking architectural triumph. With unprecedented daring and innovation the imported Gothic style has been ingeniously adapted to and merged with the Venetian tradition to produce in its distinctive ground-floor portico, in the admirably designed loggia with its slender pointed arches and quatrefoil circles, and in the vast curtain wall above of pink Verona marble and white Istrian stone in a diamond pattern, one of the most original and forever fascinating secular façades in Europe.

The Frari, Zanipolo and Santo Stefano are Built

About this time, under the auspices of one or another of the monastic orders, which had arrived in Venice the previous century, began the

Interior of the 14th-century Frari church with its Gothic spaciousness, pointed arches and ribbed vaulting.

construction or reconstruction of three of the city's largest churches, each decisively influenced by the new Gothic style. Perhaps the most impressive is La Chiesa de la Santa Maria Gloriosa dei Frari, the church of the Friars Minor of St. Francis (Franciscans), soon called simply the Frari. Many basic Gothic features were employed there: an open, spacious interior, pointed arches, lofty vaults and a multitude of windows to provide better lighting. However, as in most other Italian Gothic churches, the full exploitation of the style is lacking: tracery, pinnacles and crockets are missing or restrained, flying buttresses are non-existent, stained glass is of secondary importance, and the interior verticality is compromised by the heavy wooden tie beams between the columns, which were necessary for lack of sufficient exterior buttressing. Moreover, traces of Byzantine influence persist in some of the column capitals and in the campanile.

The same years saw another major undertaking on the other side of the city by the Dominican brotherhood with the construction of the Church

The Gothic church of Zanipolo, another monastic construction similar to the Frari.

of Saints John and Paul—Santi Giovanni e Paolo, conveniently contracted in the Venetian dialect to "Zanipolo." Similar in size, architecture and materials as the Frari, it is laid out as a basilica with its wide nave merging into transepts and apsidal chapels at the east end, which is slightly raised for the use of the monks, and it has the same luminous atmosphere, thanks to its many windows.

Concurrently, the Augustinian order started construction on their church of Santo Stefano. Not as well-known as the other two, it is also built on Gothic principles and has an especially interesting wooden beam ceiling, one of the best of its kind. The ceiling recalls an inverted ship's hull and the derivation of the word nave.[5]

Unlike the church of San Marco, the exteriors of these three buildings, which have mostly plain surfaces of brick, boast little in the way of integrated,

---

[5] From the Latin *navis*, or ship, to which the church was often likened.

decorative features (e.g. dressed stone or marble sheathing, columns, balustrades, carvings, etc.) and are similar to many other northern Italian churches of the period that were erected by the mendicant orders. But for Venice, they represent a major departure and were important undertakings, not only for their great size, but as a reflection of the city's stronger links with the *terrafirma,* to which the Republic was gradually cementing its future.

Paolo Veneziano and the Beginnings of Gothic Influence on the Arts

The interiors of the Frari, Zanipolo and Santo Stefano, unlike that of San Marco, never received any overall, coherent decorative plan. The mosaic tradition was hardly used at all, neither was the mainland practice of telling the Biblical stories in great fresco cycles. Rather, emphasis was laid on individual works of art, especially the altar polyptychs—brilliantly painted religious scenes within richly carved and gilded frames. The earlier ones were still done in the conventional Byzantine manner, but with the arrival of Paolo Veneziano (active from 1325–1360) there appeared in Venice, for the first time, an artist with a distinct personality, and one who introduced a few Gothic motifs into his later works.

It was at this time that the Pala d'Oro, San Marco's sumptuous altar screen, was being elaborated into the form we see today. That is, the older Byzantine enameled plaques and the Venetian ones in the same style were being rearranged and incorporated into a magnificent gold and silver setting studded with a wealth of precious stones—pearls, rubies, sapphires, emeralds—and surrounded by a frame of pure Gothic design, to produce one of the city's most treasured possessions.

Aside from its artistic merit, the sheer richness and extravagance of the Pala d'Oro, with its shimmering surfaces of gold, is a fitting symbol of 14th-century Venice, both for its costliness and as an example of the early link between the artistic traditions of east and west.

In 1345, the doge commissioned Paolo Veneziano to paint the wooden cover that would enclose this magnificent altar screen. The 14 paintings (now removed to the San Marco museum) that make up Paolo's cover are still mostly in the Byzantine spirit, but here and there is a hint of a new understanding of space, perspective and atmosphere. Another example of this transitioning style is his great polyptych of the Coronation of the Virgin (1354–1358), which is now in the Accademia. Again, Paolo's manner remains essentially Byzantine, especially in the side panels where the figures are still elongated and flat, with stereotypical and expressionless faces. But the new Gothic influence can also be detected not only in the obvious carving of the frame, but in the large central panel of the coronation itself. A new rhythmical sense of drawing and a new humanity now dominate the painting. This reflects the more intimate approach to religious worship that was encouraged by the mendicant orders, as opposed to the older and more austere, hierarchical tradition.

There seems, though, to be an uncertainty in the artist as to his preference between the two styles. The problem, however, appears to be solved in Paolo's successor, Lorenzo Veneziano (no relation, active 1356–1372), whose work reveals a decided turn toward the controlling Gothic influence. A good example of this is the so-called Lion Polyptych (1357),[6] also in the Accademia. Figures are more realistic, expressions more human and narrative content more lively and graphic. In addition, volumes are built up to imply a three-dimensional quality, and, more strikingly, color and line take on a new refinement and agreeableness. Although the work of the great Giotto (1270–1337), a precursor of the Tuscan Renaissance, at nearby Padua was well known at the time, his pervasive influence—solid-looking figures arranged realistically in space—is not evident in Lorenzo's paintings. For the next century, this remained true of the Venetian school of painting, which, taking the direction set by Lorenzo and sustained by growing influences from the mainland, continued to embrace the developing florid Gothic idiom that came to be known variously as the decorative or International Style.

These same influences from the west can also be seen in the more traditional Venetian artistic medium of mosaic. Good examples of this are in the complex scenes taken from the lives of Christ and of St. John the Baptist in the lunettes and domes of San Marco's Baptistry, works commissioned by Doge Andrea Dandolo around 1345. In these mosaics, elements of the Byzantine heritage remain, especially in the iconography of the episodes illustrated, but more interesting are the Gothic innovations. For instance, in the scene of the Crucifixion, the basic arrangement of the figures of Mary and John at the feet of Jesus goes back to innumerable Byzantine mosaics, but the portraits of the donors (the doge, his wife and the chancellor) are of Gothic inspiration. This influence can also be seen in the panels devoted

---

[6] Executed on a commission from a Venetian Senator, Domenico Lion.

to the life of the Baptist and especially in the lithe figure of Salome, who is dressed in spangled red and dancing for Herod.

Following the lead of the mosaicists, the sculptors were also giving expression to the new style, as can be seen at San Marco in the statues that line the iconostasis, which is itself composed of panels and columns of the most beautiful marble. These imposing sculptures of the Virgin, St. Mark and the 12 Apostles, carved and signed by the Delle Massegne brothers in 1394, reflect little or nothing of traditional Byzantine formulas, but constitute a full acceptance of the Gothic approach to art.

The Plague and Another War with Genoa

It was during these years, amidst the most flourishing period in the city's history, that an event occurred that drastically, though temporarily, interrupted its forward progress: the Bubonic Plague of 1348. Known forever after as the Black Death, this dreaded and recurring disease, carried and spread by flea-infested rats, swept out of the Crimea and entered western Europe through the port of Venice, where its effects were especially severe. Many fled the city for the countryside to escape the contagion, the source of which was not known at the time, and, for most of a year, a large part of the Rialto's enterprise was slowed to a halt. Some have estimated that the city lost about a third of its population, and although this number is probably exaggerated, its prosperity, along with those of many other urban centers, was dealt a staggering blow.

Even before the pestilence, Venice was experiencing a shortage in its most vital occupational need: able-bodied men willing to undertake the rigors of life at sea. Following the plague, the situation was even worse, and attempts were made to encourage foreigners, especially Slavs from the Dalmatian coastal ports, to enter the merchant service. This was successful to a degree and the city was just able to provide the necessary crews for its fleet when the third war with Genoa broke out in 1350. Trading rivalries and Venice's gradual reconciliation with the Byzantines, to the disadvantage of the Genoese, were the causes. However, a series of large-scale naval battles, fought from the Tyrrhenian Sea to the Aegean Sea to the Black Sea, including the bloody Battle of the Bosphorus in February 1352, in which a great many on both sides were either slaughtered or drowned, failed to tip the balance either way. In 1355 the two powers reluctantly agreed upon peace through the intercession of the Visconti of Milan, although nothing important was settled.

Venice's Mid-century Troubles

During this period the dogeship was occupied by Andrea Dandolo (1343–1354), one of the youngest and most learned to hold the office. Not yet 40 when elected, he was a humanist and teacher of the law. One of his closest friends was Francesco Petrarch, famous in his own lifetime and often referred to as the father of the Renaissance. An occasional resident in Venice who occupied a home given to him by the government, Petrarch is known to have urged the new doge to assume a leadership role for Italy in an attempt to bring some unity to the peninsula. This sound advice was premature, however, and was mostly ignored. The Venetians were apparently more interested in solutions to their more immediate problems closer to home. Dandolo's election had at first been greeted with optimism, but events proved otherwise to its early promise. Seldom did a reign suffer so many catastrophes: the plague, the five-year-long indecisive and costly war with Genoa, uprisings in Padua and in several Dalmatian cities and even a severe earthquake. Government expenses mounted, taxes increased and contention developed among the nobles. Worn out by his troubles, Dandolo died young in 1354 and was replaced by a much older, more experienced man, Marino Falier. But unfortunately this change was for the worse and the Republic's troubles were not yet over.

The course of events during the year after Dandolo's death is somewhat unclear and in dispute by historians. All that is certain is that Falier was executed for treason on April 18, 1355. He had been accused of attempting to overthrow the government and establish a dictatorship, like so many other tyrants had done on the mainland, and apparently had confessed to the charges. At the time, strong feelings were running against the establishment. The people, exasperated with the conduct of the war with Genoa, were as close as they ever came to open revolt, while the patricians were split into two hostile camps. It may never be known whether Falier actively planned a coup d'etat with the backing of some of the nobles and popular leaders, or whether he was simply the scapegoat and victim of the opposing faction, which had used force to obtain his confession. In any case, the Ducal Councilors and the Council of Ten tried and convicted the alleged conspirators between April 15 and 17 and had them all, except Falier, speedily executed by hanging them from the loggia of the palace. The doge instead was taken to the exact spot where he had earlier sworn the constitutional oath and beheaded. His death, however, did not terminate the run of misfortunes for the Serenissima. The following years saw the loss of much of Dalmatia to the King of Hungary, return visitations of the plague, an uprising in Crete in 1363 and another by the Carrara of Padua in 1369, which required much money and many troops—mercenary as well as Venetian—to put down.

On top of all this, the slave trade, an important source of income for Venice, was slowly being curtailed in western Europe. For centuries Slavs and Caucasians from beyond the Black Sea, supplemented by Greeks from the Aegean area, had been rounded up and shipped off in chains by Italian merchants, especially Venetians, for a variety of purposes. Cypress and Crete needed slaves for plantation work, Egypt for the military, European cities for domestic service and so on. But as the threat and proximity of the Turks increased, resistance developed, particularly from the church, against enslaving fellow Christians and the slave auctions on the Rialto were finally closed in 1366. By then, the public debt (the Monte Vecchio) had reached 1,500,000 ducats and was to double within a decade as the city prepared to face one of its greatest trials—the fourth, last and most perilous war with Genoa, known as the War of Chioggia (1378–1381).

The War of Chioggia

Throughout this difficult period of the mid-1300s, however, Venice had managed, to the detriment of Genoa, to hold on to most of its shipping advantages in the eastern Mediterranean, especially for cargoes moving to and from the Anatolian and Black Sea ports. Not surprisingly then, it was at a key entrance to the Dardanelles, where the Venetians had forcibly occupied the strategic island of Tenedos and threatened the free passage of Genoese ships, that once again war broke out. Several attempts to retake the island were rebuffed, so Genoa, deciding to carry the conflict closer to the enemy's home territory, ordered its battle fleet up into the Adriatic. On May 7, 1379 it met a smaller Venetian force under Admiral Vettor Pisani off the coast of Istria. The ensuing engagement, uneven from the start, ended in defeat for Pisani and the loss of most of his galleys. He was lucky to escape across the gulf and into the lagoon with his surviving ships. Incredibly, for the first time, a foreign naval force had gained control of Venice's home waters.

The news traveled fast. Within a few weeks, the king of Hungary, together with the ruling Carrara family of Padua, seizing the opportunity presented by Venice's predicament, attempted to blockade the overland approaches to the lagoon through the Veneto in order to cut off supplies and trade with the mainland. Venice was surrounded and open to attack from all sides, since its other large fleet, under Admiral Carlo Zeno, was far away raiding Genoese shipping in the eastern Mediterranean.

In command of the northern Adriatic, the Genoese fleet, coordinating their plan with the Paduans, abruptly appeared off the Lido on August 6 and proceeded to sail through the southern entrance into the lagoon, occupying the town of Chioggia. The Venetians were astounded. Suddenly they were faced with an unprecedented emergency; since Charlemagne no enemy had ever penetrated so close to home. Fortunately, however, they had not been idle. Since May they had been busy refitting a defensive flotilla and conscripting a military force. Again entrusting the leadership to their still-popular admiral, Vettor Pisani, a plan was quickly formulated to trap the Genoese fleet inside the lagoon by blocking all the channel entrances with sunken barges, while counterattacking on land in order to open up the supply routes to the west. Both undertakings were speedily implemented and, despite many attempts by the enemy to thwart the Venetians, the channels remained closed and supplies came in from the mainland. A factor in this success was the return of Zeno's fleet in January 1380, which reestablished Venetian control over the Adriatic and prevented the Genoese from reinforcing or supplying their men at Chioggia. By springtime their trapped contingent was starving and helpless; in June they surrendered.

The final peace treaty awarded Venice practically nothing. Most of Dalmatia remained in Hungarian hands, Padua continued to be semi-independent under the Carrara and Genoa retained most of its overseas colonies. However, Venice was confirmed in its manifold trading rights in the Adriatic and beyond and quickly regained its commercial prosperity. Genoa, on the other hand, torn by factionalism at home, started to decline, and was no longer able to support an aggressive foreign policy, eventually losing its independence. By simply managing to survive, Venice had achieved the real victory and never again had to contend with Genoese expansionism.

Immediately following the peace, as a response to promises made during the crisis, 30 prominent Venetians—those who had contributed the most to the war effort—were newly admitted to the ranks of the Patriciate and to the Great Council. This broadened its base and weakened the older, entrenched families' hold on power. Thereafter, for some 250 years not one of those families—Dandolo, Michieli, Morosini, Contarini, Gradenigo—which had supplied so many doges in the past, again managed to elect one of their own to that office.

Byzantine Empire Contracts as Venice Expands

In the same year the war ended, the Monte Vecchio had reached 5,000,000 ducats and the price of government bonds, which had held quite well throughout the century at around 80 to 90 (the face value was 100), suddenly plunged to 18 when interest payments were suspended out of necessity. However, when payments were resumed the following year at four percent the price gradually recovered, reaching 66 by the end of the century, at which time the public debt had also been reduced to about 3,500,000 ducats. This stabilization was indicative of a return to general prosperity and optimism. While the old enemies, Hungary and Genoa, were distracted by dynastic struggles, Venice purchased the island of Corfu in 1386 and, shortly thereafter, the Adriatic ports of Scutari and Durazzo and the port of Lepanto on the Gulf of Corinth as substitutes for the lost Dalmatian bases. In addition, a number of Aegean islands and cities in the Morea were taken over from the Byzantine Greeks, who were no longer able to defend them from the Turks. The Ottomans had achieved a great victory in 1396 at Nicopolis on the Danube against an army of some 60,000 Crusaders from all over Europe (the so-called Last Crusade). The inauspicious outcome of this battle confirmed Muslim ascendancy in the Balkans, even as it sounded the death knell for the Byzantine Empire. Only the Turks' preoccupation with their eastern frontier and their perceived lack of an effective navy saved Constantinople and its immediate surroundings for another half century.

By the year 1400, Venice had re-established its supremacy in the Adriatic and in much of the Aegean and its trading activity throughout the Mediterranean was again second to none, albeit partially at Turkish sufferance. At the same time, the domestic social and political system, stratified and tradition-bound as it was, had shown an amazing resiliency and stability. When one considers the vicissitudes the city had suffered—

papal excommunication and interdict, plague, rebellions in the colonies, an abortive coup d'etat and long costly wars with Genoa—it had demonstrated a remarkable ability to recover and rebuild its commerce, its fleets and its treasury—and at a swifter pace than its rivals. Moreover, the constitution as it had evolved was generally accepted by the majority of the inhabitants, most of whom had their roles as members of a guild, a *scuola*, or some other commercial or professional association.

The trecento, however, had been a turning point, a period of transition. Venice had entered the century as a Byzantine city in architecture, art and thought, with its principal contacts in the east. By 1400, it had firmly commenced the process of incorporating western art and ideas into its culture and increasingly shifting its focus of attention toward the mainland of Europe.

9 MAINLAND CONQUESTS OPEN VENICE TO THE RENAISSANCE: THE 15TH CENTURY

Venice had always maintained an intimate and productive relationship with its *terrafirma*—the Veneto or adjacent mainland. Much of the city's food and raw materials, especially timber and stone, came from there. The area was also the key to the Alpine routes over which the vital trading commodities passed. Earlier, the Veneto, like Lombardy as a whole, had been cut up into many small, competing towns, no one of which dominated its neighbors. But by the quatrocento the situation was rapidly changing. Increasingly aware and fearful of the growing power of France, whose Alpine border kept edging to the east, the ambitious Visconti family of Milan and the Carrara of Padua each began a program of expansion and by the turn of the century, had carved out sizable enclaves.

Venice had sometimes interfered tentatively to maintain its European alliances and commerce, but it had been cautious, even reluctant, to antagonize the Lombard cities, especially Milan. It had seemed wiser to leave a semi-independent Paduan state in between as a buffer. However, in the year 1402, the aggressive Gian Galeazzo Visconti, who had pushed Milan's borders south and east into the Romagna and even over the Apennines into Tuscany, died while fighting near Florence, leaving behind him three young sons and a long period of dynastic rivalry. For a time this limited Milanese unity and power and curtailed their potential for aggression, thereby permitting the Venetians to adopt a more expansionist policy of their own on the *terrafirma*. Accordingly, when the ambitions of the Carrara family tempted them to annex the entire area between the Adige and Brenta rivers and prompted a plea for help from the citizens of Vicenza, Venice at last felt the need to act decisively. In late 1404, negotiations having broken down, Venice sent an army against Padua, which it captured after a protracted siege. The despotic Carrara family was apprehended and executed, and the cities of Vicenza and Verona, as well as Padua, which together controlled the most vulnerable approaches to the lagoon, were brought under direct Venetian rule for the first time.

This was indicative of things to come. For Italy as a whole, the first part of the quattrocento was to see the gradual consolidation of most of the peninsula into five major power centers: the Duchy of Milan, the Republics of Venice and Florence, the Papal State, and the Kingdom of Naples.[1] The process was one of unending and bewildering intrigue, treachery and war. Within the Venetian patriciate the period was marked by two opposite and contentious points of view. One side, fearing the expense and risk of adventures on the mainland, advised a policy of rebuilding the fleet and concentrating on eastern trade and accommodation with the Turks. The other side urged an aggressive stance in the Veneto in order to command the resources there and safeguard the western commercial routes. The final decision, however, was not made until 1423. In the meantime, the Venetian government was dominated by an elderly doge with a conservative bent, Tommaso Mocenigo (1414–1423), who advised caution in upsetting traditional priorities. He accordingly cultivated the navy, eastern trade and peaceful relations on all sides. He also reduced the public debt, which had reached some 10 million ducats during the war with Padua, cutting it almost in half.

But the question persisted within the Great Council as to how Venice would survive if Milan, once again on the move under Gian Galeazzo's surviving son Filippo, should conquer the plain of Lombardy, and the Turks should continue to expand in the east. Arguing for aggression westward was Francesco Foscari (1423–1457), senator and procurator of St. Mark's, who was elected to the dogeship in 1423 upon the death of Mocenigo. Foscari soon resolved the issue by signing a treaty with Florence aimed at containing Filippo Visconti's ambitions by offensive action against him. Under the new doge, some three decades of sporadic warfare with Milan began on the mainland along with the tacit abandonment of the Byzantine Empire, which proceeded on its downward course as it was progressively dismembered by the Ottomans.

The Condottieri

At this time, wars on the Italian mainland were fought mainly by hired soldiers under mercenary captains called *condottieri* (from the *condotte,* or

---

[1] There were of course still a number of minor city-states, such as Lucca, Modena, Genoa, Mantua, etc.

contracts, they signed with their employers).[2] These were the true soldiers of fortune, who worked for the highest bidder, frequently changed sides and carefully avoided unnecessary bloodshed or decisive victories against their opposite numbers. Often refusing to fight in bad weather or during winter, they frequently prolonged their campaigns on one excuse or another, which caused costs to escalate since keeping troops in the field for long periods in an unproductive reserve capacity was an expensive proposition. Also costly were the scores of ships required that had to be specially built of shallow draught to carry armaments and supplies on the rivers of the Po Valley. To raise the money, the Venetian government increased the traditional taxes on commodity transactions and also resorted to new direct taxes, first on real estate and then on income. Finally, forced loans were reintroduced in the form of a new government bond issue paying five percent interest, henceforth called the Monte Nuovo.

Offsetting the burdens, however, were the rewards arising out of this expansionist policy and the acquisition of new territory: official positions to be filled by Venetians in conquered cities, new sources of tax revenue, estates and farm lands taken away from the former owners, the control of vital resources. So successful were these campaigns that one after another, the ancient cities of Lombardy fell to Foscari's mercenary captains, including Cremona, Brescia and Bergamo and their surrounding territories, the last being precariously close to Milan's home ground. By mid-century Venice controlled a large part of northern Italy, extending as far as the Adda River, which flows out of Lake Como southwards into the Po.[3] But, in spite of the fact that the Venetians exercised their new sovereignty with moderation and considerable local autonomy, Venice, not Milan, soon became the source of worry for the rest of Italy and caused a reshuffling of alliances. Florence switched sides and supported Milan in an effort to put a brake on Venetian aggression, and there were other re-alignments.

---

[2] The most famous *condottieri* working for Venice at one time or another during the 15th century were Carmagnola (executed for dealing with the enemy), Gattamelata (honored by an equestrian statue set up by the Venetians in Padua), Colleoni and Francesco Sforza. The last had fought for Milan, Lucca and Florence in addition to Venice, before marrying Bianca Visconti, daughter of Filippo, and later succeeded to the Visconti dukedom.

[3] Formal title to these regions was bestowed on Venice by the western emperor in 1437. They were to remain in Venetian hands to the end of the Republic.

The Fall of Constantinople

More than ever, the focus of attention for most Italians was on the kaleidoscopic shifting of enemies and allies, political intrigue and sporadic warfare up and down the peninsula. As they fought among themselves, few were concerned that the Turks, who had taken Albania in 1414 and Thessalonika in 1430, were becoming ever more menacing. Unless something was done, the ultimate collapse of what remained of the Byzantine Empire was all but inevitable. In a desperate attempt to ward off this eventuality, the eastern emperor, having pleaded for a meeting with the pope and the western princes, set off with the patriarch of Constantinople and a vast retinue of clergy and retainers to solicit military support against the Ottomans, in return for which he was willing at last to subordinate the Orthodox Church to the papacy. All the parties were to assemble in Ferrara, after traveling first to Venice in February 1438. Since this was the only time a Byzantine emperor had ever visited the city in person, elaborate celebrations were held that lasted more than three weeks before the company went on to Ferrara and later to Florence as guests of the Medici. Although a crusade was promised, it never materialized. Neither did the hoped-for union of the two churches that had been tentatively agreed upon. By the spring of 1453, the sultan's army had surrounded the city of Constantinople with some 80,000 men and was preparing to attack its imposing fortified walls. Venice at last sent out a token battle fleet (the others did nothing), but it was a half-hearted effort and too late to help. The ships did not arrive in the Sea of Marmara until after the city had been overrun and sacked by the Turks on May 29, 1453, following a 53-day siege in which more than 500 resident Venetians had been killed, along with thousands of Greek defenders, their emperor and most of his court.

Thus ended the thousand-year history of the Byzantine Empire, as well as Christian control of the Bosporus and the Black Sea trade routes. Under the circumstances the Venetians had very few choices and so began a series of long, drawn-out negotiations with the sultan conducted by ambassadors that had conveniently accompanied the fleet for just such a contingency. It required most of a year to reach an agreement. Venetian prisoners and ships were released, treaties reaffirmed and trade once more permitted to flow, though now subject to Muslim control, taxes and competition. Never again would Venice, or the West for that matter, enjoy the freedom of access, ancient trading advantages or decisive maritime superiority in the eastern Mediterranean.

The fall of Constantinople, however, shocked Italy into some semblance of unity. This materialized the following year in an agreement known as the Peace of Lodi, whereby an equilibrium was formalized between the five major peninsula powers. The treaty was especially advantageous to Venice in that it confirmed all its recent conquests on the *terrafirma*.

Late Gothic Influence on Sculpture

While Venice was thus expanding and consolidating its mainland territories, it was also experiencing a major influx of western artists and Gothic artistic influence, best represented by the carvings on the façade and column capitals of the Palazzo Ducale. These are not the inspiration of local Venetian craftsmen—few of the important sculptors working there in the first half of the century were native born—but of the Lombard school, which established an active *bottega* in Venice in the early quattrocento. The column capitals at the southeast corner of the portico continue westward to the southwest corner and around to the seventh (and larger) column facing the Piazzetta, where the building itself ended at that time. All these carvings—a total of 24—were apparently completed between 1404 and 1419 and reflect the Gothic style of Lombardy. Here in this original series are the favorite subjects of the later Middle Ages: heads of emperors, knights, crusaders, wise men; animals and birds; allegorical figures of the months, planets, virtues and vices; the differing human races; daily rituals and occupations. Here also are new Gothic motifs—rather formal, courtly, stylized figures emerging in the round from their backgrounds and touched with that human compassion and sympathy that mark the style's essence.

Even better examples and easier to appreciate are two larger sculptural groups that were probably products of the Raverti workshop. Installed around 1419 just above the level of the capitals at either end of the building facing the water, these works apparently suggest not only mankind's mortal frailties, but the importance of just laws. At the far corner is the dramatic episode of the drunkenness of Noah being pardoned by his two sons (interpreted as the clemency and tolerance of good government), while on the Piazzetta corner are the figures of Adam and Eve about to be punished

At a corner of the Doge's Palace, the Gothic sculpture of Adam and Eve tempted by the serpent.

for taking the forbidden apple (pointing out the discipline required of good government). Both groups illustrate the Gothic concern for the interdependence of man's spiritual and earthly welfare by teaching a moral lesson within the framework of a Biblical event.

Additions to the Ducal Palace

It was during this same period that the large, balconied central opening on the south side of the Great Council Room was installed on the government's order to provide an impressive setting for the doge and his councilors to be seen by the people. The balcony was placed high upon the façade, with its canopy of niches, statues and pinnacles in the Gothic style. This device to show off and glorify the persons wielding the state power was not new to the world but had been employed long before by both Byzantine and Roman emperors. In the next century a second, similar window and balcony were opened on the Piazzetta side of the Ducal Palace for the same purpose.[4]

Documentary evidence seems to indicate that by about 1419 all of this work, including the decorative elements, had been completed substantially. There was a pause for a few years until, under Doge Foscari, it was decided to extend the new building farther north along the Piazzetta by another 12 arches in the same style, with construction commencing in 1424. At first glance there is little to set this new work apart, but a closer look at the carvings of the column capitals reveals a new, more mature and finished approach, even though the subject matter of the older ones has been imitated. This is the work of sculptors from Tuscany under the leadership of Niccolo Lamberti (1375–1451). Just as Venice had earlier sent its mosaic and bronze workers to Florence, the latter, in return, was now sending its sculptors and painters north to the city on the lagoon. Influenced by Donatello and the budding Florentine Renaissance, Niccolo had moved to Venice in the second decade of the quattrocento to establish a *bottega* and an alternative tradition. He and his pupils have left the earliest surviving examples of their work in these capitals, one of which has the inscription *"duo soti florentini inc se"* for two unidentified Florentines who labored there. Also from their hands is the large sculptured group on the northwest corner, the Judgment of Solomon (again referring to wise laws) variously attributed to Pietro Lamberti (Niccolo's son), Nanni di Bartolo or Jacopo della Quercia, all Florentines working in Venice. We are at once aware of a new departure in the now less awkward, more lifelike figures that are almost entirely in the round and detached from their settings. One of these—the soldier—reminds us of Donatello's more famous statue of St. George in Florence.[5]

Still a little later in 1438 and again under the initiative of Doge Foscari, the space between the newly constructed façade of his palace and the adjoining Church of San Marco was used for the erection of a formal entrance portal to the ducal complex—an elaborate gateway and arcade suitable to link the two structures. The gateway façade itself, later called the Porta della Carta after

---

[4] And was to be used again long after by Benito Mussolini when he appeared periodically to the Fascist crowds in Rome on the balcony of the Palazzo Venezia.

[5] Two other early quattrocento Tuscan works can be seen in Venice at the end wall of the right transept of the Frari church. On the left is a wooden equestrian statue, the first in the city, of a condottiere (Paolo Savelli) by della Quercia; and on the right, a terracotta and marble monument of a Franciscan brother called Pacifico; the relief carvings from Christ's life and rich profusion of leafage and angels over the arch are ascribed to Nanni di Bartolo and Michele da Firenze (1437).

The Gothic Porta della Carta, formal entrance to the palace, above which is a statue of Doge Foscari by Bregno. On the right, above the lower corner column, is the sculptural group, the Judgment of Solomon, an early Renaissance work.

the scribes who waited there (and/or the paper decrees customarily posted there), is work from yet another *bottega*, that of Giovanni Bon (died c.1443) and his son Bartolomeo (1405–1465). They followed neither the Lombard nor the Tuscan schools, but represented a continuation and culmination of the flamboyant Gothic style, as modified by Venetian tradition. This can be noted in the intricacies and flowering detail of the various elements—the niches, the quattrofoil screen, the pinnacles and crockets, and the cherubs of the pediment—many of which were at that time gilded.

The principal sculptural group right above the main door on the lintel, that of Doge Foscari kneeling before the Lion of St. Mark (a characteristic pose signifying his personal submission and obeisance to the state), is not by any member of the Bon workshop, but is attributed to Antonio of Rigesio (near Como), known as Bregno (1426–1485), whose work is superior to most of his contemporaries and seems to represent the concluding phase of the Venetian Gothic style and a bridge to the Renaissance. The figure of Foscari is now a copy, but the fine workmanship of the original can be seen in the sculptured head of the doge—wrinkled and old but full of force and strength—now preserved in the palace museum.[6]

Behind the Porta della Carta is an arcade, at the end of which is the towering and architecturally confusing Foscari Arch. Apparently this latter structure was originally conceived in Gothic terms and partially so carried out, but significant modifications in the Tuscan or Renaissance manner were made later, producing a medley of styles. It is believed that Bregno was partly responsible for the Foscari Arch, which took its name from that doge after his death in 1457 when his body lay in state there. Bregno is certainly the sculptor of some of the statues that bestride the pinnacles above.

Returning to the façade of the Ducal Palace, it appears that Bregno also executed the three archangel statues at the three exterior corners above the loggia. Raphael, protector of pilgrims and travelers, is on the southeast corner, appropriately facing the Levant; Michael, wielding his sword and personifying militant strength, is on the southwest facing Italy where so much blood had recently been shed; and Gabriel, messenger of God and exponent of peace, is on the northwest nearest the church of San Marco.

---

[6] The original sculpture was partially destroyed by Napoleon's troops in 1797 (though the head survives intact) and was replaced in the 19th century by a good copy.

Gothic Domestic Architecture

The completion of the main part of the present Ducal Palace—the south and west sides—soon had its effect on other construction projects within the city. Especially influential was the magnificent loggia of the building, with its slender columns surmounted by the characteristic ogival arches and the elegant quatrefoil openings above, as well as the novel pinnacles along the roofline higher up. Many of these striking Gothic features soon were adapted in the design of palace façades, although the traditional use of colored marble and the customary arrangement of elevations and interior spaces remained substantially unchanged.

One of the earliest examples of Gothic domestic architecture in Venice is the Palazzo Ariani, located rather inconveniently in Dorsoduro (#2376). Here, an earlier building, (its lower story remains unchanged), was remodeled in the first half of the 1400s, using the theme of the Ducal Palace loggia to articulate the new Gothic fenestration of the upper floor, including a beautifully carved screen of stone composed of a double row of quatrefoils.

More accessible and more important are several other palazzi on the Grand Canal, each conceived and carried out in the Venetian interpretation of Gothic. The Ca' d'Oro near Rialto, built between 1420 and 1434, and three others adjoining one another farther south along the Grand Canal toward the Accademia (two for the Giustiniani family and one for the Foscari[7]) are all mid-century constructions with loggias echoing that of the Ducal Palace. There is no need, however, to examine any but the famous Ca' d'Oro, which is, as mentioned earlier, not only the epitome of the style, but the most beautiful palazzo in Venice. The façade, asymmetrical to allow for the building's internal logic, is progressively lighter and more delicate from the lower floor upwards, and has a natural, organic relationship to the total structure, as do the various decorative elements—the balustrades, fenestration, tracery, cornice, colored marbles. Here is one of the best architectural expressions of Venetian opulence, taste and synthesis of cultures from that period.

As earlier noted, much of this late Gothic construction activity was carried out under the aegis of Francesco Foscari,[8] certainly one of the most

---

[7] Designed and built by Bartolomeo Bon on commission from Doge Foscari, it is now occupied by the University of Venice.

[8] His portrait by Lazzaro Bastiani may be seen in the Corner Museum.

Doge Foscari's tomb monument in the Frari, by Bregno.

important doges in the city's history. He held the ducal office longer than any other and ruled during difficult times—retreat in the east and conflict on the mainland—that saw a permanent shift of focus for Venice. But despite his dedicated leadership, he was criticized in his last years for military misadventures and ruinous expenditures and over his strong resistance, was forced by a combination of rivals to surrender his office and abdicate in October 1457. Only a short week after doing so, worn out, angry and embittered, the old man (he was 84) died in his new palace on the Grand Canal, while the bells of Venice rang out the election of his successor. Almost at once the government had misgivings and to make amends, he was granted a lavish state funeral and was buried with honors in the Frari church near the high altar. His monument, carved a year or so later by Bregno, is another transitional piece between the Gothic and the Renaissance periods. The overall arrangement of the sarcophagus, under the familiar canopy and surrounded by effigies of the virtues, is still Gothic, but several of the figures, as well as the two soldiers in ancient armor holding back the curtains, are of Tuscan inspiration.

Pictorial Art and the Early Renaissance

The dawning Renaissance spirit—that new way of looking at man and the world around him—was slow in coming to Venice. Largely a product of central Italy, it was a truly revolutionary development, embracing as it did the revival of learning and interest in pagan literature, law and government, as well as the new, provocative humanist philosophy and the rebirth of classical art forms. In pictorial art, for example, the introduction of novel ideas to Venice was very gradual and the older decorative style hung on. The long-standing tradition of panel painting continued mostly without interruption in the still-Gothic Venetian workshops and was only slightly affected by the Umbrian, Gentile da Fabriano (died 1427), and his pupil Pisanello from Verona (died 1455), both of whom worked in Venice in the early quattrocento and carried their art to the threshold of the coming Renaissance. Unfortunately nothing of their work is extant in the city,[9] although examples by several of their Venetian followers—lesser artists such as Jacobello del Fiore (died 1439) and Michele Giambono (died 1462)—may be seen in the first room of the Accademia.

Fresco was never a Venetian specialty and when such work was required, artists were usually imported, often from Padua or Verona where local schools existed. In the second quarter of the century Paolo Uccello (1397–1475) and Andrea del Castagna (1421–1457), both Tuscan, were employed in Venice on various projects in fresco as well as mosaic. Little remains that can be definitively assigned to them personally, but some vault frescos composed in 1442 by Castagna exist in the Church of San Zaccaria and a mosaic in the Capella Mascoli at San Marco, *The Death of the Virgin,* has been attributed to one or the other. This mosaic clearly reveals characteristics of the early Tuscan Renaissance: classical architectural features, lines of perspective receding to a common vanishing point and realistic, solid, expressive figures. Along with their contemporaries and compatriots, Donatello (1386–1466) and Fra Filippo Lippi (1406–1469), who worked off and on in Padua, the influence of Uccello and Castagna was gradually brought to bear on the local artists.

Foremost of these local artists were Jacapo Bellini (c.1400–1470) and

---

[9] Their frescoes in the Ducal Palace, considered exceptional according to reports of their contemporaries, were all destroyed without record.

Antonio Vivarini (c.1415–1484). Both established family traditions and busy workshops involving many collaborators and followers. Though Vivarini was never able to break away from the Gothic style, he was influenced by the Tuscans and occasionally a few new elements do appear in his work, such as one of his larger paintings, *The Madonna with Four Saints* (1446) for the Scuola Grande della Carita', now the Accademia, where it still hangs. Here, a consistently correct treatment of space and the human figures in it and the subordination of Gothic detail to a more realistic way of looking at things indicate a slight change of approach. But, as yet, there is no evidence of any sense of movement, drama or psychological insight, which were already clearly apparent in Tuscan work of the time. Antonio Vivarini's younger brother, Bartolomeo (1430–1499) and another fellow artist, Carlo Crivelli (c. 1430–1495), also attempted to utilize the new understanding of perspective and to introduce classical motifs in their paintings, but, strongly influenced by the Paduan school dominated by Andrea Mantegna (1431–1506), they succumbed to Mantegna's emphasis on line and artificiality of surface textures, and never really left the Gothic tradition behind. As a result the Vivarini *bottega* is not representative of the developing main stream of Venetian painting, which took its cue from the Bellini family.

Jacopo Bellini's early work, now lost, was probably in the decorated Gothic style. However, at some point he fell under the influence of Gentile da Fabriano and the Tuscan painters, as shown by the solidity and realism of several of his Madonnas. The Renaissance influence is especially evident in his emphasis on depth and perspective, which can be seen in his landscapes and in his imaginative renderings of classical architecture. These achievements were taken up and refined by his two sons, Gentile (c. 1429–1507) and Giovanni (c.1430–1516), though in different directions.

Giovanni Bellini and Venetian Renaissance Religious Painting

Giovanni, the greater artist of the two, dedicated his considerable talents to expressing in his religious paintings that combination of realism and human emotional insight pioneered by the Tuscans. Taking the open, spacious feeling of his father's work and combining it with a new infusion of light and color—no longer merely decorative, but integral parts of the picture's message—his earlier works set the pattern for the main development of Venetian painting. There is also some influence of Mantegna (who

Giovanni Bellini's polyptych (1465) at the Ferrer altar in Zanipolo: the epitome of early Venetian Renaissance painting.

married Giovanni's sister), but never to the point of dominance. Though many of Giovanni's works are now elsewhere, a good example may be seen in the Correr Museum's *Crucifixion,* where the luminous, expansive mood of the landscape unites with the anguish of the figures and the drama of the moment to produce a new and consistent unity. Also in the Correr are two other works from his early period, the *Pieta* and the *Transfiguration of Christ*, both clearly reminding us of Mantegna. Most important are the background landscapes in all three paintings. They are based on views of the Veneto countryside from his father's sketchbooks and are bathed in a new luminosity—a special quality of half-light that was to be one of Giovanni's great contributions to Venetian painting.

Of even more importance is his famous polyptych on the altar of St. Vincent Ferrer in Zanipolo, done in 1465. This work confirms the decisive and final break with the Gothic past, not only within the several paintings themselves, but also in the overall attempt to coordinate the work of art with its physical setting. The paintings incorporate all of the

Giovanni Bellini's tryptych (1488) in the Frari's sacristy reaffirms his genius.

psychology of the personages, the sweep of the background scenes, the treatment of light and color as emanating out from, not applied to, the picture surface, as well as including a concession to the Paduan emphasis on line. Even the frame, with its classical motifs in the Renaissance style, probably the first of its kind in Venice, suits the theme. After this breakthrough, a logical relationship between this new manner of painting and the architectural surroundings became not only appropriate but possible, as church interiors were redesigned to supplant the old.

As the century wore on, Giovanni progressively left behind the influence of Mantegna by softening outlines, enriching the atmospheric effects and permitting color to reassert itself in the historic Venetian tradition. Illustrating the direction of his art during this middle phase are two of his best-known works. Both are in Venice and both are in the form commonly known as *sacra conversazioni,* a conventional arrangement of a group of saints surrounding the Virgin who they communicate with in a spiritual rather than a vocal sense. One of these works is the San Giobbe altarpiece (c. 1485), which was painted for the church of that name, but is now in the Accademia; the other is the Frari Tryptych (1488) in that church's sacristy. In each we

Gentile Bellini's painting of the *Miracle of the True Cross* (it was lost in the canal and then found) provides an excuse for recording the details of the city and portraits of the citizens.

can clearly see the great stride forward the artist has made in relation to his immediate predecessors. Giovanni's subsequent work and final maturity falls into the period of the Venetian High Renaissance during the 16th century.

Vittore Carpaccio and Narrative Painting

Meanwhile, Giovanni's brother, Gentile, following more in the footsteps of their father, was carrying on a different Venetian tradition, the execution of large-scale narrative works often set in the context of Venetian city life or ceremonial occasion. Frequently painted on commission for one of the *scuole*, these had always been popular as they illustrated all the genre details of the city, its buildings, canals, bridges and *campi*, as well as depicting many leading citizens arrayed in the colorful costumes of the time. Several of Gentile's works dating from the late 1400s can be seen in the Accademia.

Finally, in this context, Vittore Carpaccio must be mentioned (c.1455–

Vittore Carpaccio's painting, also of the recovery of the true cross, still is in the Gothic tradition, but with Renaissance additions.

1526). He was apprenticed to the Bellini *bottega* in the 1480s and, like Gentile, used the city, often combined with a vivid imagination, as the raw material for his large narrative paintings, also often commissioned by the *scuole* but now mostly re-arranged in the Accademia. One cycle, however, remains in situ—his famous series for the Scuola di San Giorgio degli Schiavoni (Confraternity of the Slavs or Dalmatians) depicting scenes from the lives of the three protectors of Dalmatia, the saints George, Tryphon and Jerome.

It is interesting to compare another work by Carpaccio, *The Miracle of the True Cross,* with Gentile's painting of the same subject. Both are in the Accademia and both were produced within a few years of each other at the end of the quattrocento. Each artist faithfully recorded every detail of the city surrounding the point selected, in Gentile's case the Ponte di Lorenzo and in Carpaccio's, the Ponte Rialto. Each painting presents realistic representations of the personalities of the time, their costumes and equipage—including their gondolas—as well as an understanding of the new perspective. But whereas Gentile confined himself to a more prosaic approach in a stiffer, more formal Gothic tradition, the younger artist was able to infuse the scene with the magic of Venetian light as pioneered by Giovanni Bellini. Moreover, not content with a straightforward recordation of the scene, which would have shown only the old wooden bridge, the Fondamenta del Vin and the actual Gothic buildings on either side of the canal, he added on the left a beautiful Renaissance loggia in the new style from his own imagination.

Carpaccio was also responsible for another impressive cycle of paintings, the Legend of St. Ursula, undertaken between 1490 and 1499 for one of the smaller *scuole* dedicated to that saint, and now displayed in the Accademia. They illustrate a then-popular legend concerning the martyrdom of a Princess Ursula of Brittany in a series of episodes which serve merely as a pretext to glorify and indeed exaggerate the rich life of the 15th century in general and the Venetian environment in particular. Unlike other more literal representations of the city, these paintings evoke the spirit of the time and place. Some details derive from the Byzantine heritage—the domes, the minarets, the pennants flying; some are pure Venetian—the costumes, the ships, the bridges; while others, especially the architectural particulars, are an imaginative mixture of traditional Gothic forms with the artist's own interpretation of Tuscan Renaissance ideas.

Here Carpaccio tells the story of Ursula's betrothal to an English prince as arranged by ambassadors, the young couple's meeting and embarkation on their pilgrimage to Rome, despite being forewarned in a dream of disaster, their arrival and baptism by the pope in the Holy City, and finally their death and martyrdom near Cologne on the trip back. The ten-year period over which the work was carried out permits us to observe a marked maturation of Carpaccio's style and craftsmanship. The paintings were not, however, executed chronologically, as one of the last episodes, *Arrival in Cologne,* was actually painted first and shows a less balanced composition and a less clear approach to color when compared to the later ones, for example the *Arrival and Return of the Ambassadors* and the *Meeting of Ursula and Her Husband.* These pictures, crowded with the life and costumes of the time—the many distinctive faces were obviously portraits—are among the most sumptuous scenes with vivid colors and skillful control of spatial effects, another clear statement of the nascent Venetian Renaissance in the field of painting.

Renaissance Architecture Appears in Venice: Pietro Lombardo

For indeed Renaissance architecture had by then already been introduced into Venice. It found its earliest expression in a rather odd place—the main portal of the Arsenale designed by Antonio Gambello (active 1458–1481) in 1460.[10] The parts of the entrance that Gambello constructed—the archway, the four Greek marble columns, the entablature and pediment, portions of which were taken from older buildings—seem to have been inspired by the architect's studies of Roman triumphal arches and might be considered something of a fluke since his other works at this time were in the Gothic style. (The statues and terrace were added later.)

More important is Pietro Lombardo (c. 1438–1515), who was trained in Tuscany and who began a little later the gradual process of designing and redesigning a number of Venetian churches in the new style. An early project was the rebuilding of the Church of San Giobbe in 1470. Here, Lombardo's work transformed a recently completed Gothic building designed by Gambello (parts of Gambello's construction remain—the windows on the south side, the exterior pilasters of the apse and the bell tower) into an almost Tuscan building. Of particular merit are the fine cornices done in the manner of the Florentine, Brunelleschi, that support the main dome of the crossing. Lombardo's work also includes the chancel, side chapels and the central doorway with its carved lunette and statues of saints.

After this, in the 1480s, came the small church of Santa Maria dei Miracoli, which is considered by many to be the most beautiful church in Venice and which Pietro worked on with his sons, Tuillio and Antonio, for nine years. Constructed to enshrine a painting of the Madonna believed to have miraculous powers, it is an exquisite jewel of Renaissance architecture, both for its artistic unity and originality, inside and out, and for the superb integration of the new motifs with the traditional Venetian use of colored marble. And it achieves this despite the fact that the architect largely ignores the relationship between the external structure—the cornices for example— and the internal logic of the building. But color, texture and the play of light, both outside and in, form a classically balanced and unified whole.

In the construction of Santa Maria dei Miracoli, the Lombardi truly

---

[10] The main yards and working areas of the Arsenale had only been roofed over in the 1450's in order to speed ship construction in any kind of weather.

S. Maria dei Miracoli, Pietro Lombardo's Renaissance "jewel box" church with its varied colored marble façade.

created a feast for the eyes. The striking façade, with its dramatic display of carved pilasters, arches and cornices framing polychrome panels of red (porphyry), green (verde antique) and mottled yellow marble, is only an introduction to the amazing interior, where all traces of the Gothic style have been left behind. The plinths, squared columns, capitals, friezes and semicircular arches inside the church, which are all intricately etched with classical designs—garlands, tendrils, leaves, sea serpents—and surrounded by solid walls of veined marble, clearly announce the Venetian Renaissance. A coffered, barrel-vaulted ceiling crowns the nave, and over the altar, a small cupola is supported on pendentives, each of which bears a roundel with low relief carvings of the Four Evangelists. The altar itself, situated on a raised level reached by a steep, wide staircase in the center, is the focal point of the entire scheme and shelters the highly venerated "miraculous" painting, which was the raison d'être for the church.

A somewhat similar treatment of a secular building can be seen in the

The interior of S. Maria dei Miracoli displays all the new Renaissance elements: squared columns, rounded arches, coffered ceiling, classical reliefs and carvings.

exterior façade of the Palazzo Dario on the Grand Canal, also by Pietro (1487), where the more traditional Venetian use of colored marble and an asymmetrical arrangement is beautifully combined with the rounded arches and columns of the new style. The Miracoli and the Dario were the first buildings in Venice to make practical, architectural use of the idealized geometrical forms underlying Renaissance theory—the circle and half-circle (used in marble disks, roundels, domes, windows and arches), the square, the cube and the triangle (modular shapes and panels, linear friezes and cornices, pediments)—as well as the many motifs from classical antiquity—the capital orders, shields and plaques, swags of flowers, vines, urns and a hundred others revived by that generation of builders.

Even more sophisticated and original was Pietro's handling of the asymmetrical façade of the Scuola Grande di San Marco, which he and his sons constructed between 1487 and 1490. Although Gothic revivalists later

The late quattrocento façade of the Scuola di San Marco is the product of two architects, Pietro Lombardo, who created the original design, and Mauro Coducci, who added the upper story.

deplored it, the façade is one of the most unusual in Italy and is remarkable for its Renaissance arches and pediments, its variety of color, its carved reliefs (some executed by the Lombardi), and, especially, its novel attempts at perspective by means of marble paneling.

Mauro Coducci and Architectural Balance

The upper story of the façade of the Scuola di San Marco, however, with its harmonious lunettes across the top, was added later in 1495 by a different architect with another perspective. This was Mauro Coducci (1440–1504), who was called in to finish the building. Though he, too, was inspired by the Florentines—Brunelleschi, Michelozzo and Alberti—he differs strikingly from the Lombardi. His emphasis is on organic balance, a structural logic and the correlation of exterior architectural features with the interior spaces, rather than a major interest in the decoration of surfaces. This approach is

151

The façade of San Zaccaria by Coducci and the Scala del Bovolo.

evident in the church of San Zaccaria, which had been started in the Gothic style by Gambello, but remodeled in the Renaissance style by Coducci, who was again called in to complete a project commenced by others. The façade of this church with its triple curved crown, one of Coducci's trademarks, is considered his masterpiece.

In a similar vein, Coducci was responsible for two other important churches, Santa Maria Formosa in 1492 and San Giovanni Crisostomo in 1497. He gave both of these churches a centralized Greek-cross configuration, with a dome over the crossing, harkening back not only to Eastern tradition, but also to Brunelleschi and the other humanist architectural theorists who ultimately came to favor this over the basilican plan. In these two cases, he was able to start from the beginning with a unified concept and the exteriors of both these churches are the logical expression of their internal arrangements.

Coducci's secular architecture also left its imprint on the city, for near the end of the quattrocento, he designed a number of impressive palaces that

Gentile Bellini's procession painting, our earliest exact view of the Piazza San Marco as it was in 1496.

decisively influenced his successors. The two most important, both on the Grand Canal, are the Palazzo Corner-Spinelli and the Palazzo Vendramin-Calergi. Although traditional Venetian characteristics remain in the overall fenestration and the general lightness of both buildings, the earlier brick façades are now replaced by Istrian marble and several Florentine Renaissance features are introduced: the double windows contained within hemispheric arches, the prominent columns and cornices of classical inspiration, and, in the Corner-Spinelli, the heavy rustication of the lower part of the building. Most importantly, the emphasis, especially in the Vendramin-Calergi,[11] has subtly been diverted from the vertical, as it is, for example, in the Palazzo Dario, to the horizontal line of the canal.

During these same busy years, Coducci somehow found time to also design two of the most familiar landmarks in the city, the Procuratie Vecchie and the adjoining clocktower, which together form the north side of the Piazza San Marco. The earliest authentic view we have of this area is from Gentile Bellini's remarkable painting, *The Procession of the True Cross* (1496),

---

[11] Like many other Venetian palaces, this impressive building, originally constructed for the Loredan, changed hands many times. For awhile it was owned by the Calergi and later by the Vendramin, both wealthy families, who were among those admitted to the patriciate following the Chioggia war. Eventually it housed the notorious and extravagant Duchess de Berry (mid-19th century), as well as Richard Wagner who died there in 1883. It is now used as the Municipal Casino.

now in the Accademia, which clearly depicts in minute detail the northeast corner of the Piazza as it was then. The old residences of the Procurators of St. Mark, with their Byzantine façade of porticos and loggias, can be seen on the left, but the clocktower did not yet exist. Then, in the next few years, Coducci introduced to the scene that elegant Renaissance building with its spectacular clock, its colored marble, its winged lion of St. Mark and, surmounting the entirety, its famous figures of the two Moors hammering the great bell at the top. All of this was completed in the year 1500, four years after Bellini's picture, and can be seen in Jacapo de Barbari's engraving of the city.

The two side wings to the tower do not appear in the engraving since they were not added until a few years later by Pietro Lombardo. Also, Barbari's view of the Procuratie Vecchie still shows the older medieval building, which was not altered on Coducci's designs into a Renaissance façade with an additional story above until the next decade.

Perhaps one of the last notable examples of quattrocento architecture, and certainly the most unusual, is the curious rear façade of the Palazzo Contarini (near Campo San Luca) with its Scala del Bovolo (spiral staircase) apparently built in 1499 by Giovanni Candi, a follower of Coducci. The stairs are enclosed in a cylindrical tower pierced with a series of Renaissance arched openings. As each of the five stories of the palace is progressively reduced in height toward the top, the gradient of the stairway is ingeniously made to accommodate itself so as to not only properly meet each landing, but also to appear aesthetically correct. The building is difficult to locate, as it is tucked behind others and down a narrow alley, but worth the trouble seeking out.

Renaissance Sculpture: Antonio Rizzo

We have seen earlier the first incipient evidence of Renaissance sculpture in the façade carvings of the Ducal Palace by Florentine workers (e.g. The Judgment of Solomon) and in the statues high up on the Arco Foscari by Bregno. Also mentioned was the beautiful tomb of Doge Foscari in the Frari, which, conceived and carried out by Bregno, perhaps assisted by his pupil, Antonio Rizzo (1430–1498), also reveals a few Renaissance characteristics. More obviously Renaissance in style is the vast scheme directly opposite Foscari's monument, the tomb of the Doge Nicolo Tron, which was carried

The tomb monument of Doge Nicolo Tron was carried out in 1473 by Antonio Rizzo in Renaissance style albeit with a few Gothic holdovers.

Antonio Rizzo's lifelike statue of Eve (c. 1480), influenced by Tuscan and north European work, is his masterpiece.

out somewhat later in 1473 by Rizzo. There are a few remnants of the Gothic remaining—for example, the stance of the figures in the upper tier, executed by Rizzo's assistants—but the overall architectural arrangement, the figures in the round including the doge himself, the decoration of the pilasters, the reliefs—all confirm the triumph of the classical revival in Venice.

Rizzo's two masterpieces, however, are the twin marble statues of Adam and Eve (c.1480), which once stood outside in niches in the Foscari Arch, but are now replaced by bronze copies while the originals are kept in the Ducal Palace. These lifelike figures, certainly impressive in the history of Venetian sculpture, derive their inspiration from Florentine work, but the basic lessons of Donatello—realism, classical *contraposto*, psychological insight—have been slightly modified by a north European influence in treating the human figure—for example, the narrow shoulders and wide pelvis of the Eve—rendering a less ideal but more natural result.

Opposite the Foscari Arch where the bronze copies of the statues now stand rises the so-called Giant's Staircase, which serves to connect the axis of the Foscari Arcade with the entrance to the doge's quarters. These stairs, together with the façades added on either side of the old eastern wing (one façade faces the courtyard, the other faces the canal known as the Rio di Palazzo), were constructed from designs by Rizzo, who was put in charge of the palace works following a serious fire that damaged the building in 1483. At the time a complete demolition of the eastern wing was considered, but instead it was rebuilt to conform to its original layout and the new façades were made to fit the existing structure, as the window arrangements testify. This building, the original Palatium Ducis, had always housed the doge's apartments and his small chapel, as well as anterooms, waiting rooms and meeting rooms for the various government bodies.[12] Together with the adjacent old Torresella at the southeast corner, the remainder of the east wing was used as an armory where weapons of war and defense were kept and as a depository for precious municipal treasures and archives, such as enemy trophies, papal and imperial edicts, illuminated manuscripts and codices, sea charts and maps.

It seems the canal façade was completed first and incorporates some of the elements of Rizzo's Tron Monument, a severe but consistent

---

[12] For example, the Sala del Collegio where ambassadors were received, the Sala del Senato, the Sala del Consiglio dei Dieci, etc.

Canaletto's painting shows the Giant's Staircase, so called for the two oversized statues of Mars and Neptune at the top, leading to the doge's apartments.

Right: The tombs of four doges at Zanipolo, three by Pietro Lombardo, illustrate the progress of Renaissance sculpture: Malipiero's (upper left), Mocenigo's (upper right), and Marcello's (lower left). Vendramin's tomb (lower right) is by his son, Tullio.

Renaissance design when compared to the overdone exterior facing the courtyard. The latter façade, with its extravagant use of classical motifs and excessive ornamental reliefs that were all grafted to a Gothic building, is perhaps more the legacy of Pietro Lombardo, who took over as supervisor in 1498 when Rizzo, accused of embezzling construction funds, was forced to flee the city.

Pietro Lombardo as Sculptor

Like Rizzo, by whom he was influenced, Pietro Lombardo was equally renowned as a sculptor. His greatest achievements in that medium—three tomb monuments for as many doges—are all concentrated at Zanipolo and each of them shows a more decided commitment to the new style. The earliest, created for Doge Pasquale Malipiero (mid-1460s), can be compared with the Foscari tomb and still contains the Gothic canopy (for the last time). But, it also exploits the Florentine spirit in the general arrangement of the tabernacle, the reliefs and the decorative carvings on the corbels, pilasters and entablature. In addition, Pietro's north Italian heritage (more specifically, the influence of the Paduan, Mantegna) can be seen in the somewhat harsh linear modeling of the figures in the relief under the arch at the top of the monument.

Next in point of time is the tomb of Doge Pietro Mocenigo, constructed between 1476 and 1481. In Mocenigo's tomb all Gothic influence has been left behind and the sculptures and motifs, though combined in a traditional Venetian arrangement, are of a markedly Renaissance character. The fine quality of the reliefs, the realism and individuality of the several figures, as well as their relationship to the architecture of the tomb as a whole, mark this as an impressive step forward. This work should be compared to Rizzo's slightly earlier Tron Monument in the Frari.

Lastly, Pietro's tomb for Doge Nicolo Marcello, probably created a little later, is the artist's culminating achievement in this medium. All the humanist ideas and lessons from the Florentine Renaissance are nobly expressed in the arrangements and proportions of the overall composition, the elegance of the reliefs and the modeling of the figures, so that this work has been extolled as one of the most impressive sculptural groups in Venice. On the other hand, critics point out that it also represents an overly conscious awareness of the demands of classicism, which was to steadily influence

Venetian culture in the next century.

Pietro's sons carried on their father's tradition and one of them, Tullio, is also well represented at Zanipolo by several tombs. The most important of these, his masterpiece, is the one for Doge Andrea Vendramin (1492) and is of exceptional size and quality. Again, as in his father's Mocenigo monument, elements of which he borrowed, the reliefs and statues, especially those of the two warriors in Roman armor, are impressively carved. Beyond that, the logic and balance of the entire architectural composition presents an even more convincing statement than the earlier one.

The Statue of Bartolomeo Colleoni

Not surprisingly, it is to a Florentine, and not a north Italian sculptor, that we owe by far the greatest of Venice's 15th-century monuments, the majestic and imposing equestrian statue of the condottiere Bartolomeo Colleoni, placed on a high pedestal just outside the church of Zanipolo. Here, in bronze, is the embodiment of the age, a symbol of the city in its most triumphant posture, the Renaissance spirit in martial trappings.

The story of the statue is well known. Colleoni, born in Bergamo, was a foreigner like most mercenary captains, but he had served the Republic faithfully for many years and died there in 1471. In his will he left some 216,000 gold ducats plus lands and other property to the Republic on the condition that an equestrian monument be erected to him in a space adjacent to San Marco. Since no one, not even the greatest of the doges, had ever been so honored, it was an impossible request. However, it would have been equally impossible for the government to turn down such a large gift. Accordingly, the thorny problem was neatly circumvented by assigning his memorial to the *campo* at the Scuola (not the Church) of San Marco, which is discreetly removed from the city's center.

The sculptor assigned to Colleoni's monument was the Florentine Andrea del Verrochio (1435–1485), the teacher of Leonardo da Vinci. With this commission and in his last years, he produced his masterpiece. Horse and rider are as one, both responsive and alert, disciplined and powerful. Together, they personify those qualities the city sought to convey to its enemies, and also sought, sometimes in vain, in its condottieri: strength, confidence and determination.

But in a sense the statue is really out of character for Venice, which had

The equestrian statue of the condottiere Bartolomeo Colleoni, Andrea del Verrochio's masterpiece.

no cult of personality, no subservience to a dynasty or a tyrant. Even though it considered itself imperial, the Republic was never in the same category as other capital cities such as Constantinople or Rome. Venice had few manifestations of power or grandeur, no imposing circuit of walls, no grand avenues, no triumphal arches, no amphitheaters in which to rally the crowds and no other equestrian monuments. Even the few doges honored by public statues are shown not as commanding figures but as more humble men, like the carving of Francesco Foscari kneeling before the lion of St. Mark.

Nevertheless, the Colleoni statue provides us with a striking glimpse into the 15th-century world of the mercenary captains and their importance to the community, and constitutes a work of art of which such a severe critic as Ruskin could say, "I do not think there is a more glorious sculpture existing in all the world."

An Unstable Balance of Power at the End of the 15th Century

Most of the nine doges that followed Foscari to the end of the century were in office for relatively short terms. It was a period of almost continual struggle against the Ottoman Turks. Although Venice had occasional support from Hungary and Poland,[13] as well as from some of the other Italian states, there were few victories. In the 1460s Venice made a valiant effort to take over the Morea (Peloponnesus), but by late century it had not only given this up, but had also lost Negroponte and its other bases in the northern Aegean. However, Venetian ships were still able to trade and occasionally raid there, and its control of the Adriatic and Ionian Seas, including the key islands of Corfu, Cephalonia and Zante, was unimpaired. Crete remained a colony, and Caterina Corner, heiress of an old and very wealthy Venetian family, became the queen of the Island of Cyprus, long valuable for its sugar and cotton plantations, which was to lead to its acquisition by Venice in 1489.[14] But even

---

[13] The Kingdoms of Hungary and Poland were two of the largest states in Europe during the 15th century and both were directly contiguous to the Ottoman Sultanate.

[14] In 1468 Caterina Corner (in Venetian dialect, Cornaro in Italian) had married with great pomp the King of Cyprus, whose family had acquired the island in 1192 from the Knights Templars. On ascension to the throne after her husband's death, she was persuaded by the Council of Ten to abdicate and authorize the annexation of the island to the Venetian Empire. In return she was awarded the fief of Asolo in the Veneto and an annual income of 8,000 ducats. She was the only female ever to rule over a territory of the Republic.

though Venice controlled these assets, on balance the Turks had become the masters of the eastern Mediterranean.[15]

On the *terrafirma*, the last half of the century witnessed a measure of stability, thanks in part to the Peace of Lodi and to the continuing efforts of the Sforza of Milan and the Medici of Florence, who acted together to thwart any serious aggressions or upset of the status quo by the other powers. At the same time, however, no common political objectives ever materialized among the five larger states of the peninsula. The governments of Naples and the Papal State were still tyrannical feudal regimes, while Milan and Florence, though more progressive, were too nationalistic to consider surrendering any degree of their sovereignty. Venice itself, the richest and most liberal, whose "republican" institutions were often admired by others and which was a logical nucleus for Italian unity, never made the slightest effort to encourage any trust among its neighbors. Francesco Barbaro, humanist, statesman and one of the city's most admired citizens, dreamt of a new alliance of Italian powers, much as Machiavelli did of a new prince to unify the peninsula. But with all the internal rivalries, the mutual suspicions and the dependence on mercenary armies, Italy could neither unite nor defend herself, and the stage was set for domination by foreigners in the next century.

---

[15] By now, their rule had consolidated itself south of the Danube, throughout the Balkans and the Greek Peninsula. Even the island of Rhodes, occupied by the Knights Hospitallers of St. John for almost two centuries, came under assault. An attempted invasion in 1480 by the Turks was repulsed and they were held off for a time. Finally, however, the Knights were forced to leave and were resettled at Malta in 1522.

10 THE GOLDEN AGE OF VENICE: THE 16TH CENTURY

The 16th century has been called Venice's Golden Age, not because the city grew more prosperous in relation to its competitors, but because of its great cultural achievements, especially in the field of painting. Venice did enter the year 1500 wealthy, proud and self-confident, but it would soon face a combination of economic and political challenges over which it could exercise progressively less control. The rounding of the Cape of Good Hope and the discovery of America were to induce the world's major trade routes, traditionally centered in the Mediterranean, to shift gradually elsewhere. Spain and France had not only acquired, for the most part, their modern geographic scale, but also both had forged military powers that were out of proportion to all their neighbors. Meanwhile in the east, the Ottoman Empire continued to encroach on European territory. All these factors were to have an adverse effect on Italy and particularly Venice.

It was France that first upset the status quo by mounting a series of invasions of the peninsula around the turn of the century in an attempt to perfect a royal claim to the throne of Naples. But this only served to aggravate the Spanish, who also held a claim, and led to a struggle between the two powers that conveniently took place not on their own territories, but up and down a disunited Italy that was helpless to control the situation. Several years of chaotic fighting were followed in 1503 by a Spanish victory in the south. The Kingdom of Naples was placed under a Spanish viceroy, but the French were allowed to retain control over parts of Northern Italy, including Savoy and parts of Lombardy.

During these same years the Turks had been applying increased pressure on land and at sea and had won several important battles. By 1503 the Venetian strongholds of Modon and Coron in southern Greece were lost, as were several others in Albania. Accordingly, to hold what was left of its colonies, especially the newly acquired island of Cyprus, the Great Council grudgingly concluded that war in the East was too problematic and expensive and that negotiation might bring greater rewards. Reluctantly the Republic sent out a delegation to arrange peace with the Ottomans and obtained a treaty.

The League of Cambrai and Spanish Triumphs

The decision not to continue the struggle against the Turks but to make a deal with the Muslims did not go down well with the Christian West. Moreover, this alleged breach of faith was further compounded by a brazen and poorly timed move by Venice to enlarge its dominion to the south by taking over a sizable area in the Romagna, including the cities of Ravenna, Rimini, Cervia and Faenza, traditionally vicariates of the Papal State. Together these affronts brought on the combined enmity of Venice's neighboring European states, an antagonism formalized a few years later in 1509 as the League of Cambrai.[1] The avowed purpose of the League, forged by the fiery Pope Julius II, was to punish Venice for its treaty with the Turks and aggressions on the mainland and to strip the Republic of its Italian possessions. Besides the not-unexpected excommunication and interdict, the most frightening aspect for Venice was the number of powers arrayed against it: Spain (which was promised several Venetian enclaves in southern Italy, as well as formal confirmation by the pope of its claim to the Kingdom of Naples), France (which wished to enlarge its territory in Lombardy), the Hapsburg emperor (who wanted to repossess long lost imperial fiefs in the Veneto and Friuli), and Julius (who would reimpose the church's sovereignty over those areas in the Romagna claimed by the papacy).

Had the allies stuck together they would have easily accomplished their purposes, especially after the Venetian army was routed at the bloody Battle of Agnadello near Milan (May 14, 1509). But the survivors fell back to defend their lagoon, quickly raised a citizen militia and prepared for a siege. At the same time, the towns of Brescia, Verona and Padua, which had been forcibly occupied by the French and Germans, rose in revolt. And before long, the pope had second thoughts about serving up a large portion of Italy to foreign powers and the alliance fell apart. The League's very scope, made up of such diverse interests, was its fatal weakness. Conniving with the Spanish and even the enemy—Venice had diplomatically sought a reconciliation—Julius was soon at war with the invading French. By 1512, he had them in retreat and the Venetians reoccupied almost everything they had lost, with the exception of the cities in the Romagna, which were returned to the papacy. Venice had narrowly escaped, but its chances for Italian leadership and ultimately, for

---

[1] Cambria, France where the parties met to sign the treaty.

Italian unity, were gone.

This, however, was not the end of the matter. In 1515, the French, now led by their dashing young king, Francis I, tried once more to enlarge their rule on the peninsula. But this time they were up against an even more formidable opponent in the newly crowned Charles V, the most powerful man in Europe. Charles was King of Spain and Naples and soon to be elected Holy Roman Emperor, heir to both the Hapsburg dominions and those of Spain. The ensuing struggle was long and arduous, but the French defeat was inevitable. By 1529, following the disgraceful sack of Rome by imperial troops (the papacy had again switched sides), all of Italy, with the notable exception of Venice and its territories, was either directly or indirectly in the hands of the Spanish. At the same time, the Ottomans, having overrun most of Hungary and the Danube Valley, as well as Egypt and the North African coast, had managed, by means of an almost invincible army and a renewed fleet, to expand their dominion to its maximum extent.

Thus, within a few decades, Italy, which had in many respects been the commercial center of Europe and the well-spring of its culture, suddenly found itself occupied by foreigners and pressed on all sides. The meteoric rise and domination of the Spanish and Turkish states, the new opportunities in America and East Asia reached now by new routes, the growth of rival trading cities in the north of Europe, the impending Protestant revolt—all these inexorably put the Italians on the defensive and undermined their confidence and prosperity. Only Venice survived independent, and it was wedged in between the two colossi of the Hapsburg and Ottoman Empires. The Serenissima's only hope was through alliances—now with France against the Spanish and later with Spain against the Turks. Remarkably, Venice managed these alliances for the rest of the century by means of its fleet, its money and especially by its tenacious diplomacy. Venetian diplomacy, in fact, became legendary and its ambassadors, posted regularly to all the courts of Europe, renowned.

The Final Evolution of the Venetian Constitution

Equally admired was the Venetian constitution, which was by now firmly cast into its permanent form and little changed in its historic structure. The Great Council, always the source of all power, continued its exclusive, hereditary character, but by the early cinquecento had reached a membership of more than 2,000 nobles. The council was too large for the daily conduct of business, but met regularly to elect the various intermediate bodies and to confirm their acts. One of these was the Senate, of primary importance in the hierarchy, but it too was rather large, made up of 120 members. So to expedite business brought before it, some 16 Savii (sages or wise men) were selected and each delegated a specific area of responsibility—commerce, the navy, the colonies, etc. The Savii, in turn, were required to meet on a regular basis with the Signoria and together formed a kind of Council of Ministers called the Collegio, which worked out specific proposals to be voted on by the Senate as a whole.

At the same time the Council of Ten, originally established to deal with limited but urgent matters that threatened the government, had gradually expanded its jurisdiction. For example, it now supervised the domestic police, the suppression of dissidents and factions and the disciplining of officers acting beyond their authority or any patrician involved in treason or other high crime. Occasionally the Ten had even attempted to encroach into foreign affairs and finance, traditionally the purview of the Senate, but this invariably provoked a reaction within the Great Council, which was wary of the Ten's invasive propensities and jealous of its own prerogatives.

While there was no separation of legislative, judicial, or executive powers—all three functions were exercised by each of the various bodies—the overlapping of authority insured a check on power and discouraged its concentration in any one branch. In theory all the nobles sitting in the Great Council were eligible for the important offices (the Ten, ambassadors, *proveditori,* governors, fleet admirals, etc.), but in practice most were filled by members of wealthy well-connected families. The actual method of nomination and election by lot and by secret ballot was so complicated as to defy description, but cumbersome as it was the Venetians continued to put their trust in it. Although bribery and undue influence were ever-present, power was never permanently concentrated in one or a few noble families.

Since most terms of office were limited, expertise in running the government usually devolved upon the permanent civil service, the secretaries and notaries, whose tenure was more or less continuous and independent of the shifting political forces around them. Required by law to be of Venetian birth and proud of their status, these men exerted considerable influence, especially their highest officer—the Chancellor—who held office for life and took precedence in all ceremonial functions.

As we have seen, Venice had never fallen under the heel of a tyrant as did so many other Italian city-states of that age—such as the Visconti in Milan, the Borgia in Ferrara—nor did it fall under the effective control of one family as Florence did under the Medici. Its constitution and political leadership did, however, have some similarities with those of the Tuscan capital prior to the Spanish dominance. Both demanded that no man put himself above the law and both required rotation in office, limited terms and accountability by the office holder. While Florence permitted more men of humble birth to rise to the top, in practice the wealthy generally provided the leadership in both cities. At the same time, the theory of republicanism as each defined it was highly praised and defended, as were those aspects of a liberal education—the study of the classics for example—that broadened the view and provided the semantic tools to carry on the nation's business and politics. This was the civil humanist's real goal—to use the new learning not just as an end in itself, but as a means for safeguarding the republican ideals of freedom and independence.

By the 16th century, the Venetian constitution was universally recognized and admired by scholars all over Europe, even by the proud Florentines who at various times tried to adopt some of its features. But the Florentine republic had finally succumbed to Spanish power, while La Serenissima miraculously managed to survive and preserve its independence.

Venetian Financial Advantages and Increased Competition

To a degree the survival of Venice was due to its fabled wealth, the envy of all. Not only had the Venetian gold ducat become one of the primary monetary standards of Europe, but it has also been estimated that by the year 1500, annual government revenues amounted to about 1,000,000 ducats and were to double as the century progressed.[2] The income of the larger polities exceeded this (the Ottoman and Spanish Empires and France), but compared to the vast majority of the smaller European states (Milan, Naples, Florence, Burgundy, Portugal, England) this was two, three and four

---

[2] Derived from direct and indirect taxes on the citizens, salt sales, payments from mainland jurisdictions and overseas colonies.

times the amount their rulers were able to collect.[3] Moreover, Venice was able to reduce its bonded debt dramatically during the 1500s, though often at heavy discounts to holders.

Much of the government's business was carried on with the aid of the *giro* banks. Just as merchants were no longer required to make payment for their many transactions in coin or bullion, but simply received a debit to their account with a reputable banker, similarly, the government could order goods and services from suppliers and pay them with credits to their respective accounts. The mechanics of this were simple. The merchant or government official making payment appeared in person before a banker—if in Venice itself, always at one of his benches under the portico at Rialto—where the transfer was noted down in his ledgers. Credit with a sound *giro* bank was literally as good as gold.

Venetian trade in the 16th century did not contract sharply because of the new trade routes, as is popularly thought, but its nature changed. For example, the Portuguese ships that rounded Africa and captured part of the pepper and spice trade from India cut into Venetian shipments via the Red Sea and Egypt. However, this was only temporary and, in any case, the European demand for these items doubled during these years, so that by the 1560s Venetian traders were actually shipping more than they had a hundred years earlier. Similarly, while certain commodities proved more difficult for Venetians to deal in through the Ottomans, others such as Turkish carpets and Persian silks, which were exchanged for woolens and metals from Europe, were readily available. And again, while sugar from Cyprus and Crete was eventually supplanted by the Portuguese product from the newly discovered Madeiras, where it could be grown for less, the Venetian farmers in the eastern Mediterranean switched to cotton, which, when shipped to Germany and England, proved even more profitable.

In general, the growing prosperity of Europe as a whole and the increasing demand for special cargoes sustained Venetian commerce. And

---

[3] To get some idea of the value of the Venetian ducat around mid-century, the following are approximate annual incomes earned within the city: lowest paid (boy apprentices, female cloth workers) 10 ducats; unskilled construction and Arsenale workers 20 ducats; semiskilled 30; skilled craftsmen 40 to 50; ship's masters, key Arsenale personnel, cittadini (lawyers, small merchants, lower officials) 80 to 150; leading artists and architects 200; nobles holding important offices 200 to 500; the doge 4,800. In addition, the annual income of the wealthier nobles ranged from 1,000 to 10,000 ducats.

even though cities like Lisbon, Antwerp and London diverted some of the carrying trade, they were also flourishing centers of consumption.

Much of this long distance trade would have been more difficult and less efficient without the parallel development of marine insurance. In fact, the 16th-century Rialto became the primary European center for arranging coverage for ships and cargoes. There, near the bridge, brokers went the rounds signing up merchants and bankers willing to underwrite (literally sign their names under the contract) a given share of the values at risk, customarily from 100 to 500 ducats each. And not only were local ventures insured there, but many foreign ones were also, as, for example, the Medici of Florence, who often used their Venetian branch to obtain insurance on their far-ranging shipments across Europe.

Changes in Shipping

One important aspect of heightened commercial competition was the further change in the size and efficiency of cargo ships. Even though oared galleys, long used commercially in the Mediterranean and for the Atlantic convoys, had increased in tonnage, Dutch and English shipbuilders were not only enlarging capacity, but were also improving the design, defense and rigging of their oarless round ships. Known as carracks, these vessels were now built in the 600 to 900 ton range with additional deck space made available for heavier and more numerous cannon. In addition, their sail capacity increased; many carried three masts, taller and with more yardarms, replacing the smaller one- or two-masted cogs. Compared to the galleys, relatively fewer crew members could safely transport much larger cargoes, and gradually the older, oared ships, with their narrow beams and costly manpower, proved uneconomical for long-range trade. The last of the Venetian merchant galleys were seen in the English Channel in the year 1533, and even in the Mediterranean, much of the carrying trade was lost to the northerners in the decades that followed.

While over time the Venetians and the other Mediterranean powers were reluctantly forced to accede to the advantages of the carracks for commercial enterprise, they stubbornly refused to give up their oared galleys for military purposes. There were plausible reasons for this. For one, the heavy guns required for the defense of the larger vessels and cast from imported metal were expensive; for another, a conversion to round ships demanded the rebuilding of practically the entire war fleet since the two types did not always operate well together. Moreover, oared galleys were more maneuverable and since the Turks continued to employ them, practical considerations and military tradition enforced their retention. Orders, therefore, continued to go out to the Arsenale for ever larger war galleys, which now ranged up to almost 200 tons. Some were powered by as many as 150 oarsmen, either arranged two or three on a stepped bench, each with an oar, or later, three or four men to a straight bench sharing a single, much heavier oar.

In the long run, however, this policy proved to be a mistake. Not only were the galleys incapable of competing during peacetime as cargo carriers and thus earn their keep, they ultimately could not stand up in combat to the ever larger and more heavily armed carracks from the northern seafaring nations that increasingly operated in the Mediterranean toward the end of the century.

A New Emphasis on Agriculture and Manufacturing

The combined effect of the Turkish domination in the East and the growing control of long-distant trade by other Europeans in the West tended to place more emphasis for the Venetians on commerce in the Adriatic and business activity closer to home. In particular, agriculture in the Veneto began to assume an ever greater importance, especially after grain shipments from the Black Sea ports were completely cut off by the Ottomans in 1551 in order to feed their own growing populations. The number of people in Venice was also increasing rapidly, multiplying from about 115,000 in 1509 to some 180,000 in 1575, according to official census figures, which by the 16th century were relatively accurate for the first time.

To insure an adequate supply of staple foods, always a concern for a city surrounded by water, was the responsibility of the municipal grain office in charge of Venice's two warehouses, one at Rialto and one near San Marco. As wheat prices continued to rise throughout the century and other sources of supply in Sicily, Crete and Cyprus failed to meet the demand, more extensive planting in the Veneto, not only of wheat, but of maize and rice, both introduced into Italy at this time, was encouraged by the grain office. This often required large-scale reclamation projects—the draining of marshes, the building of canals and bridges—and demanded substantial outlays of capital, some of which was subsidized by the government. Accordingly many wealthy Venetians turned away from the hazards and risks of commerce to more secure investments on land and, not incidentally, a more leisurely, comfortable life. It has been estimated that about 250 substantial country villas were built or enlarged in the Veneto during the cinquecento by the Venetian upper class, who gradually transformed themselves from merchant princes to landed gentry.

Concurrent with these developments was a sharp increase in the industrial life of the city, especially in the production of woolen cloth, a business formerly dominated by Tuscany and the low-countries, among others, and of minor importance in Venice. But after the disruptive effects of the Italian wars, many artisan refugees had sought stable conditions in which to practice their trades and found them in Venice. Each year until the end of the century saw an average increase of about 10 percent in the city's textile production. Similarly, the more traditional Venetian manufacturing industries—glass, silk, lace, soap and other chemicals—showed a marked expansion. Traditionally the government had always encouraged commercial capitalism (investments in ships, warehouses, port facilities, etc.), but had put restrictions on industrial capitalism; for example, it limited the number of textile-weaving looms one man could own. In the cinquecento, however, this policy was altered, especially with respect to the wool industry, and larger groupings of capital and guild organization were promoted. In fact, after 1539, when the guilds established along occupational lines were required to supply most of the manpower for the war galleys, guild membership was practically obligatory, and by the middle of the century about 100 were in existence. Not only did the guilds provide the usual social and economic advantages, supplying protection and security for their members, but, by demanding the highest skills, they also enhanced the quality and artistic value of Venetian products.

Immigrants and Printing Presses

Partly for its commercial reputation and partly for its general tolerance, Venice had always attracted foreigners and many—silk weavers from Lucca, artisans from Lombardy, German traders, Tuscans, Greeks, Armenians, Jews—were induced to settle there during the 16th century. A Jewish colony, mostly employed as bankers, merchants or doctors, had long been established in Venice on the island of Giudecca (apparently named after them) and had been accepted by the community on a mutually advantageous basis. In the cinquecento, however, with an influx of Jews from the Levant, their situation became more complicated. The curtailment of western trading rights by the sultan provided an advantage to those Levantine Jews still able to maintain contacts there, which gave them a competitive edge over their fellow Venetians. This, combined with the religious tensions of the Reformation, produced a certain anti-Semitism, which expressed itself in a decision in 1516 to move all Jewish residents from the Giudecca to a confined area in the *sestiere* of Cannaregio known, then and now, as the Ghetto,[4] with various restrictions placed upon them. In spite of this, however, the social climate in Venice favored an ethnic and religious pluralism, when compared with the rest of Italy, a fact proved by the size of the foreign colonies voluntarily resident there.

Of all the important enterprises in 16th-century Venice the one owing most to foreigners was that of book printing. Movable type, invented in Germany by Gutenberg, had been brought by northerners to the lagoon city, which soon became an important center of printing and publishing. By the early 1500s, more than half the books printed in Italy and about one-quarter in all Europe were produced in Venice. The city was rich, it had many skilled craftsmen who could fabricate the molds for casting type, paper was cheap and of good quality, and it was still the hub of the most extensive distribution system in Europe for selling the finished product. More importantly, Venice enjoyed a relatively liberal political climate where censorship and interference by the church was at a minimum. Almost overnight the cost of books—in the past tediously copied by hand, expensive and affordable to only a few— dropped dramatically. At the same time, in addition to the traditional religious works, titles in many new fields—medicine, music, geography, literature, now printed in the vernacular—began to appear in quantity.

The largest and most famous printing firm in Venice, known as the Aldine Press after its founder Aldus Manutius (1450–1515), an immigrant from the Romagna trained in Latin, Greek and the classics, thrived and prospered, especially under his son and grandson, throughout the cinquecento. The company's greatest achievement—aside from Aldus's invention of what is

---

[4] The name meant "casting" in the Venetian dialect because of the foundries located there, but has come to signify any area of segregation. Some of the tallest buildings in Venice are located in the Ghetto—up to seven stories in order to house so many within a limited space.

called *italic* type, the small gauge of which permitted him to compress books into pocket-size volumes called *octavos* (about one-eighth the dimension of the large *folio* additions)—was the publication over many years of almost the entire body of the Greek classics,[5] making them available for the first time in the original to a large number of Europeans. To accomplish this, Aldus employed many of the refugee Greek scholars living in Venice, but others formed their own publishing firms. With their homeland overrun by the Turks these firms became and remained the principal source of printed books in the Greek language for the entire Orthodox world. And with so many educated Greeks in the city, the ancient Hellenistic culture became, as it had earlier in Florence, the object of intense interest by a growing number of local humanist scholars, who formed an institution to study the classics called the Neacademia (New Academy) of which Aldus was a member.

Pietro Bembo and the Growth of the Humanities

Another Neacademia member was Pietro Bembo (1470–1547), the most prominent and cosmopolitan of Venice's 16th-century men of letters. Though he was born in Florence, he was of a Venetian family and studied Greek in Sicily and philosophy at Padua. He matured intellectually in the company of the Borgia family in Ferrara between 1498 and 1506. His reputation as a humanist scholar was made first in the sophisticated court life of Urbino—which was described and romanticized in one of the greatest books of the Renaissance, Castiglione's *Il Cortigiano* (The Courtier)—and later, between 1516 and 1520, in the worldly court of Leo X's Rome. After that, he returned to his family's homeland to write and study, to collect art and to become Venice's official historian (the last he achieved in 1530). Finally, in his declining years, as a crowning honor, he was made a cardinal in 1539.

Perhaps Bembo's most lasting influence was on the Italian language itself. Schooled in the Tuscan idiom of Dante and Petrarch and drawing from his experience in the princely courts across Italy, he consciously set about obtaining the general acceptance in Venice and northern Italy of the

---

[5] Hesiod, Aristophanes, Herodotus, Thucydides, Sophocles, Euripides, Demosthenes, Plato, Aristotle. In 1507 Aldus's friend, Erasmus, wrote to him praising his work on the Greek philosophers, "not by your printing alone or your splendid types, but by your brilliance and your uncommon learning."

Tuscan vernacular as the standard for literary communication. This version of Italian, which eventually was to become the basis of the modern language, gradually took the place of the old Ciceronian Latin, in which Bembo himself had earlier written his Venetian history. In fact, when he decided to translate his work for a broader public, he did so into Tuscan, and not into the Venetian dialect, which thereafter gradually lost acceptance for serious or scholarly works. In his retirement, Bembo was appointed custodian of one of the world's greatest collections of Greek manuscripts that belonged to a distinguished Greek scholar, John Bessarion, who, along with many of his countrymen, had fled to Italy before the Turkish advance, joined the Roman church (he was later made a cardinal) and then bequeathed his collection to Venice upon his death. It was later to form the nucleus for the city's great library, the Biblioteca Marciana.

Compared to the bibliophiles of Florence and other Italian courts, the Venetians were slow to take up the humanist penchant for collecting classical manuscripts, codices and other antiquities, but the practice caught on rapidly in the 16th century. Neither had Venice pioneered in the development of its own official institution of higher learning within the city, but after Padua was acquired, its university, one of the oldest in Europe, became the exclusive training ground for the sons of the Venetian nobility and was liberally supported financially by the government. Its faculties of law and science, especially medicine, and later its humanistic studies, including the Latin and Greek authors, attracted students from all over Europe and its reputation was second to none.

One of the reasons for the University of Padua's excellence was the Venetian tradition of excluding any excessive influence of the church over its institutions, including those of higher learning. This was especially important during the disruptive years of the Inquisition, which so paralyzed liberal thinking elsewhere during most of the 16th century. As a result, scholars seeking a haven for free discussion and experimentation were readily attracted to Padua. The study of human anatomy, for instance, by means of dissection was encouraged there though vigorously opposed by the Church. Also encouraged was the study of Aristotle's writings in the original Greek, much different from the heavily interpreted versions propounded by the Latin scholastic tradition. And it was at Padua that Galileo, despite censure from many quarters, accomplished his greatest achievements in experimental physics and astronomy.

Humanism and Venetian Painting

Altogether, the many new enquiries and ideas coming to the fore were the direct results of Renaissance humanism, which is roughly defined as that change in emphasis of thought and concern away from matters of faith and dogma toward man, his achievements and his immediate environment. Inevitably, this fresh approach as revealed in the Venetian educational process, in the intellectual life of the city and in the private pursuits of the nobility had its effect on the artists, influenced by and dependent as they were on their patrons from the *scuole,* the government and the wealthy families. This in turn opened up a wider range of subject matter for art: historical themes, pagan mythology, civic exaltation, portraiture and landscape painting. The last, no longer subordinated simply to stylized background, became a realistic and integral part of the pictorial message and an end in itself. Biblical stories and religious art were not abandoned, but these works now were less ethereal, less spiritual and more reflective of humanity. At the same time the newly developed painting techniques—linear and atmospheric perspective, advances in the study of anatomy, modeling and the role of light—were ready at hand and all waiting to be exploited.

So followed a proliferation of secular paintings now released from the traditional limitations with a new freedom to indulge the eye in a feast of color and the play of light. From time-honored religious scenes framed in idyllic settings came forth bucolic pastorals, mythic and allegorical themes, riotous bacchanals—some more pagan and erotic than even pre-Christian art—all celebrating the beauty of earth, sky and nature. From the Venetian vantage point on the isolated lagoon islands, the countryside and *terrafirma,* now more important than ever, had a special appeal. Perhaps these romantic settings were an escape from the realities of life, and from underlying fears for the future.

In prior centuries Venetian painting had existed primarily to serve religion and was the reflection of a relatively confident and conservative state of mind, the product of material success and spiritual certitude. But as the cinquecento wore on, tensions increased as the Italian political, military and religious situation deteriorated. The states of the peninsula had proved no match against the larger powers, the center of attention (and much trade) was moving from the Mediterranean to the Atlantic, and the Reformation was challenging the Roman Church's authority. It is not surprising that there followed a loss of conviction and a degree of self-doubt among Italian intellectuals and artists, which sense is clearly expressed in the writings of Machiavelli and in the work of Michelangelo and the Florentine mannerists that followed him. This feeling of unease took longer to reach Venice since the city was still rich and proud and nominally independent, but inevitably the painters and their patrons were affected. In some ways the portrait paintings of the time, soon produced in great quantities to immortalize the fame, piety or rank of the patron, unveil this concern, revealing in the faces a pensiveness, an anxious awareness, a need to be cautious. In the same way, serious religious painting, which never lost sight of the promised possibility for ultimate salvation beyond the grave and life's uncertainties, continued on a parallel course. At the same time, there existed an unspoken understanding that the city's great ambitions had been largely achieved and that it was appropriate to turn and admire all that had been built and to glorify the Republic's history and mythology, partly for its own sake and partly for fear that it might not last.

Giovanni Bellini and Giorgione

As mentioned earlier, the single most important Venetian painter at the turn of the century, one whose work and influence acted as a hinge between the artistic innovations of the quattrocento and the coming of the High Renaissance, was Giovanni Bellini, by then in his 70s. He had now arrived at the full maturity of his style, which was to set in motion artistic forces that would culminate in one of the greatest achievements in the history of European painting. The essence of this late style, which lent 16th-century Venetian painting its unique quality, was the retention of his predecessor's traditional emphasis on color and surface pattern, but now expressed through a more advanced visual approach to nature. That is, he moved away from the then-current Florentine and Roman concern with line, linear perspective and sculptural forms in space toward a reaffirmation of color planes on a surface, or as we seem to see nature on the retina of the eye. Shapes, shadows and details are unified by a softening of contours and by an all-encompassing aerial haze, called *sfumato* by the Italians. Two famous examples in Venice attest to this: Bellini's *Virgin and Child* (c.1504) in the Accademia and his *Madonna and Saints* (1505), another *sacra conversazione* known as the San Zaccaria Altarpiece in the church of that name. Both

Giovanni Bellini's San Zaccaria altarpiece (1505) represents the artist's ultimate contribution to the advancement of Venetian painting into its golden age.

masterfully express the luminous fusion of material forms and spatial values in a mood of calm and piety.

Bellini's influence evolved not only from his actual paintings, but also from his studio where many of the next generation of painters studied, including Giorgione, Titian and Sebastiano del Piombo. Giorgio Barbarelli of Castelfranco (1477–1510), known as Giorgione, was the first to capitalize on Bellini's lead, applying his talents not only to religious and mythological subjects, but also in a novel direction with the invention of a new kind of art, the mood painting, one that illustrates no definite theme or story, but suggests some inner or subjective feeling. Little of Giorgione's authenticated work remains extant and most of it is scattered, but one painting, perhaps his most famous, is still in Venice, and in the Accademia. Known as *The Tempest*, it is an example of this new idea expressed in the manner of Bellini. Here the subtle gradations of color values from one to another, the soft contours and dense atmosphere of the *sfumato* technique are used to express no known theme, but instead convey a feeling of tension, the obvious one in nature—the threatening storm itself—and an inner, psychological one. While in Giovanni Bellini's work the message is always clear, Giorgione leaves us wondering what is going on in this cryptic scene suspended in time—a moment of stillness, like the calm before the deluge. But the specific message doesn't really matter as the picture, once seen, though provoking different reactions, is never to be forgotten and resolves itself into the essence of all great art—the mystery of nature and man's place in the scheme of things.

Such a novel painting had an immediate and wide affect, appealing to a new type of humanist collector seeking art for art's sake, and influencing other artists, who took up the outward, more literal idea—that of expressing a newfound relationship between man and nature, if not always the inner feeling—in the production of what came to be known as Giorgionesque painting.[6] One follower, however, caught the full meaning of Giorgione's message and, with his prodigious talents, went on to become the most famous Venetian of them all, Tiziano Vecellio, whom we call Titian (c.1480s–1576).

---

[6] See the work of Palma Vecchio, Lorenzo Lotto, Gianbattista Cima and Marco Basaiti in the Accademia.

180

Giorgione's mood painting called *The Tempest* took art in a new direction, away from a clear religious message toward the enigmatic.

Titian

Giorgione and Titian had worked together in 1508, just before the former's early death, on a series of frescoes (now unfortunately destroyed) on the exterior walls of a building called the Fondaco dei Tedeschi (q.v.). Engravings of the frescoes made later indicate a final maturity in Giorgione's style and the point of departure for the younger artist, whose subsequent work falls into several broad periods. In the earliest, ranging through the 1530s, Titian combines the elements of Giorgione's method with his own personal approach, as yet relatively unaffected by outside influences, to produce some of his greatest masterpieces and to make his European reputation. As with his mentor, few of his paintings remain in Venice. One that does, perhaps his greatest and certainly his most monumental, is his *Assumption of the Virgin* (1516–1518) painted for the Franciscans at the Frari Church, where it remains to this day over the high altar. About 12 feet by 22

Few, if any, pictures ever painted have made such an astounding impact on the public than Titian's *Assumption of the Virgin* when it was unveiled in 1518.

Titian's *Presentation of the Virgin* combines a religious event with all the contemporary Renaissance themes—classical architecture, drama, nature, portraiture.

feet in size, this striking picture, intended to focus attention down the whole length of the building, perfectly illustrates the developing maturity of the Venetian school as well as the great genius of the artist.

Here most of the goals of the painter's art are approached more closely than ever before. The virtuosity on the technical side—the balance and harmony of the formal composition, the masterful drawing, the opulent color—combines with a sublime achievement on the emotional side—the rendering of dramatic action, the expression of psychological insight, the fusion of reality as man sees the world with the glorification of an event ideally conceived—to produce a picture that has few, if any, rivals in the world. Even the vainest and most self-confident critics have been loath to censure. Here, too, is the logical culmination of the long Venetian tradition stretching back to the Byzantine mosaics with their shimmering surfaces, lustrous golden light and brilliant color.

Titian followed this a little later in the 1520s with another altarpiece, his *Pesaro Madonna*, also for the Frari, a revolutionary picture that broke the custom of showing the Madonna in a placid, balanced and pyramidal arrangement in favor of a more animated, asymmetrical one. Here, the emphasis shifts away from the spiritual/religious theme toward an accurate portraiture of the various members of the Pesaro family, who are being warmly commended to the Virgin by St. Francis. The donor, seen kneeling on the left, is Jacapo Pesaro, who ordered the work to celebrate a victory he fought against the Ottomans. His triumph is symbolized by the armored knight behind him holding two Turkish prisoners, while St. Peter, whose strongly colored robes form the central core of the painting, benignly looks on. Although the subject matter involves religion, the thrust of the work clearly centers on a worldly opulence that was to set the future pattern for much of Venetian painting.

Besides these two masterpieces, Venice retains one more of Titian's important canvases, the *Presentation of the Virgin*, also still located in its original site, in the Scuola della Carita, which houses the Accademia.[7] Painted in 1534 and one of his last works before his attention was diverted by mannerist influences and patronage from outside Venice, it follows the older predispositions of the *scuole*. It is a large, narrative scene with conventional groups of figures and genre details. But, by virtue of Titian's genius in expressing the beauty of life and nature, as well as by the originality of the composition, the painting advances well into the context of cinquecento art. Many of the faces depicted are portraits, an art form in which Titian was to excel during his long life, while the background reflects not only the rugged Dolomite mountain peaks of his birthplace, but also the artist's conception of the new Renaissance architecture, which at last was beginning to make its mark on the topography of the city.

Renaissance Architecture

The earliest and most extensive architectural innovations of the cinquecento in Venice took place with a major rebuilding effort in and around the commercial center of the Rialto. First came the complete reconstruction of the Fondaco dei Tedeschi, the German trading headquarters on the Grand Canal by the eastern end of the bridge, carried out by Giorgio Spavento (c.1440–1509) between 1505 and 1508. With the emphasis on the horizontal, the building is of a rather unusual design for Venice. It is in the form of a huge free-standing cubical block that surrounds a central courtyard and presents fewer and smaller windows on its several wide façades than is customary, along with a greater expanse of solid wall, which Giorgione and Titian were called upon to decorate, as already mentioned.

A little later in 1520, at the western end of the bridge, the entire area

---

[7] At some time, incredibly, a piece was cut out of it on the left side to make room for a doorway.

The impressive façade of the Scuola di San Rocco completed in the first half of the cinquecento well illustrates the abundant resources of the confraternities.

around the old church and *campo* of San Giacomo di Rialto was marked out for modernization. The work continued through to mid-century, starting first with the Fabbriche Vecchie by Antonio Lo Scarpagnino (1505–1549), which forms, with its long, narrow arcades, a continuing axis of the bridge itself, and ending with the Fabbriche Nuove by Jacopo Sansovino (1486–1570) which runs along the Grand Canal. Both buildings are somewhat utilitarian in appearance, though the latter incorporates some handsome Renaissance features. These buildings housed the officials that governed commercial and tax matters.

During the same period, just behind the Giacomo church and opposite the Fondaco dei Tedeschi, the interesting Palazzo dei Camerlenghi (1525–1528), reserved for the city's treasury and financial magistrates, was constructed. Unusual in Venice for having all four (really five) of its façades exposed to view and with its brilliantly white Renaissance decoration, it is one of the most noticeable buildings as one proceeds along the Grand Canal. Picking up the Florentine theme, the emphasis is toward the horizontal, marked out by the entablatures with their elegant friezes, the pilasters and the round-headed windows. Still, a number of traditional Venetian characteristics remain: the narrowness of the fenestration, for example, and the inlaid colored marbles.

A little further away, two other important structures in the new style made their appearance (work continued on each throughout the first half of the cinquecento): the Church of San Salvadore, begun by Spavento and completed by Sansovino and one of the more impressive Renaissance churches in the city; and the Scuola di San Rocco, destined to hold some of Tintoretto's greatest paintings.

The original plan for San Rocco was designed in 1515 by Bartolomeo Bon (the Younger) (1450-1529) as headquarters, chapel and meeting hall for the confraternity and he carried it out as far as the lower floor with its double windows in the style of Coducci. However, the building was later completed between 1527 and 1549 by Scarpagnino, who is responsible for the main doorway, the pediments and the jutting columns and cornices of the upper floor, as well as the grand stairway inside. It is an impressive structure with its generous use of marble and a good example of the wealth and taste of one of the larger Venetian *scuole*.

Sansovino and Sanmicheli: Reviving Classical Roman Architecture

Central Italian influence can be seen in all these buildings, especially through the authority of the architect Jacopo Sansovino. Born in Florence, where he was trained, and then working in the Rome of Julius II and Michelangelo, he came to live in Venice in 1527. Although he was careful to accommodate conventional Venetian ideas in the final synthesis of his designs, the monumental nature of ancient Roman architecture predominates. His genius lay in his ability to combine diverse traditions in particularly sensitive areas of Venice to produce some of the most dramatic buildings in the city in the full Renaissance style, while at the same time avoiding any discord with existing structures.

Sansovino's earliest work was for the *scuole* and for private families, the most impressive example being the huge Palazzo Corner della Ca' Grande (another Cornaro house started in the 1530s). Taking the essentials of size and arrangement from Coducci's Ca' Vendramin-Calergi, he proceeded to

Sansovino's Libreria is one of the city's most powerful buildings, able to complement and balance the much larger Doge's Palace across the Piazzetta.

build up the façade on the Grand Canal with monumental impact. Both Florentine and Roman influences can be seen in the heavy rustication of the lower level, the balconies that provide the horizontal thrust, and especially the coupled columns with their chiaroscuro effects on the upper floors. Here are the early manifestations in Venice of the plastic or sculptural approach to architecture, the precursor of Mannerism and the Baroque.

This was soon followed by his work at the Piazza San Marco, first in some restoration projects within the church itself, and then in his masterpiece, the Libreria (started in the 1540s and often called the Sansoviniana) built to house the Biblioteca Marciana. The challenge here was to provide an opposing and balancing counterweight to the most important civic building in Venice, the Ducal Palace. He cleverly juxtaposed a radically new architecture against that of the older building to create between them the Piazzetta—a space previously cluttered with ramshackle inns and shops—a new and magnificent main gateway to the city. One should note how well the library's two stories complement the portico and loggia of the Ducal Palace and how satisfactory their respective proportions are, even though the latter is on a more massive scale.

The original and dramatic architecture of the Libreria, taken by itself, was an enormous and immediate success. All the features of the Palazzo Corner are more strongly emphasized here: the long, horizontal expanse of the eastern façade (it is 21 arches wide), the pronounced chiaroscuro of the multi-coupled columns, the rich plastic relief of the frieze decorations, the crowning terrace with its statues. Now, instead of the traditional windows interrupting or piercing the wall and the pillars subordinated to the building itself, we have arches and engaged columns making up the essence of the structure in the classic Roman manner. Wall surfaces as such have all but disappeared. And yet the building seems as natural a part of Venice as its neighbors.

At the about the same time, Sansovino, who by now had been appointed head architect for the city, was also designing and constructing the adjacent building on the Molo, the Zecca, or mint, for the Republic's bullion reserves and where the Venetian coinage was to be struck. Later it became an annex of the Libreria. The Zecca has a heavy, ponderous look—perhaps intended—due to the heavy rustication and the stout, banded columns of the façade, which were first introduced here.

It would seem that the Signoria could rely on no one else, for soon after Sansovino was again called upon to design the small, elaborate structure at the base of the nearby Campanile. Aside from housing the guard, the purpose of this building, known as the Loggetta di San Marco, was to glorify the history of the Serenissima. Finished in 1549, with its free-standing, purposeless columns, its oversized frieze and its many carved allegorical reliefs and statues,[8] some executed by the architect himself, the Loggetta is a good example of the Mannerist style, which was just then emerging out of central Italy. The Loggetta was smashed to pieces with the collapse of the Campanile in 1902, but was re-assembled later, much of it from the original materials.

In a similar vein, Sansovino was commissioned a little later in 1557 to design and build a grand new interior stairway inside the east wing of the

---

[8] The four bronze figures of Apollo, Minerva, Mercury, and Peace, symbolizing respectively the Republic's power, wisdom, eloquence, and dedication, are by Sansovino, while above are three relief panels. The center one personifies Venice as the figure of Justice seated above the river gods of the Veneto; the side panels represent Jupiter and Venus, allegorical figures symbolic of the two most important island colonies, Crete and Cyprus.

At the base of the unadorned, brick campanile stands the ornate Loggetta, designed by Sansovino to glorify the city and its empire.

Ducal Palace. This stairway was to provide ceremonial access to several important rooms (the Senate, the Collegio, etc.) as well as to the doge's private apartments. Known as the Scala d'Oro (Golden Stairway) because of its elaborate gilded stucco reliefs glorifying the myths and history of the Republic, its theatrical style is in keeping with that era's need to impress and exalt. The same can be said of the two giant statues of Mars and Neptune (also by Sansovino and done in 1566) just outside at the top of the Scala dei Giganti, which was named for them. Oversized and melodramatic, they dominate the official entrance to the palace, as they were intended to do, at the place where the doge always took the oath of office[9] and where all important civic ceremonies were held.

Another architect working at about the same time was Michele Sanmicheli (1484–1559) from Verona. While most of his work is found

---

[9] A newly elected doge, after receiving the standard of St. Mark at mass in the Basilica and after being carried around the Piazza for all to see, would take the oath of office at the top of the stairs where the ducal cap was placed on his head by the senior councilor.

elsewhere throughout the Venetian Empire (the Veneto, Crete, Corfu), he was responsible for two important palaces within Venice itself, both of which are mid-century constructions: the Palazzo Corner-Mocenigo on the Rio San Polo and the Palazzo Grimani, on the Grand Canal. Like Sansovino, Sanmicheli was concerned with adapting elements of classical Roman architecture to the Venetian tradition, but not in as consistent a manner. Both of the aforementioned palaces are monumental and imposing, both achieve chiaroscuro effects and employ Roman motifs, but in the end product, they hardly seem to be designed by the same man. The Palazzo Corner-Mocenigo stands on a heavily rusticated basement, almost like a fortification (Sanmicheli was a successful military architect), and, with its rather narrow windows, slender pilasters and interrupted cornices and balustrades, has a pronounced and traditional verticality. On the other hand, the Palazzo Grimani appears to emphasize the horizontal with its wide arches, its generous classical-style pilasters and columns, and especially the dominating cornices and balconies that step back as they ascend. The first seems stately and elegant; the other, stately and ponderous.

Palladio's Great Churches

Curiously, all the names of the great Venetian architects of the 16th century begin with the letter *S:* Serlio,[10] Spavento, Scarpagnino, Scamozzi, Sansovino, Sanmicheli. The exception, of course, is Andrea Palladio (1508–1580), the most famous of them all. Like Sanmicheli he studied in Rome and left most of his works in the Veneto, not in the capital. His numerous country villas, scattered all over the *terrafirma*, had a global influence, as did his architectural writings based on the theories of Vitruvius. But the three churches and the adjacent buildings he designed in Venice are of utmost importance to the city and to the history of his art. All three, planned and undertaken between 1559 and his death in 1580, can be encompassed in one sweep of the eye while standing on the Piazzeta and looking south across the Bacino di San Marco. From left to right, they are San Giorgio Maggiore, the Zitelle and the Redentore, the latter two on the Giudecca.

The church of San Giorgio Maggiore, situated on its own little island and attached to a complex of monastic buildings constructed over many

---

[10] Sebastiano Serlio, a writer on architectural theory studied by his contemporaries.

Palladio's San Giorgio Maggiore cleverly integrates the façade components of a classical temple with the basic structure of a Christian basilica.

centuries, is most impressive, especially when viewed from across the water. The work on the church itself was commenced by Palladio in 1566, but not finished until after his death. The design of the façade was considered at the time unique and exerted wide influence, both aesthetically and practically, as it provided a solution to the old problem of adapting architectural forms from the Classical Age to the physical requirements of a Christian church. That is to say, he needed to reconcile a classical façade with the traditional arrangement of a basilican church interior, which has a high central nave and lower side aisles. To do this, he ingeniously superimposed two interlocking temple fronts—one with a high central pediment supported on four tall columns corresponding to the structure of the nave, and a wider, lower one resting on pilasters and corresponding to the aisles on either side. This clever resolution of two differing concepts is carried forward inside, where he combined an apparently longitudinal aisled nave with a centralized plan under a dome—the length of the nave and the width of the transepts are about the same—lending a great openness to the interior space. Yet the eye still is drawn forward past the crossing to the high altar and choir beyond, an important element in celebrating the Eucharist and Catholic liturgy. The overall spatial effect is one of lightness and clarity with the details of the Renaissance forms subordinated to the basic concept of the structure. All this had been worked out in accordance with mathematical theories of ratios and proportions, as first conceived by the Florentines.

The adjoining brick buildings, originally a Benedictine monastery, were also redesigned by Palladio, who rebuilt the first cloister and the magnificent refectory leading off it, one of the most monumental dining rooms in the world. Subsequently these buildings suffered from many vicissitudes (for a time they were a military barracks) and finally fell into ruin in the 19th century. In recent years, the entire complex was rescued by Count Vittorio Cini, who was responsible for beautifully restoring the structures for the use of the Cini Foundation, which is dedicated to the study of Venetian civilization.

Close by on the neighboring island of Giudecca, only one stop away by waterbus, Palladio's other two churches, built a little later, may be studied. The first, as one proceeds west along the *fondamenta*, is the Church of the Zitelle (Virgins) with its rather plain façade and generous dome over a centralized plan. It was essentially built as a chapel to serve the adjoining convent and hostel for poor orphaned girls that surrounds it on three sides.

Farther on we come to the Church of the Redentore (Redeemer), another of Palladio's masterpieces built in gratitude for the city's deliverance from another recurrence of the plague in 1576. In contrast to the Zitelle, which is hemmed in by its surrounding structures, the building stands out detached and freestanding, which emphasizes its distinctive architectural merits. The façade, raised above a broad flight of steps and often compared to Palladian villas on the mainland, is an elaboration of San Giorgio's and has a more complex integration of pediments, four in this case (including a small one over the main door), superimposed on one another and reflecting the church's interior arrangements. That is, the highest and deepest set pediment on the façade is echoed inside by the choir at the far end, which is also elevated; the next highest pediment reflects the nave vaulting; the next that of the aisles. More importantly, the architect has skillfully combined the essentially linear, classical theme with the supple curves of the approaching baroque style; both outside and in, the rectangular and triangular lines of the façade and the buttresses and pilasters of the nave give way gradually, as

The façade of the Redentore Church is a later and more complex attempt by Palladio to relate the columns, pilasters and pediments of a Roman temple to the interior logic of the building.

the eye moves down the building, to the graceful roundness of the dome, the minarets (a Byzantine touch), the semicircular transepts and the curved colonnade behind the high altar.

Here, as at San Giorgio, the success of the spatial feeling of the interior is dependent on the relative proportion of every facet of the structure. But neither of these buildings, the products of research and logic and purity of design, reflected the time-honored ambience of Venice's traditional churches. Gone were the paintings and tombs, the mosaics and frescoes, the clutter of centuries that characterized the older Byzantine and Gothic periods. Instead the Venetians were presented with a stark revival of classicism with its clean lines and mathematical proportions, the ultimate in rational design and balance that defines the high Renaissance. But this orderliness and sparsity of ornament was only temporary as the coming years were to prove. The Italians, and especially the Venetians, were unable to resist the coming appeal of the Roman Baroque in its full maturity. Gradually the carving and gilding, the color and sumptuous décor, and all the old emotional panoply were steadily reintroduced during the next two centuries.

The Battle of Lepanto

The last decade of Palladio's life, the 1570s, was a difficult one for Venice. It opened with yet another war against the Turks waged by a combination of Christian allies known to history as the Holy League that fought under the sponsorship of the pope and included besides the Venetians, Spanish, Neapolitan, Genoese and other Italian forces. Though the final outcome of the war was a stalemate, two positive results could be claimed for the West. For one, a great naval victory was won by the allies at Lepanto; for another, the Turks thereafter gave up further aggression into eastern Europe and their frontier with Austria and Poland became stabilized.

The Battle of Lepanto, the last great sea fight between oared galleys, took place October 7, 1571 in the Gulf of Patras. The allied fleet of some 208 ships (about half of these were Venetian under the command of Sebastiano Venier, former governor of Corfu and Cyprus and later a doge) had assembled earlier at Messina and sailed east with the determined aim of confronting the sultan's somewhat larger navy, which was known to be resupplying at Lepanto on the gulf, in a final showdown. The Turks, underestimating the strength of their opponents, left the safety of the harbor in the early morning to give battle. Together comprising more than 100,000 men, the two fleets approached each other over a two-mile front on a collision course and sighted one another around noon. The first contacts, which proved crucial, were shots fired from six heavily armed Venetian galleasses[11] that were posted ahead of the allied fleet and whose cannon out-ranged the enemy and inflicted severe damage to its center. Neither side faltered, however, and within minutes were locked together in a savage life-or-death struggle. Attempts to ram the nearest ship gave way to exchanges of crossbow and arquebus fire, grappling and boarding. No quarter was given by either side and when it was over about four hours later the Turks had lost some 35,000 men, either dead or captured, and more than half their galleys.

---

[11] Generally defined as oversized galleys, similarly rowed and rigged, but slower and with gun platforms fore and aft to accommodate heavier cannons.

The remainder escaped to the protection of the forts at Lepanto. The Holy League, though having lost about 9,000 men, had won the battle and some 15,000 Christian galley slaves were freed from Turkish captivity.

Unfortunately, by no fault of Venice, the League fell apart within a year. The naval victory was never followed up and Cyprus, which had been overrun by the Turks despite a valiant resistance, was permanently lost; Venice gave up its claim to the island and made peace in 1573. Even so, a Muslim fleet would never again threaten control of the central Mediterranean.

A Visit from the French King

This last treaty with the Turks simply set the seal on a situation that had been developing for some time—the gradual withdrawal of Venice as an important power in the eastern Mediterranean. Well before the Battle of Lepanto, Venice had begun its decline as a maritime power. Money that formerly would have gone into overseas trade and the navy was now spent to improve local fortifications, pay mercenary armies on the mainland and finance the estates and villas these armies were meant to protect. In addition, money was now, more than ever, spent on embellishments to the city, on palatial new homes, on art, luxuries and endless pageantry. A perfect example was the lavish ten-day reception in July 1574 that the city provided for the young French king Henry III on his progress through Italy. Even the mainland cities extended him a regal welcome as he and his retinue proceeded on to La Serenisima, where he was sumptuously installed in the Palazzo Foscari for most of his stay. Elaborate barges carried the king and his entourage daily along the canals or across the lagoon to the Lido for receptions, galas and feasts. He spent hours touring the Arsenale and watching acrobatics in the Piazza or the traditional Guerra dei Ponti (mock fights on the bridges). He was introduced to Venice's greatest artists—Tintoretto did his portrait—and to the city's most beautiful courtesans. At night, it was said, he enjoyed strolling incognito through the back alleyways of the city.

The climax came with a banquet in the Great Council Hall at the Ducal Palace, where a golden throne was erected for him on a raised platform surmounted by a baldachin draped in yellow and blue satin. Guards of honor in resplendent uniforms attended the king, while the nobles and their ladies, dressed in gorgeous Venetian or oriental costumes, crowded the hall. A sumptuous feast was elaborately presented and punctuated by toasts, speeches and the exchange of gifts. Even a play was written for the occasion, while afterwards music and dancing went on into the night. Venice outdid itself and the king was full of joy and enthusiasm. Never would he forget that stay in the lagoon. And that, of course, was what the Venetians hoped, since France was an important counterweight to Hapsburg and Spanish power.

Venetian Prosperity Begins to Decline

But all this extravagance and apparent well-being hid a less sanguine reality that was slow to be recognized. The strain and cost of the Turkish wars, capped by the tragic loss of Cyprus, and the gradual obsolescence of the Venetian merchant fleet as it gave way to its competitors' larger capacity ships plying the new Atlantic trade routes, were silently undermining the city's prosperity. To these unseen problems were now added several costly and more obvious calamities. Beginning in 1574, soon after the French king departed, a series of devastating fires broke out in the city's center, two of them in the Doge's Palace. Major parts of the building were destroyed, including the interiors of the Collegio, the Senate and the Great Council, along with their wall paintings by some of the most celebrated artists in the city's history—the Vivarini, the Bellini, Titian and others. While the damage to the structure was repairable, albeit at great expense, the loss of so many renowned works of art at the very seat of government was an inconsolable and disheartening blow to Venetian pride and, to some, a threatening omen of things to come.

Then in 1576 the plague returned, this time so severe that it killed at least 40,000 people in Venice alone. One of those was the painter Titian, who died August 26, 1576, although he might simply have passed away from old age, having lived into his 90s. He had been productive to the end; at his death he was working on still another painting for the Frari, where, as he requested, the Venetians buried him with all the pomp of a state funeral.[12] Few artists can rival the career or accomplishments of Titian. He had lived and worked within the traditions of his city, exploiting the social, intellectual and business opportunities around him, dressing in magnificent clothes and enjoying the fruits of humanism and the revived paganism of the times. His

---

[12] His neoclassical mausoleum was not erected until the 1830s and may be seen in the nave.

long life not only paralleled but exemplified the Venetian High Renaissance. Starting with little, he accumulated much: wealth, the honor of his city, a worldwide reputation, and the friendships of the powerful and the great, from his fellow artists to kings and emperors. His paintings express it all: the richness, the apparent confidence, the pageantry and the color of his native Venice in the full flush of its maturity.

Titian's Legacy

This is not to say that during the consummate phase of his career—the last 40 years—Titian's approach to painting remained aloof to outside artistic influences. In fact, he had resided at the Vatican between 1545 and 1546 as a guest of the pope and had been exposed to that emphasis on sculptural values in space, so prized in central Italian art. Titian, however, was able to digest these influences in his stride and use them to supplement, not override, his work. But the tensions that had manifested themselves up and down the peninsula following the 1527 sack of Rome and the subsequent Spanish domination also had their effect in Venice, even though its territories and independence remained relatively untouched. This is obvious in Titian's later works, which often reflect scenes of agitated unrest, characteristic of Mannerism. These paintings, some mythological, some religious, peopled with groups of anguished figures in dramatic confrontations or conflict, and usually set in the context of a stormy background, reveal the tension. And it was during this period that he developed his original and distinct free or summary style through spontaneously executed brush strokes, which suggested rather than precisely detailed the subject matter. This was the so-called painterly technique that his contemporaries were soon to emulate.

Little of Titian's later work remains in Venice, scattered as it is through the museums of Europe. But this is not the case of his immediate successors, Jacopo Bassano (1518–1592), Jacopo Tintoretto (1518–1594) and Paolo Veronese (1528–1588), many of whose paintings may be seen in the Accademia and throughout the city. Of the three, Bassano is the least important and the most Mannerist, though in his later years he followed Titian in re-emphasizing color and chiaroscuro.

Tintoretto's highly dramatic painting of St. Mark freeing a slave was his first acclaimed success.

The Dramatic and Painterly Works of Tintoretto

Bassano's exact contemporary was Jacopo Robusti, called Tintoretto because he was employed as a youth in his father's dye works. Compared to Titian, his success did not come easily. He was 30 before he received his first important commission to paint a legend concerning St. Mark for the Scuola di San Marco. Tintoretto had carefully studied the best of Venetian and central Italian painting and in this work, entitled *St. Mark Freeing a Slave*[13] (now in the Accademia), he attempted to combine the sculptural aesthetics of the Tuscans with the rich colors of his native school. In neither direction

---

[13] The painting, commissioned by the *scuola*, is based on the story of a slave who escaped to Venice to pray before the relics of St. Mark, is captured and condemned to be blinded and maimed. As his punishment is about to take place, the saint appears from above while the instruments of torture disintegrate before the terrified onlookers.

is the effort fully successful from a critical point of view—space is not clearly defined by the crowded, frantic figures and the paint tones exaggerated—but as a dramatic and eye-catching picture, it was immediately popular and made his reputation.

Following this, for more than 40 years, Tintoretto went on to literally cover the walls of Venice with his art. Taking up Titian's lead, his style became ever more personal, more summary, more rapidly executed—in a word, more painterly. No project daunted him. At the church of Madonna dell' Orto,[14] he filled one entire wall with paintings, some over 40 feet high. In the Palazzo Ducale, after the fires, he was commissioned to redecorate vast areas, including the end wall of the Sala del Maggior Consiglio above the Signoria's podium, where he and his assistants executed the huge *Vision of Paradise.* Inspired by Dante's Divine Comedy, this is probably the largest oil painting in the world, embracing some 500 figures from Christ and the Virgin through angels, archangels, the church fathers and innumerable saints, all arranged according to rank. But it was in the *scuole* where he exerted his major efforts, especially in the Scuola di San Rocco. This *scuola* had been dedicated to the French martyr St. Roch, whose relics were enshrined in the adjoining church. Born into a wealthy family in Montpellier in the 13th century, as a young man he had given up his inheritance to follow Christ and tend the victims of the plague. He became the patron saint of the sick and of the hospital that the confraternity maintained.

Tintoretto obtained the commission to decorate the spacious interior rooms of San Rocco by submitting a finished painting instead of the mere design that was called for in the competition. His rivals claimed this was unfair, but apparently the complaints were overlooked, and he was awarded the task of telling once again in paint the sacred Christian story. This he did almost single-handedly over a period of more than 20 years, devoting the lower floor to the life of the Virgin Mary and the upper to Christ. Of the many paintings, the largest and best known is the *Crucifixion,* perhaps his masterpiece. In this work, all the artist's special means of expression are combined: the multitude of crowded figures and naturalistic detail; the large scale, dramatic narration and rapid, painterly brush strokes; the glowing color and nuances of light. By such means he accelerated the trend away

---

[14] He was later buried in this church.

Perhaps his masterpiece, Tintoretto's *Crucifixion* is one of the many he painted for the Scuola di San Rocco.

from the older Venetian approach—calm, decorative and composed—into dramatic spectacle. Christ on the cross is surrounded by the frenzied actions of the many human figures, who, with the exception of a few, bear witness to this agonizing and climactic scene with cold indifference. The whole arrangement is disturbingly cut up by the daring juxtaposition of dark and light in various areas across the picture surface, but by the skillful placement of the principal groupings he manages to unify the many diverse incidents illustrated.

He has been faulted by critics for the coarseness of his figures, the cluttered confusion of his compositions, the overly dramatic violence of his themes and the lack of finish in his technique. But while all this is true to a degree, these were his personal means of interpreting the Christian story. Few painters have ever incorporated such a wealth of human life in all its variety within the context of sincere religious belief. Tintoretto's works are spread generously around Venice and have become an integral and essential aspect of the city's ambience and personality.

Venice Exalted in the Paintings of Veronese

The last of Titian's successors, Paolo Veronese, though ten years younger than Tintoretto, came to the fore around the same time. Much less moody in temperament than his rival, his paintings expressed the lighter side of life. Tintoretto had insulated himself from society and painted humanity in all its trials and tribulations through heartfelt devotional

Veronese's famous and controversial painting, supposedly of the Lord's last supper, but more like a lavish pagan banquet, was renamed *Feast in the House of Levi*.

messages. Veronese, on the other hand, emulated the Venetian nobility
with whom he associated and painted a classically idealized version of its
environment—the palaces, the heroic figures, the voluptuous women and
their splendid garments of silk and velvet—as though it were a part of the
Greek pantheon.

The most famous example of this is his great painting in the Accademia,
later entitled *Feast in the House of Levi,* which was one among the many pictures
of banquets commissioned by the Venetians. The subject is purportedly
Christ's last supper, but in reality is a pagan extravaganza. Assembled here
are all the particulars Veronese loved so well—the magnificent architecture,
the gorgeous costumes, the numerous servants, the spirit of revelry and
good living. The artist was scarcely concerned with religious propriety or
moral values—no more so than with historical accuracy—and Christ's figure
is simply one among many in the crowd. Instead, he painted to dramatize
an episode, to impress the viewer and to exploit the painter's art by creating
a feast for the eyes. The painting was commissioned and approved by the
monks of Zanipolo for their refectory—an implicit comment on their
worldliness. It was finished in 1573 while the Inquisition was in full swing
and the artist was called before one of its tribunals to explain the work's
many irreverent aspects. With clowns and dwarves, drunkards, animals, birds
and rich hedonistic paraphernalia, this was hardly the setting of the Lord's
last meeting with the disciples. It seems he was required to modify the work,
but it is not clear what, if anything other than the title, was ever changed.[15]

Both Tintoretto and Veronese, following Titian, had taken up the technique of working rapidly, roughing details and leaving their work with a less finished effect than had been the usual practice. Both, too, produced highly original, dramatic compositions, combining many figures in daring juxtapositions. But while both pursued the Venetian flare for color and luminosity, Tintoretto placed the emphasis on contrasting light and dark in close proximity. Veronese, on the other hand, minimized chiaroscuro, avoided black or inky pigments and sought to relate each color with its complementary one.[16]

Further Embellishments at the Ducal Palace

The distinction between the two artists can best be noted in the Ducal Palace, where Veronese literally began and ended his career. At the far end of the Room of the Great Council hangs Tintoretto's vast *Paradise,* which as mentioned is a confusion of lively figures portrayed by the chiaroscuro technique in a highly dramatic arrangement, but in an overall context of reverence and religious conviction. This is not the case in Veronese's equally great work, *The Apotheosis of Venice,* the centerpiece of the magnificently carved and gilded ceiling, painted just before his death in 1588. The picture, depicting the elevation and exaltation of the Serenissima amidst the gods of Olympus, harkens back to Roman imperialism as filtered through the Venetian heritage. The whole feeling and symbolism is not only irreligious, but a triumph of pagan sensuousness. Although both paintings depict the majestic and the celestial, Tintoretto's seems believable and convincing, a scene filled with real people suffused with faith, while Veronese's is a surface dream inhabited by heroic and larger-than-life figures that can only exist in the imagination.

Nevertheless, the grandeur of Veronese's picture encompasses a triumphant scene of unprecedented pomp, and was conceived for the self-glorification of the artist as much as for the nobles who occupied the hall. It is probably more appropriate, however, to the arrogance and splendor of

---

[15] On two of the pilasters in the painting have been added the words, "Fecit d. covi magnum levi" and "Luca cap. v," which translates, "And Levi made him a great feast in his house" and "Luke Chapter V."

[16] For those who have the time and energy, the Church of San Sebastiano, near Veronese's home, contains some of his greatest works, and is his last resting place.

Ambassadors and other notables assembled in this imposing room, the Hall of the Four Doors, while awaiting an audience with Venice's leaders.

Renaissance Venice, which was not yet seriously affected by defeat or decay, than Tintoretto's more spiritual display of faith. Both artists also employed their talents in other rooms of the Ducal Palace, the most noteworthy being those on the upper floor at the top of the Golden Stairway. All these rooms were reconstructed and redecorated in the late 1570s following the fires, several of them by Palladio. The actual work was then carried out by his many assistants (woodcarvers, sculptors, stuccoists, etc.) under the direct supervision of Antonio Rusconi. Altogether, they reflect the glorification of past traditions upon which the Venetian state was by then living.

The first of the reconstructed rooms in the Ducal Palace, the Hall of the Four Doors (accessible through the southwest portal from the Golden Stairway) is an imposing entrance and contains a large, important painting of Henry III's arrival in Venice escorted by the doge through a triumphal arch erected for the occasion. Here in this hall, notables (foreign and Venetian ambassadors, rectors of dependent cities, admirals of the fleet, etc.) paused before being summoned to one or another of the governing bodies within, whose chambers can be reached through the other three doors. All

Tintoretto's painting of Venus uniting Venice (Ariadne) with the Adriatic (Bacchus) underscores that historic and vital relationship.

of these impressive portals, with their columns of precious marble and statues above, were designed by Palladio. The one on the northwest (with sculptures by Alessandro Vittoria (1525–1608)) leads to the Anti Collegio Room where several of Tintoretto and Veronese's greatest paintings are to be found, including the former's *Bacchus and Ariadne Crowned by Venus*[17] and the latter's *Rape of Europe,* both executed around 1578. The statues and stuccos of the room's elaborate fireplace, as well as the vaulted ceiling's complicated gilded patterns (probably the work of Vincenzo Scamozzi), all combine with the beautiful colors of the paintings to produce a very sumptuous effect.

The Anti Collegio chamber served as the last stop for envoys and officials before their presentation to the members of the Collegio who occupied the

---

[17] The presumed allegorical message of the painting: the Goddess of Love (Venus) joining Venice (Ariadne) with the Adriatic (Bacchus)—symbolizing that all-important relationship for the Republic's well being.

Veronese's mythological painting called the *Rape of Europe* illustrates, in spite of the title, a rather cooperative group of females during one of Jupiter's arranged abductions, here in the form of a bull.

adjoining room. In addition to receiving ambassadors and reports from the colonies, the Collegio prepared the agenda and reviewed the proposals that were to be placed before the Senate, which met in the larger room just to the east.

These two stately chambers are imposing indeed and have many features in common. Both include a raised dais or tribunal at the north end, carved wooden paneling and seats around the other sides, as well as huge back-to-back matching wall clocks. Both have flat (as opposed to vaulted) ceilings of richly carved and gilded frames into which are set numerous paintings by Tintoretto, Veronese and others. Seldom has any government occupied such luxurious, if not ostentatious, quarters, surrounded by masterpieces from the hands of some of the world's greatest artists.[18]

The walls and ceiling of the Senate Hall, one of the most luxurious rooms in the Doge's Palace, are covered with paintings by Venice's greatest artists.

The Senate Hall opens back into the northeast portal of the Room of the Four Doors, which is opposite the fourth door leading into the Sala del Consiglio dei Dieci or Hall of the Council of Ten. This room together with the two smaller adjacent chambers on the south side—one was for the three senior members of the Ten (the Tre Capi) and the other was the Sala della Bussola—were in an area that escaped severe damage from the fires of the 1570s and so date from a few decades earlier. Their decoration is accordingly a little less elaborate.

The Hall of the Bussola is so named for the unusual three-sided wooden entrance screen *(bussola)* shielding the corner access to the room from the several narrow passageways and stairways leading to the prison cells. Here the accusers, the witnesses and the accused himself were assembled prior to their appearance before the dreaded Council of Ten. The prisons themselves

---

[18] One of the most impressive is the canvas above the dais in the Hall of the Collegio by Veronese. The subject is Sebastiano Venier, the hero of Lepanto and later doge, giving thanks to Christ for victory against the Turks, a vivid expression of Venetian dedication to both the state and religion.

had long been located within the Ducal Palace. The oldest cells were in the basement areas running along the southern side of the palace below the Room of the Great Council and others were added later under the central portion of the east wing. All are accessible by stairs from the Hall of the Ten several stories above. Divided into narrow, windowless cubicles, they were known as the *pozzi,* or the wells, because of their dark, confined, damp nature. A few of them can still be visited.

Still later, midway through the 16th century, more cells were needed and were constructed high up under the roof rafters above the Hall of the Ten. This place, sweltering hot in the summer months, soon became known as the *piombi,* or the leads, after the leaden material sheathing the roof. Adjacent to these and immediately above the Sala dei Tre Capi was the Room of the Rope, where prisoners were trussed up to an overhead beam during questioning or otherwise subjected to torture. These areas too were directly accessible by stairs running down to the Hall of the Ten.

Late-Century Architecture

Apparently, even these additions were insufficient to accommodate the many criminals and enemies of the Serenissima, so plans were formulated for the construction of an entirely separate building directly across the Rio di Palazzo, henceforth known as the New Prisons. Some existing ancient structures were demolished and the building proceeded in three successive stages: the first part at the rear, where the darkest and most cramped cells are to be found, was completed about 1570 under Palladio's assistant, Rusconi; the middle portion a few years later; and the last section, facing the Basin of St. Mark, completed in 1577 by the architect, Antonio da Ponte (c.1512–1597). This final part of the building, used mainly by the police officials, has a handsome façade of Istrian stone, wide arches and a solid appearance. With these features, it provides a balancing support to the neighboring bulk of the Ducal Palace, but gives little indication from the outside as to its true and foreboding purpose.

During the same period, Antonio da Ponte was also put in charge of rebuilding the Hall of Scrutiny, also destroyed in the fires and the second largest room in the Doge's Palace after the adjacent Great Council Hall. It originally housed the Republic's library before the collection was transferred to the Sansoviniana. Later the hall was used primarily as the balloting place

A view by Canaletto of the Rialto Bridge, designed and built by Antonio da Ponte. On the left is the Fondaco dei Tedeschi and on the right the Camerlenghi Palace.

for all official elections, not only for the doge, but for the other important offices as well. Accordingly, elections were held here almost weekly. All the paintings around the walls and in the massive ceiling were done by followers of Tintoretto and Veronese and depict various Venetian battle victories. The frieze contains the portraits of the last 42 doges.

Even while supervising this work and that of the New Prisons, da Ponte submitted the winning design for the new stone bridge that the Great Council had finally determined must replace the ancient wooden one at Rialto, at that time the only one across the Grand Canal.[19] It was commenced in 1588 and finished in 1591 under da Ponte's supervision with the aid of his nephew, Antonio Contino (1566–1600). The arch of the span itself is graceful enough, but the arcade of shops that line both sides is generally considered out of proportion and top heavy. Nevertheless, the Rialto Bridge

---

[19] Designs by Michelangelo, Palladio, Sansovino and Scamozzi were rejected.

The Bridge of Sighs (left) connecting the Doge's Palace with the new prisons; and (right) the Procuratie Nuove where Florian's cafe has long been located.

has become a key feature of the Venetian scene and a kind of symbol of the city's commercial and maritime associations.

Da Ponte died in 1597 and his nephew took over as supervisor of the work at the Ducal Palace and the New Prisons. When it was decided that a direct bridge connection was needed between the two buildings, he was selected to design and build it. From the beginning this bridge has been known as the Ponte dei Sospiri, or the Bridge of Sighs, presumably named after those mournful utterances that were heard from the doomed prisoners as they caught sight of the lagoon and the surrounding sky through the bridge's narrow windows, perhaps for the last time, during their passage from the court of justice to their incarceration. Completed just at the turn of the century, the bridge is entirely enclosed on all sides; the interior is separated into two narrow, parallel passageways, each connected separately to stairways leading from the *pozzi* and the *piombi* prison cells in the Ducal Palace. On the exterior, Contino has given us the full flavor of the coming baroque style with the original and pleasing curves of both the upper and lower arches and the decorative scrolls and volutes.

At about the same time, the Balbi family was building an important palace at a strategic point on the Grand Canal where it makes a sharp turn to the south, and which can be easily identified by its two pyramidal ornaments at the roof line. It was designed by Alessandro Vitoria, who was better known as a sculptor than as an architect. Its façade displays less linear and more plastic early baroque features, particularly in the broken pediments above the windows and doors, the sculptured armorial plaques and the slender, disengaged, paired columns. All these became standard components in later architectural programs.

Finally, in the last years of the cinquecento, still one more of Venice's great architects was also working, Vincenzo Scamozzi (1552–1616). His principal contribution was the design of the Procuratie Nuove, the long building that forms the southern side of the Piazza San Marco. Modeled after Sansovino's Library but with an extra baroque upper story, it was originally the residence of the nine *procuratori* in charge of San Marco and its endowments. Today it houses the Correr and Archaeological Museums.

11 THE LONG DECLINE INTO DECADENCE: THE LAST YEARS OF THE REPUBLIC — 1600–1797

So ended the great achievements of the 16th century and the Golden Age of Venice. The city had nurtured some of the most famous artists of all time and had given them the scope, the encouragement and the means not only to embellish, but literally to transform the fabric of the city itself. On the surface things appeared as stable as they had ever been. Hospitals and charitable societies provided aid to rich and poor alike. Beggars and foundlings, it was said, made up only one percent of the population, which, at about 140,000, was again approaching its historical maximum and still growing. The census of 1563 had counted about 168,000 before the plague of 1575. Festivals and pageantry punctuated every month. Few other cities could rival the luxury of the new palaces along the Grand Canal, to say nothing of the interiors of the Ducal Palace itself. The public debt was under control and, while trade was declining, local industries like glass- and lace-making were coming into their own. Moreover, a great deal of inherited wealth was still intact and had not yet been eroded away. All in all the worldly reputation of the Serenissima remained generally unimpaired.

At the same time, by the turn of the century, a decisive change had taken place in Venetian life and culture; increased leisure, centering for part of the year around the country villa, permitted the upper class to involve itself less with business and more with pleasure. Men, whose grandfathers had been sea captains and traders, now wrote sonnets and engaged in witty or learned conversation. Much time was devoted to the sports of hunting and hawking and to musical entertainments. Collecting became the rage: manuscripts, incunabula, codices, antique finds. Of course, original sculptures and remnants from the Classical Age were scarce and expensive so copies, usually in bronze or stone, were commissioned by the thousands. Concurrently, the demand for paintings of all kinds surged, the subject matter no longer devoted so much to the glorification of Christianity or the State, but of a lighter concern: portraits of family or contemporaries, pagan gods or myths, mood pictures. Whereas admirals and adventurers once captured the popular imagination, it was now the turn of artists, architects and men of letters. The emphasis was on ever grander buildings, on art and music and on luxuries of every kind. Venice could never deny the riches of the East and the need for beautiful things and lavish ceremonies. But while earlier there had been some attempt by the sumptuary laws and other legislation to restrain or control excesses and immoderation, the government now actually encouraged them.

Maritime Vulnerability and Piracy

In any case, by the year 1600, a competent observer would have detected some underlying negative constraints that together threatened the very existence of Venice as a viable, independent state. Much of the eastern empire, including Cyprus, was now gone, swallowed up by the aggressive Turks. And although the *terrafirma* remained, that dependent territory was completely surrounded by acquisitive Spanish and Hapsburg jurisdictions that far outranked the Serenissima in resources and power. The years 1579 to 1589 had seen the revolt in the Netherlands against Philip II of Spain and his doomed armada against Elizabeth's Britain. As a consequence, more and more Dutch and English privateers, deep-keeled and heavily armed carracks, entered the Mediterranean not only to trade (often under more favorable concessions from the Ottoman sultan), but also to prey on Spanish merchantmen and their allies, which frequently included the Venetians. At the same time, the Republic's navy and merchant galleys, once second to none, were fast losing their military and commercial effectiveness, and were less able to withstand attacks from enemy ships and marauding pirates. The latter had long been a problem, especially those known as the Uskok buccaneers, who operated out of Dalmatia, and the Barbary Corsairs, based at a number of North African ports. Venice was in continual conflict with these pirates, but considering such concessions beneath its dignity, stubbornly refused to negotiate or pay ransom money. Accordingly, expensive convoys, partly financed by reluctant merchant shippers, had to be organized from increasingly limited naval resources.

Over many decades, Venice made repeated attempts to eradicate these marauders through special punitive expeditions. In addition, Venice sought cooperation from other Mediterranean powers whose merchants were equally vulnerable to attack—the Spanish viceroys of Naples and Sicily, the Tuscan grand duke's naval Order of St. Stephen, even the Knights of St. John at Malta. Occasionally these forays met with success and the predators were tracked down and apprehended, in which cases the pirate crews were given no quarter and every last man taken alive was immediately put to the sword, beheaded or hanged from a yardarm.

But by the early 17th century, with fewer native citizens willing to undergo the rigors of shipboard life, convicts and slaves chained to their benches or Greek and Dalmatian substitutes, paid by the guilds, were manning many Venetian merchantmen and even some of the war galleys. At the same time, fewer sons of the nobility were willing to be trained for command at sea or for merchant enterprise. A contemporary, Antonio Foscarini, the Venetian ambassador to England at the time, commented that the Republic's maritime trade was rapidly collapsing due to "bad crews and worse captains, so that any petty pirate can plunder them, because they will not fight."[1] It is not surprising, however, that such crews, who were often mistreated and who were not Venetian citizens with a stake in the venture, were demoralized. Conditions aboard open-decked galleys could be severe, especially in bad weather, and many died of exposure, disease or exhaustion. Little wonder they had no heart to resist when attacked, and that by the third decade of the century, fewer and fewer Venetian convoys ventured out beyond the Adriatic. One consequence was that the great traditions of Venetian seamanship slowly began to fade, a condition reflected in average contemporary rates of insurance for Venetian maritime ventures, which were about nine percent as compared, for example, to Dutch rates of five percent.[2]

There were a number of reasons why the Republic was reluctant to rebuild its merchant marine. For one, although overall European trade increased, a general contraction occurred in the volume of certain cargoes, such as sugar and cotton, that were important to Venice, as production in the Mediterranean was replaced elsewhere. Even the traditional spice and wine trade was being partially diverted and carried to Northern Europe by the larger and more efficient English and Dutch ships via Gibraltar or directly from the Far East around Africa. For another, shipbuilding at the Arsenale became relatively more expensive as the forests in the Veneto had been depleted and wood for construction was scarce and had to come from greater distances. Research has shown that both building and operating costs

---

[1] Foscarini was later tried and executed for treason by the Ten during a plot to overthrow the government. Afterwards, it was proved that he was wrongly accused and convicted. The Ten thereupon issued him a public apology and exoneration and he was reburied with a state funeral in 1622.

[2] These figures are for comparison purposes. Actual rates varied considerably with seasonal weather conditions, routes, types of cargo, number of armed escorts, etc., sometimes by two or three times. On occasion ships could not sail for lack of underwriting capacity as insurers withdrew their capital from the market.

of Dutch ships, for example, were less than two-thirds that of Venice.

Moreover, there continued a general rise in prices and wages, especially in Southern Europe, aggravated by the massive influx of silver from Spanish America. The stagnant Venetian economy could not keep up, nor could the ducat avoid a progressive devaluation. A galley that could have been built at the Arsenale for 4,500 ducats in the 1560s, cost three times that by 1620. Accordingly, shipyards closed down, Venetian mariners went elsewhere to work and vessels lost to pirates, privateers or shipwreck were simply not replaced. Instead, foreign carriers, usually English carracks, some as large as 700 tons and able to travel alone without the need or expense of a convoy, were often hired to transport long-distance cargoes. It has been calculated that the total tonnage of the Venetian merchant marine reached its maximum in the mid-1500s and had contracted to less than half by the early 17th century. Little by little the city became more of a local center for Italian and Adriatic trade and for luxury crafts, such as glass blowing and silk weaving. Even some traditional staples of local industry fell, including the production of woolen cloth, which declined by more than two-thirds between 1600 and 1625.

Renewed Conflict with the Papacy

Further aggravating the whole situation, another difficulty faced the city. Venice's relations with the Vatican and the rest of Catholic Europe had been steadily worsening after its unpopular treaty with the Ottomans and the collapse in 1573 of the Holy League. The root of the trouble had really begun long before with the antipapal attitude of the merchant-banker class, and later with the Renaissance humanist movement. Both were at odds with the older religious traditions which the invention of printing and the wider circulation of new ideas only helped to magnify. Social innovation and religious pluralism in places like Venice had created a psychological distress among European conservatives, both inside and outside the church, who sought to re-establish a philosophy of final truths and a return to the unity of a revived Catholicism by means of the Holy Inquisition. All along, Venice had maintained its usual independence from Rome and had offered only a minimum of cooperation with the Counter Reformation, which was dedicated to rooting out secularism and Lutheran heresy. While the Inquisitors were occasionally allowed to conduct heresy trials within the Veneto, all of their decisions had to be confirmed by Venetian lay officials, which in practice rendered the proceedings ineffectual. Similarly, Jesuit schools in Venetian territory were severely limited and hedged about with numerous prohibitions. And from the pope's standpoint, more offensive still was the University of Padua, where all young Venetian noblemen were educated and where Galileo had been given a professorship to pursue his astronomical research that was at odds with Catholic doctrine. The university had been in the forefront of the new humanistic and scientific studies and a bulwark of religious pluralism against papal or Jesuit authority. One occupant of St. Peter's chair at the time had actually complained aloud, "I am pope everywhere except in Venice."[3]

Such a flamboyant disregard for the established religious, political and moral convictions of the age created tension and helped to isolate the Republic from the general experience of the rest of Catholic Europe. The resulting strains finally came to a head in December 1605 when His Holiness, Pope Paul V, became infuriated by the Republic's stubborn enforcement of local laws, which restricted the church's ownership of land within the Veneto, and by its refusal to hand over several clerical offenders for trial in the papal courts. In combination, these two challenges to the pope's authority proved unacceptable and the city, with all its territories, was excommunicated yet again and put under a papal interdict requiring that the churches be closed and any form of religious worship forbidden. Far from complying, the Most Serene Republic refused to accept or even permit the publishing of the papal orders and instead declared any interruption of normal priestly duties punishable by death. In general, the government was obeyed, the pope threatened war and the situation continued to be tense for a year.

During this difficult time, the Venetian point of view was ably argued in a series of official papers and letters issued under the authority of the Venetian Senate. These treatises, which attracted wide attention throughout Europe, were written by a Servite friar named Paolo Sarpi, trained in legal theology and renowned for his learning.[4] For months polemics were exchanged on either side and the stalemate continued. Finally, realizing

---

[3] To quote a well-known comment once made by a visitor: "The Venetians love St. Mark very much, God somewhat and the papacy not at all."

[4] So important was Sarpi's role in the confrontation with Rome that several attempts were made to assassinate him. However, he died peacefully in his bed in 1623. A statue of him stands today in the Campo Santa Fosca.

that Venice would not give way and that the situation was undermining the Church's prestige, the pope, with the mediation of the French king, agreed to lift the excommunication and grant absolution. No one had actually been executed, although some Jesuits had been expelled from Venetian territory and forbidden to return. The Serene Republic had gambled again and the papacy had backed down. It is interesting to note that this was the last interdict ever issued in the history of the Catholic Church.

Foreign Dangers

Although apparently having won a moral or diplomatic victory, Venice could hardly be taken seriously on the military front. Fortunately for the Republic, Europe as a whole became deeply preoccupied with the Thirty Years War, which endured for most of the first half of the century and diverted attention away from the island city's increasing vulnerability. The Dutch had broken away from Spain to form their own republic and there were uprisings in Portugal, Catalonia, Naples and Sicily against the Spanish. Austria was tied down by religious wars in Germany and the Protestant campaigns of Gustavus Adolphus, who was aided by France under Louis XIII and Cardinal Richelieu. Venice managed to get through the period with only a couple of minor confrontations with the Hapsburg armies. These were of little consequence when compared to another appalling return of the plague in 1630, which this time wiped out almost a third of the city's population, cutting it back to about 100,000.

More or less successful in maintaining a position of neutrality in the west, Venice attempted the same policy in the east. This, too, was viable as long as the Turks were preoccupied with Persian problems, but by 1645 they had turned their eyes westward once again, determined to conquer Crete, the last major island denied them in the Eastern Mediterranean.[5] Venice's largest island possession for so many centuries, Crete was exceedingly important, not only economically but also psychologically, and the Republic put up a stout

---

[5] In the year 1645, John Evelyn wrote in his diary: "There being at this time a ship bound for the Holy Land, I had resolved to embark intending to see Jerusalem . . . but after I had provided all necessaries, laid in snow to cool our drink, bought some sheep, poultry, biscuit, spirits, and a little cabinet of drugs in case of sickness, our vessel happened to be pressed for service of the State to carry provisions to Candia (Crete) now newly attacked by the Turks; which altogether frustrated my design, to my great mortification."

resistance to the sultan's navy that continued on and off for an incredible 23 years. But once the Turks had obtained a sizeable foothold on the island, the war resolved itself into defensive actions and efforts to interrupt enemy supply convoys at sea. Venice won a number of naval engagements and gained the admiration of all Europe with its long and tenacious defense of the island's capital, Candia. But the Turks proved equally determined, and year after year gradually wore down the defenders, who ultimately were unable to withstand the repeated assaults against the city's battered ramparts. Vast sums had been spent on ships, supplies and fighting men and the records are full of numerous acts of heroism, both at sea and within the besieged capital. But in the end, all was to no avail. This painful loss effectively ended the Venetian presence in the eastern Mediterranean, although control was maintained in the Adriatic and Ionian Seas with the possession of Corfu.

Influence of the Baroque

Thus hemmed in by unfriendly states on all sides, yet struggling to maintain its pride and independence, the Serenissima also found itself surrounded by pressures on its cultural traditions and identity by the overwhelming and irresistible influence of the Roman Baroque. This stylistic revolution, developing out of Mannerism in central Italy, was early employed by the Church during the Counter-Reformation (mid- to late 1500s) in countless religious works meant to inspire the faithful and attract worshippers back to a rejuvenated Catholic faith. But it soon extended far beyond that, spreading into all facets of life and art, whether ecclesiastical or secular, Protestant or Catholic, public or private. The essence of the style embodied a break from the manifest restraint and classical balance of the Renaissance into new forms and patterns—whether spiritually, morally or politically motivated—of emotionally charged energy, flamboyant action and theatrical illusionism. This was expressed in visual art—especially in paintings, statues and reliefs of saints and martyrs—by excited or exaggerated gestures, fervent, ecstatic facial expressions, flying drapery, a dramatic juxtaposition of figures; and in architecture, by sculptured façades with deep, shadowed recesses, prominent colonnades, projecting cornices, broken or staggered pediments and entablatures, elaborate interiors richly carved and gilded and a generous use of colored marble. Not all this was imported into Venice without local modifications, but the essence and spirit of the Baroque eventually dominated.

This stylistic surrender can best be seen architecturally in the magnificent votive church of Santa Maria della Salute on the Grand Canal. This church was by far the most important addition to the city in what was to become the final period of the Republic's existence. Designed and built by Venice's last great architect, Baldassare Longhena (1598–1682), a follower of Palladio and Scamozzi, to fulfill the people's vow of thanksgiving for deliverance from the most recent recurrence of the plague, it was begun soon thereafter and required some 50 years to complete.

From a variety of angles, the building presents to the eye a dramatic and imposing silhouette that has become one of the most famous landmarks in the city. Palladio's influence is obvious not only in the centralized plan, but also in the interlocking columns and pediments of the main portal. These were derived, as in San Giorgio Maggiore, from a Roman temple front and are theatrically elevated above a flight of steps. But the architect's main achievement was to exploit the new baroque style in a restrained way so as not to offend local sensitivities, especially at such a central and key position in the heart of the city.[6] For example, the massive baroque volutes that act as buttresses to the great octagonal drum are subordinated to the overall clustering of the several cupolas in a form reminiscent of San Marco and the Venetian-Byzantine tradition. It is true that some of the architectural members do not always have a structural or logical purpose and are only decorative, but taken together the beautifully balanced proportions of the entire building constitute one of Venice's most memorable sights.

This building alone would have assured Longhena's reputation, but he was to make many more contributions in other parts of the city. He worked on numerous churches and *scuole*, for example the Scuola dei Carmini and that order's church of the Scalzi in the 1660s.[7] More important, however, are the two massive baroque palazzi he designed on the Grand Canal: Ca' Rezzonico (begun in 1667) and Ca' Pesaro (begun in 1679), both of which were finished by others after many years of construction. The façades of the two buildings are similar; both have generous proportions, substantial,

---

[6] Santa Maria della Salute in effect forms a counterweight at one point of an equilateral triangle connecting it across the lagoon with two other of Venice's most pivotal monuments—the Doge's Palace and San Giorgio Maggiore.

[7] Known as the Barefoot Friars (Scalzi), the Carmelites did not come to Venice until 1633, but were held in high esteem for their missionary work during the Turkish wars.

heavy rusticated lower floors, two upper floors of columned and balustraded windows with deep chiaroscuro effect, projecting cornices and decorative and bizarre carvings. Here is the full flowering and culmination of the Venetian Baroque in domestic architecture as expressed in the massive use of Istrian stone, the depth and rhythms of the colonnades and the sculptural treatment of the façades as a whole. At the same time the interiors were embellished with magnificently painted trompe l'oeil ceilings, dramatic, often gilded, stucco work, elaborate mantelpieces, Murano chandeliers and glass mirrors and monumental furniture—some lacquered, some carved and gilded. All are in the spirit of the new style.

The Baroque Overdone: Santa Maria del Giglio

Although the Ca' Rezzonico and the Ca' Pesaro are the best examples of the forceful introduction of the Baroque into the city's secular architecture, a degree of restraint and good taste is evident. This is not the case with a number of contemporary religious buildings designed by other architects. Most garish, if not downright ugly, is the Church of San Moise[8] (built in the 1660s) whose heavy-handed façade, overloaded with festoons, statues and garlands, has become a nesting place for pigeons and an object of general derision. The dark interior, with its clutter of baroque and rococo sculptures, monuments and paintings, is not much better.

Nearby is the similarly controversial church of Santa Maria del Giglio or the Zobenigo,[9] which was rebuilt in the 1680s when the façade was added. Systematically disparaged by writers, critics and tourists from Ruskin to Baedecker, it serves as an example of a 17th-century proclivity for converting a religious building into the funeral monument of a rich patron. In this case, the man who bequeathed the money (30,000 ducats) and the design for the façade (by Giuseppe Sardi, 1630–1699) was one Antonio Barbaro (1627–1679), a victorious admiral and diplomat who had served his country in numerous capacities, including service in campaigns against the Turks in Crete and the Morea. Shortly after his death and in conformance with his will, the work of reconstruction was speedily carried out during the next

---

[8] It is not recorded whether Moses was ever sainted, but that is how the Venetians term it.

[9] Named for the giglio (lily) presented to the Virgin by the archangel Gabriel; later nicknamed Zobenigo after a corruption of the family name of Jubanico, who were early patrons of the church.

The excessive baroque façade of S. Maria del Giglio reflects the egotism of the church's patrons.

few years. The most striking feature, the façade, devoid of even the slightest religious reference, is wholly given over to the glorification of Antonio and the Barbaro family. In the center is a statue of the admiral himself, standing on his own sarcophagus and theatrically posed with the symbols of his office—helmet and baton—while above him is the luxuriant Barbaro coat of arms. Surrounding the statue and alluding to his fancied excellence are figures of Fame, Glory, Wisdom, the Cardinal Virtues, etc. and below are those of Antonio's four brothers. The most interesting features of the façade, however, are the carved relief maps along the base. They represent areas of Venetian and Barbaro involvement—Candia, Padua, Spalato, Corfu, Zara, etc. Above on the frieze, other reliefs depict sea battles against the Turks with their details of war galleys. Altogether, the whole ensemble mirrors the temper of the times; it is a flamboyant statement of exaltation, both of the family and the city itself, still proud and wealthy, but now more inclined to overstate its achievements and past glories. The Baroque was, of course, the perfect medium for expressing the attitudes of the patrons, wherein the basic architecture of the building, to say nothing of its purpose, was mostly subordinated to a program of secular sculpture and decoration.

Inside, fewer modifications from the earlier church were made, and a less secular tone is set by the white *marmorino* walls and an abundance of religious works. Famous is the Giglio's 17th-century organ (fabricated in the 1690s). The organ's case is decorated with several panels by one of Venice's best baroque painters, Antonio Zanchi (1631–1722),[10] who also was responsible for a number of other paintings in the nave and sacristy. However, the church's most treasured possession, the pair of pictures of the Evangelists by Tintoretto hanging behind the high altar, just below the organ loft, is from an earlier period.[11]

Between 1672 and 1680, Sardi designed another façade, the one that is attached to Longhena's church of the Scalzi. This work is a further example of baroque ostentation, but is a little more successful. Much easier to appreciate is the Palazzo Surian-Bellotto (built in the 1690s) on the Rio di Cannaregio. This structure is also sometimes attributed to Sardi, but its restrained motifs and wide, horizontal lines seem to indicate a break with the

---

[10] His tomb is here in the Giglio.

[11] The organ, as well as the entire interior and exterior of the church, have been extensively restored between 1969 and 1972 by the International Fund for Monuments.

architect's predisposition and the era's overriding style.

Venetian painting in the 17th century was on the whole relatively unimportant. The special qualities of painterliness and color, which had characterized the city's greatest achievements, were either poorly imitated or subordinated to outside influences and the most important artists were indeed foreigners who took up residence in the city.[12] Of Venetians themselves, only Palma Giovanni (1544–1628), a pupil of Titian in his last years, is worthy of special mention. Uneven though prolific—his work is scattered throughout the city's churches—Palma strove to emulate his mentors, Bassano, Titian and Tintoretto, but the theatricality of the all-powerful Mannerist/baroque influence dominated his compositions as it did those of his contemporaries.[13]

Venice Attempts to Maintain Its Character

Potent as the cultural shock wave from outside was, Venice did attempt some resistance, just as it also made efforts to disregard the dominant political, moral and religious dogmas of its neighbors. It had held the Hapsburgs at a distance and never considered adopting any aspect of their system of governance. Venice had also rebuffed the popes and refused to comply with the demands of the Counter Reformation. But this certainly did not mean that the Venetians had forsaken the Catholic religion and there was never any possibility that the Republic would surrender to Protestantism, the austere and puritanical aspects of which were utterly foreign to the Venetian character. Nor was the city ever a refuge of tolerance in declared principle, even though there existed a general sympathy for the Reformation. Many diverse believers and non-believers—Protestants, Jews, Orthodox Christians, even Muslims—managed to live there, worshipping as they pleased without serious interference. Venetians expressed their Christianity not so much by conforming to Catholic ideology or papal governance, but through visible, tangible, external forms. They demonstrated their piety in the innumerable

---

[12] Domenico Fetti (from Rome), Bernardo Strozzi (Genoa), Jan Liss or Johan Lys (Germany), Sebastiano Mazzoni (Florence), Nicolas Regnier (Niccolo Renieri as he translated his native Flemish name)—all of whose works can be seen in the Accademia and in the Galleria Querini-Stampalia.

[13] The Church of San Giuliano (Venetian: San Zulian) contains some of his, and also Zanchi's, best work.

sacred relics preserved in scores of churches, the holy shrines scattered throughout the city, the extravagant processions and religious rituals, the ostentatious display of pious sentiments in the art assembled by the parishes, the monasteries, the *scuole* and other civic authorities.

Carnevale

Moreover, Venice was always anxious to maintain all its ancient Catholic festivals, especially that of Carnevale. Originally an agricultural rite to propitiate the gods and encourage fertility, this seasonal festival had merged during the Middle Ages with the Christian celebration of Easter. Always given over to heavy eating, drinking and carousing with the church's sanction, there still had been limits so as not to seriously corrupt morality or carry over into the rest of the year. But with the growth of cities during the Renaissance and increased prosperity, the festivities lengthened and became more compelling, eventually starting in Venice as early as St. Stephen's Day (December 26) and lasting through the spring until Lent. Acrobats performed amazing feats in the public squares, bear and bull baiting drew large crowds, oxen were sacrificed, actors declaimed on open-air stages, menageries of exotic wild animals were displayed, ritual dancing went on for hours and fireworks filled the night skies.

The diarist John Evelyn, writing in 1646, was impressed

> When all the world repairs to Venice to see the folly and madness of Carnival, persons of all conditions disguise themselves in antique dress and with extravagant music and a thousand gambols, traverse the streets from house to house. . . They have a barbarous custom of hunting bulls about the city which is very dangerous. They fling eggs filled with sweet water, the comedians have liberty, witty pasquals (lampoons) are thrown about and the mountebanks have their stages at every corner. . . It is impossible to recount the universal madness of this place during this time of license."[14]

---

[14] But no written description can ever capture the color, the intrigue, the drama of Carnevale better than Giandomenico Tiepolo's painting entitled The Minuet, unfortunately no longer in Venice, but in the Louvre.

From the beginning Carnevale provided a diversion and a release of frustrations for the lower classes. In Venice particularly, disguises in the form of ritual costumes and masks played a vital part in the festivities, permitting people to take on an assumed identity, to mock and satirize authority and to free themselves of everyday restraint. A typical Venetian costume was the *domino*, a long hooded garment like a monk's robe, or the *bauta,* a black silk cape covering head and shoulders, over which a mask, usually white, and a tri-cornered hat were worn, a disguise favored by all classes so that a person's rank or status was unknown. Another was the *moretta,* a long black velvet cape and hood with an oval opening for the face mask, worn only by women.

Government Regulation of Excess

Attempts were made by the government to control the use of disguises, but by 1700 so many exceptions were made that the laws were meaningless. Even outside the carnival season, when these traditional costumes were not worn, the upper classes were to be seen wigged and perfumed in the most sumptuous and colorful regalia, day and night, throughout the year. The younger nobles' outfits were the most astonishing. Their clothes were made from velvet or damask or linen trimmed with lace and studded with gold and silver buttons and ornaments, to which some added embroidered sashes, striped stockings and brightly colored shoes with polished buckles. Even the older patricians, required by their rank to appear in prescribed outer gowns (crimson for senators, red for the *Savii,* black for the members of the Ten; the colors probably stemmed not from the Roman past but from the Byzantine connection), often left them open or doffed them completely outside the council halls, revealing garments hardly less luxurious than those of their juniors. The women, especially the courtesans, outdid the men with their elegant parasols, preposterous ribboned hats, painted fans, handkerchiefs of colored silk, furs and muffs, as well as the heavy use of cosmetics on faces, necks and bosoms. And by mid-century, powdered wigs in the French style came into fashion for both sexes.

Even from earlier times, the need to restrict display, pomp and vanity was often recognized and the so-called sumptuary laws were repeatedly imposed and in theory enforced by the aptly sounding Proveditori alle Pompe. Not only were strictures instituted on clothing, especially those of women (e.g. the length, material and color of dresses, the number of jewels, etc.), but limits were also put on the use of brocades and wall-hangings, the size of dowries, the color of gondolas (black only) and even the details of domestic architecture (eaves could not project too far, statues on façades and roofs were prohibited). In addition, there were continual attempts by the government and the *scuole* to discipline the population by regulating working hours, wine consumption, gambling, taverns, brothels, swearing and cursing. But no matter how often restraints were attempted, ways were found to avoid them.

A good example of the difficulty in governing behavior were the mountebanks mentioned so often by foreign travelers. These hucksters were the subject of municipal regulations that tried to control their numbers time and again. But in the 1600s, they were everywhere in Venice, dressed in bizarre costumes, singing and jesting from their wooden platforms, while attempting to foist their patent medicines and other remedies on a credulous and intrigued public.

Rise of the Performing Arts

Especially popular were the open-air puppet shows, which often portrayed uncouth caricatures of the traditional participants in the *commedia dell'Arte*. The latter were year-round entertainments staged by troupes of actors portraying certain stock characters. Sometimes called Commedia Improvisa, because the spoken lines were largely improvised to suit the occasion, hardly anything was written down, except for a *scenario* or outline of the plot. With this, each of the actors worked out the stage mechanics and invented his own lines. According to Casanova, if one of them "stopped short for a word, the gallery would hiss him mercilessly."

These plots had evolved out of street plays based on hundreds of profane or ribald variations on humorous themes or comic domestic relationships. Invariably the same stock characters appeared: Pantalone, a typical Venetian merchant—shrewd, calculating, cautious to the point of miserliness (from which, by the way, came Shakespeare's Shylock); the daughter who gives him trouble and worry; *il dottore,* a pompous parody of the half-educated intellectual whose elaborate orations, embroidered with Latin quotations, are invariably absurd; the *zanni* (servants or peasants)—Arlecchino (Harlequin, playing the acrobatic clown or buffoon), Brighella, Pulcinella; and always the romantic young lovers. Some of the characters wore masks and usually delivered their lines in the crude dialects of Venice, Bergamo or Bologna, all the better for low comedy, while the lovers spoke in the purer, literate Italian (Tuscan).

Originally rustic, coarse and performed in the open on movable platforms, the *Commedia Dell'Arte* had become more sophisticated and racy by the 17th century and was now regularly staged indoors and patronized by the upper classes. Accordingly, a number of privately owned buildings that were designed specifically as commercial theatres appeared in Venice.

Opera in Venice

Although it was invented in Florence around 1600, opera, too, was soon perfected in Venice, which became its center under the leadership of such musicians as Giovanni Gabrieli (1557–1612), Claudio Monteverdi (1567–1643) and Francesco Cavalli (1602–1676). The first two were choir-masters at San Marco and pioneered baroque-style innovations in church music. Beyond this, Monteverdi became the most successful composer of opera of his time, moving away from its earlier recitative mode onto a more melodious plane.

The world's first public opera house designed for that purpose, San Casciano, was opened in Venice in 1637 and nightly attendance by the patrician class quickly became routine. As with the *commedia dell'arte*, the usual behavior of those in the audience was by our standards incredible. They spent as much time gossiping, flirting, playing cards and eating as they did listening to the drama itself. But their critical reaction, serving as a foil to the actors, was all important and quickly and emphatically determined success or failure. As many as 388 operas were produced in Venice alone between 1637 and 1700. Cavalli was the first to use the word *opera,* from the phrase *opera scenica* to denote a scenic work, in describing the new art form. As the origin of the phrase *opera scenica* would suggest, staging soon became as important as the words or music. The technique of painting scenery and shifting it rapidly about for dramatic effect became a Venetian specialty, exported abroad along with the operas themselves. Throughout the 17th century, Venice became the unquestioned European center of music, not only for opera, but for instrumental concerts, cantatas, and especially for the choirs of young girls from its internationally renowned conservatories.[15]

Again we hear from John Evelyn who often attended the opera during his stay in Venice (1645–1646). He was impressed by these performances:

> ...Where comedies and other plays are represented in recitative music by the most excellent musicians, vocal and instrumental, with variety of scenes painted and contrived with no less art of perspective, and machines for flying in the air, and other wonderful notions; taken together it is one of the most magnificent and expensive diversions the wit of man can invent.

One opera he writes "held us by the eyes and ears til two in the morning, when we went to see the noblemen and their ladies at basset (cards), all in masquerade." On another occasion he dined at the English consul's home where they were entertained by one of the best known singers

> so late at night that, conveying a gentle woman who had supped with us to her gondola at the usual landing, we were shot at by two carbines from another gondola in which were a noble Venetian and his courtesan unwilling to be disturbed, which made us run in and fetch other weapons, not knowing what the matter was, til we were informed of the danger we might incur by pursuing it farther.

Gambling and Other Diversions

Parallel with the development of opera was an obsession with gambling, originally conducted in the homes of the nobles, who acted as croupiers and bankers and sometimes combined their resources to operate as gambling syndicates. At first these casinos were not open to the general public but functioned as private commercial enterprises for upper-class Venetians and foreigners of both sexes seeking excitement and diversion. Although they were opposed in the beginning by the authorities, the casinos were impossible to control. This led to the official approval of a public gaming

---

[15] There were four that were noteworthy. Commonly called the Pietà, the Ospetaletto, the Incurabili, and the Mendicanti, all were state-financed charitable institutions for orphaned or dowryless girls.

house near San Moise in the *ridotto* (annex) of a house belonging to the Dandolo family, that soon came to be known simply as the Ridotto. With rooms for refreshments and games of chance—faro, biribi (forerunner of roulette), basset—it acquired a wide reputation and operated continuously almost until the end of the Republic.

A painting of the interior of the Ridotto by Guardi, now in the Ca' Rezzonico, immortalized the place, as well as the mood and temper of the times. It also illustrates the elaborate dress of upper-class Venetian women in the 17th and 18th century, including the mandatory masks that were customary in the casinos. These ladies certainly did not go unnoticed by foreign visitors, but were in fact one of the incentives for going to Venice. John Evelyn remarked that

> their garb is very odd, as seeming always in Masquerade, their petticoats coming from their very armpits, so that they are near ¾ apron, their exceedingly wide sleeves commonly tucked up to the shoulders showing their naked arms . . . totally different from other nations.

Another Englishman, Fynes Moryson, was astonished to see "their naked necks and breasts bound up and swelling with linen and their skin white as chalk." Many travelers commented on how the women, especially the courtesans, painted their faces and scented their breasts, clothing and bedding. Also noted was their novel custom of dying their hair blond and then spreading it out to dry on the wide brims of special crownless hats.

Surrounded as they were by a continent undergoing the extremes of a repressive moral code imposed by Catholic and Protestant reformers, the Venetian lifestyle, involving theatergoing, gambling, elaborate dress, sumptuous dining and every other display of sensuality and licentious frivolity, soon became the talk and fascination of all the courts of Europe and an important diversion for young men on the Grand Tour.

The Patriciate and Economy Weaken

In other respects, however, the center of European attention was moving northward away from Venice and Italy. Reformed Catholic theology and morality forbade new departures and the dogmatic rigidity of the Counter-Reformation in the Mediterranean countries actively suppressed scientific innovation or experiment, as it also discouraged any changes in the organization of government, business or agriculture. Intellectually, the Italian universities began to lose preeminence to centers of scientific inquiry in France, Holland, Germany and England, although the University of Padua still commanded respect for its medical school. Italy remained divided into many entrenched local or foreign regimes that became ever more inflexible, while the church establishment and the monastic orders grew larger and more expensive to maintain. This was certainly the case in the Veneto where in the late 1700s the Republic dissolved a number of Benedictine and other monasteries, whereby some 35,000 acres were turned over to the nobility and to local landlords. But the antiquated and oppressive agricultural system stemming from medieval feudal arrangements, combined with a growing rural population, kept the peasantry poor, while protectionist policies and high taxes discouraged commercial development and the increase of the middle class.

Fortunately the Venetians managed to stay out of the War of the Spanish Succession (1701–1713),[16] which embroiled most of Europe, but their policy of semi-armed neutrality, though less costly than full scale war, was financially burdensome. They also had to contend with the never-ending conflict with the Barbary pirates and sporadic forays against the Turks.[17] In any case, the government debt increased from eight million ducats in 1641 to 50 million by 1714.

The concerns of the Venetian nobility inevitably followed their money, which they increasingly invested in farmland or government bonds. Accordingly, they concentrated on agriculture and, of course, politics. The political constitution, long since frozen into its unique form and providing a large measure of domestic peace, was generally admired by the rest of Europe, which was still suffering from religious strife and was beginning to feel the effects of modern political faction and revolutionary turmoil. Venice, benign, stable, non-monarchial and arriving at decisions by debate

---

[16] This war was fought to determine whether Louis XIV of France would inherit the throne of Spain, contrary to the wishes of England, Holland and Austria. Defeated at Blenheim and elsewhere, Louis was forced to renounce the inheritance at the Treaty of Utrecht (1713), while Austria obtained Naples and Milan.

[17] Venice actually retook parts of the Morea between 1683 and 1699 but lost them to the Ottomans by 1715. However it managed to hold on to Corfu despite an attempted Turkish invasion in 1716. By then a mutual exhaustion on both sides at last resulted in a treaty in 1718 that settled the status quo for the rest of the century.

and balloting, seemed the perfect model for republicanism. But in fact, this became less and less true. Political parties never developed in Venice and power tended to concentrate more and more in the Ten, the Savii Grande, and the three State Inquisitors, which offices were occupied in rotation by an ever diminishing number of nobles. The total number of Great Council members contracted from more than 2,000 in the 16th century to about 1,000 by the end of the Republic. This decrease was due partly to the consequences of the plague and partly to a deliberate policy of restricted marriage and fewer children in order to prevent the dispersal of inherited wealth, which became progressively more concentrated in a smaller number of families. By the 1700s well over half of the male members of the Patriciate remained bachelors and numerous ancient lineages died out completely. And this was true despite efforts after 1645 to augment the class by the sale of seats in the Great Council. From that time until around 1718, the names of 127 wealthy individuals were inscribed into the Book of Gold on payment of at least 100,000 ducats each—a very large sum in those days. Of these, a number were Venetian citizens by birth (*cittadini*), or local patricians from the mainland cities, but most were simply successful businessmen who could financially afford the honor. Emulating the older families, these new members often gave up their bourgeois occupations and invested what was left of their assets in land. Other offices were also sold—for example, that of Procurator of St. Marks went for 20,000 ducats.[18]

Not only the nobles but practically everyone else in Venice had come to acquire their respective position or occupation, from artisan to chancery official, by inheritance, handed down from father to son. This inflexibility insured a vested interest in the status quo, but did not encourage a dynamic internal economy. Employment in the silk and woolen mills fell drastically; cargo shipments declined as Trieste and Ancona captured more of the traffic; porters had no work and even the number of printing presses, still a Venetian specialty, dropped by a third by mid-century. In addition, unlike Europe as a whole, the city's population did not expand, but stabilized at around 150,000. In the meantime, even while commerce and industry were languishing and tax revenues were falling, the government spent vast sums

---

[18] It is interesting to note that later in the century (1775) 40 memberships in the Patriciate and the Great Council were offered to approved families, but only 10 were taken up. The price had become too dear and the honor dubious.

on repaving the Piazza and the *campi,* on street lighting (heretofore almost nonexistent), on deepening the ship channels and on rebuilding the sea wall along the *lidi,* (vital for the preservation of the lagoon).

The simple fact was that by the 18th century Venice could no longer afford the status of a major European power. With much of its empire gone and with it, the trade, Venice's tax base was inadequate. The navy was gradually cut back in size and the army, though never very large, practically disappeared. Moreover, the once famous Arsenale, no longer essential to the government, was in an advanced state of decay. Without even the pretense of real military power and relying more and more on negotiation and luck for its safety, the Serenissima's declared policy of "armed neutrality" eventually became "neutrality by any means." Under such conditions national pride had to be tempered with reality. As an example, in 1763 Venice concluded a treaty involving tribute money with the Barbary pirates, a concession it would never have considered in its prime.

The Final Artistic Revival: Religious and Monumental Painting

Remarkably, despite these weaknesses, enough private wealth and church patronage remained in Venice to indulge still a last surge of artistic expression and a few more architectural monuments. A great deal of diverse and somewhat unexpected cultural activity continued—a sort of final flowering, a last burst of glory.

The most striking and prolific phase of this period is to be found among the city's painters, who somehow returned, after a hiatus in the 17th century, to the great coloristic and painterly values of Venice's golden age. Two artistic currents, both from the early decades of the 1700s, led to the major personality, Gian Battista Tiepolo. The first, centering around Sebastiano Ricci (1659–1734) and his follower Giovanni Pellegrini (1676–1741), proceeds mainly from the compositional style of Veronese, but shows the lighter touch and airy spaciousness that was characteristic of contemporary rococo influence. Ricci's great altarpiece *The Madonna and Saints,* still hanging in its original place at San Giorgio Maggiore, is a good example. The other artistic current is to be found in the more serious and intense paintings of Giovanni Piazzetta (1683–1754), molded from the Venetian tradition in combination with the realism and compositional drama emanating from the

G.B. Tiepolo's painting, *Christ on Calvary*, in the church of S. Alvise, reflects the artist's theatrics.

baroque influences of central Italy.[19]

From this background came the greatest Venetian painter of the period, Gian Battista (abbreviated Giambattista or G.B.) Tiepolo (1696–1770), who carried his native Venetian school on to new heights. The grand monumental manner of Tintoretto and Veronese were merged in him, along with the compositional revival by Ricci and the illusionistic drama and decorative, yet realistic, detail of the baroque/rococo style expressed by Piazzetta. Tiepolo had the prolific range of a true Renaissance artist, producing a vast amount of diverse work—religious subjects, cabinet paintings, landscapes—but it was as a large scale mural decorator using classical or mythological themes that made him internationally famous early on.

The general consensus is, however, that despite his keen observation of nature, infallible brushwork, mastery of the painter's technique and the

---

[19] Several examples of Ricci's and Piazzetta's work are in the Accademia and the Ca' Rezzonico.

The Virgin in Glory, one of many paintings at the Scuola dei Carmini by G.B. Tiepolo displaying his genius for dramatic compositions and vibrant color.

This subtle conversation piece by Francesco Guardi shows a deceptively innocent gathering in the nun's *parlatorio* at San Zaccaria.

breadth of his range and scope, he was ultimately a prisoner of his era and of his own stylistic demands, producing works more melodramatic than profound. Even in those paintings that reveal a sincere spiritual dimension, such as those in the church of Sant' Alvise, he surrenders to virtuosity and drama. While he was the perfect artist to depict the sensuality, pageantry and contrived allegories and myths of his time and place, the decadence and the lack of serious purpose of his country and his patrons are reflected in the superficiality and staged quality of his work.

Nevertheless, his art is fascinating and, although he was called away to decorate ceilings and walls all over Europe, a good selection remains in his native city. Besides the Accademia collections and the famous ceiling murals in the Ca' Rezzonico, there are his masterful Anthony and Cleopatra wall frescoes in the Palazzo Labia[20] and the cycle of religious paintings for the upper hall of the Scuola Grande dei Carmini, which reveal the artist's personal piety that so inspired his fellow citizens.

---

[20] The ballroom in the palace where they are located was a reconstruction by Giorgio Massari, who removed a floor between two levels and created a cube-shaped room some 40 feet in each direction, one of the most impressive in Venice. Covered from floor to ceiling with trompe l'oeil architectural decorations that frame Tiepolo's frescoes, the whole grand effect speaks to the extravagance, not to say the delusions, of the Labia family and the age.

Francesco Guardi's genre scene of the infamous Ridotto Casino and his masked contemporaries gambling, drinking and conducting their veiled liaisons.

Genre Painting

Among other artists represented at the Ca' Rezzonico, all of whom subtly reveal the wealth and elegance as well as the frivolity and hedonism of upper-class Venetian life of the time, are Pietro Longhi (1702–1785), Francesco Guardi (1712–1793) and Giovanni Domenico (Giandomenico or G.D.) Tiepolo (1727–1804), Giambattista's son. Perhaps the best known paintings in the palace are those entitled *La Parlatorio* and *Il Ridotto,* both once thought to be by his brother Gianantonio, but now attributed to Francesco Guardi. One pictures the interior of the reception room at the Convent of San Zaccaria, which was notorious for the immorality of the nuns, seen here behind a grill waiting to entertain their visitors. The other, the setting of which is the famous gambling hall at San Moise, depicts the participants in their masks amid an atmosphere of revelry and intrigue. Both of the houses portrayed served as trysting places and both paintings convey the feeling of jaded courtliness on the surface and of conspiracy behind the scenes.

Prominent in the Ca' Rezzonico collections are a number of genre works by Longhi. These small conversation pieces are remarkable not so much for their artistic merit, but for their gently satirical, yet incisive comments on the Venetian milieu. They show scenes from lower-class and bourgeois life, as

G.D. Tiepolo's fresco of a local crowd lining up to view a diorama of exotic places—the new world—a late work (1791) as the old world of Venice draws to a close.

well as the luxurious, though often empty, existence of the patricians.

Another painter of genre, but on a higher plane, was the great Tiepolo's son Giandomenico, who collaborated for many years with his father and almost equalled him in ability. Like Longhi, he provides a glimpse into the everyday life of the people, but Giandomenico's work is much more profound and of greater artistry. His painting known as *The New World* at the Ca' Rezzonico is a good example, along with a series depicting the festivities of carnival as seen through the figures of the white-costumed clowns and acrobats.

Vedutisti and Capricci Painting

Running parallel to this regeneration of religious, monumental and genre painting, the Venetian school at the same time produced two other categories of painters. One group, the *vedutisti,* turned out the now familiar view or cityscape paintings, the movement coalescing in the realistic work of Antonio Canaletto (1697–1768) and his nephew and pupil Bernardo Bellotto (1720–1780).

Canaletto's earlier work followed the lead of Piazzetta, emphasizing the chiaroscuro technique, but later on he subordinated this to his superb mastery of diffused light and atmospheric spatial values. Throughout his

This painting of a feast day celebration by Francesco Guardi captures 18th-century Venice's frantic efforts to entertain the world.

works, perspective balance and accuracy are meticulously calculated, but never dominate the aesthetics of the compositions. Canaletto concentrated most of his life on architectural and topographical views, especially scenes of his native Venice. Early in his career, these portraits of the city were in tremendous demand by collectors all over Europe, especially in England, and thus, practically none of Canaletto's paintings remain in Venetian museums.[21]

Canaletto's nephew, Bellotto, was strongly influenced by him, as was Francesco Guardi. The latter, however, gradually drew away from Canaletto's clear precision toward another group, pioneered by Sebastiano Ricci; these were artists producing more whimsical, fanciful and nostalgic pictures called *capricci*, often of poetic ruins in romanticized landscapes. Dramatic storms and lightning, fleeting figures seen hurrying and desperate or lethargic and disconsolate, either surviving among the remnants of ancient buildings or playing out jaded roles

---

[21] The Accademia has a couple. Most Canalettos were purchased by English collectors, including the Crown. Joseph Smith, a long time resident of Venice and later British consul, transacted many of these sales and served as a commission agent for the artist.

A typical and poignant Francesco Guardi *Capriccio* of melancholy ruins in the fading light of a civilization that had lost its way.

in archaic ceremonies—these are the recurrent themes with which Guardi described the inner mood of his contemporary Venetians. His paintings of the vast stretches of the lagoon, as well as of views of Venice itself, are all wrapped in drama and mystery and give a feeling of unreality. These pictures are so different from the orderly and tranquil cityscapes of Canaletto, as if the artist were contemplating, as indeed he was, the remnants of a lost civilization.

Guardi was the last of the great Venetian painters. And while he was only one among many to paint the topography of the city, he was the most profound. We feel we are viewing an unworldly place of the imagination, a mysterious relic from the past. This was the theme to be caught up later and exploited by the Impressionists as they and others made Venice their unrivalled place of pilgrimage.

Sculpture in the 18th Century: Antonio Canova

Meanwhile the art of stone carving was continuing in Venice, no less so than in Italy generally, as the details of innumerable palace façades, gardens and church interiors will testify. Venice had its share of talented and more than competent sculptors,[22] each moving toward a more perfect realism within the scope of the dominating rococo style, but it was not until late in the century that the city produced one of genius and international fame.

Antonio Canova (1757–1822) was recognized at an early age and taken under patronage by a patrician senator, Giovanni Falier.[23] The young sculptor promptly produced three statues superior to anything done in Venice for centuries—the Orpheus, the Eurydice, and the group of Daedalus and Icarus, all now in the Correr. Fame was immediate and he was soon called away to Rome to develop his neoclassical style, later so admired by the French and Napoleon. It can be readily recognized in Canova's renowned series of statues from Greek mythology, now scattered around Europe's museums— the Villa Borghese, the Palazzo Pitti, the Louvre, the Hermitage, but none, unfortunately, in Venice. In addition, he was responsible for several tombs at St. Peter's for as many popes and other works ordered by Bonaparte. The sculptor shuttled back and forth between Rome and Paris for most of his life, but he finally returned to Venice to work in his last years.

Venetian Architecture in the 18th Century

Throughout the 18th century, a number of architects worked alongside the sculptors, either carrying on the baroque/Palladian tradition or moving ahead to the European neoclassical style. Two of the best examples of the latter in Venice are the Church of San Simeone Piccolo and the Church of the Maddalena. Both are built on centralized plans with domes, inspired by Rome's ancient Pantheon, but designed with the clear, pure, simplified lines characteristic of the rationalist influence from France. More important, however, was the work of Giorgio Massari (1686–1766), who gathered together the many themes of his immediate Venetian predecessors and epitomizes the period. Two churches and a palace that he designed are worth considering.

Santa Maria del Rosario, better known as the Gesuati Church from an

---

[22] The best known were Orazio Marinoli (1643–1720), Andrea Brustolon (1662–1732) and Antonio Corradini (1668–1752), all of whom are represented at the Rezzonico.

[23] A testamentary monument by Canova to his first patron, Falier, may be seen in the Church of Santo Stefano.

order of friars of that name, was built by Massari between 1726 and 1736 and is situated on the sunlit Fomdamenta delle Zattere facing south on the Giudecca Canal. The columns and pediments of the façade of the Gesuati harken back to Palladio's Redentore church directly across the water, though the former has a less refined, more massively sculptural treatment, the lingering influence of the Baroque. Massari's building, along with its wealth of contemporaneous sculpture and painting inside (especially a number of altarpieces by Ricci, Piazzetta and G.B. Tiepolo, as well as several grand ceiling frescoes by the last artist, all of which remain in their original positions) is a good example of 18th-century Venetian religious architecture.

Massari's other church, the Pietà on the Riva Schiavoni, is interesting for its associations as well as its architecture. It was built between 1744 and 1760 and was a reconstruction of an earlier chapel long used by the young girls of the adjoining hostel—the Pietà—one of the city's four principal charitable institutions for orphaned girls and, as mentioned, famous for their choirs and musical concerts.[24] Antonio Vivaldi (1675–1741), the composer of some 44 operas, had been violin teacher and chorus master there for many years. Accordingly, Massari designed the new church primarily as a concert hall. He used an oval centralized plan with rounded interior walls, low domed ceiling and a buffer-like entrance hall for acoustical reasons. The sophisticated architecture is further enhanced by the woodwork of the choir stalls and altar rails and by G.B. Tiepolo's beautiful paintings, including his *The Coronation of the Virgin* (1754). Positioned at the convergence of the ceiling vaults amidst a blaze of light and color, this work depicts many of the heavenly participants appropriately playing musical instruments.

Finally should be mentioned the Palazzo Grassi, just across from the Ca' Rezzonico. Undertaken by Massari in 1748, this was the last of the great houses to be built on the Grand Canal in the final years of the Republic. No longer rococo, the severe, rather flat, neoclassical façade incorporates ideas from earlier periods, but is stretched out width-wise to emphasize the horizontal line of the canal. The more interesting interior was designed logically around a large central colonnaded courtyard, which is approached from the water by a portico that opens wider in two stages

---

[24] Among others, both Rousseau and Goethe claimed they had never heard such "exquisite, ineffable beauty" as these female voices singing in harmony.

and in turn precedes a symmetrically divided staircase and loggia above.[25] An improvement over a similar arrangement at Ca' Rezzonico, where the courtyard is too confining and the stairway seems like an afterthought, this house was especially created for the self-indulgent life of an aristocratic 18th-century family and their lavish entertainments.

Pleasure Center for the World

It was at this time, in the 18th century, that the city gave itself over to the pursuit of pleasure as Venetians turned away from the problems and challenges stirring abroad. Carnival, once confined to the Lenten season, was extended through half the year, and the other half lived in anticipation of it. With less serious government business to conduct—and any such matters handled largely by an entrenched civil service—the noble class was relatively free to engage in any frivolity. From morning until late at night, music, gambling, feasting, gossiping and theatergoing became full time occupations. Balls, banquets and water pageants punctuated every month and numerous *festivi* featuring clowns, dancers, acrobats and boxers provided an excuse to dress up in costume and to festoon the buildings on the piazza with hundreds of torches. The first coffee houses appeared when that drink became fashionable, providing yet another opportunity for social intercourse. Two such cafés on the Piazza San Marco still remain: Florian's, opened in 1720, and Quadri's somewhat later. In these cafés and in the gambling casinos, the wives of the nobles, often accompanied not by their husbands, but by a *cavaliere servente* (a younger escort, often a noble himself) could be seen listening to the latest scandals or arranging their more or less discreet assignations. These cavaliers—part gigolo, part companion, sometimes, but not always, lover—were generally known in Venice as *cicisbei*. They accompanied their ladies everywhere—to the opera, dinner parties, gambling casinos, regattas on the canals—morning, noon and night. The custom of wearing the carnival mask only served to heighten the desire for intrigue and the spirit of carefree revelry. Venice became a perpetual party, hostess to the world, playground of Europe. And the tourists flocked from every country, especially from England, loving it and reporting on it in detail.

---

[25] The palace is open to visitors as it is now used for art exhibitions.

The beautifully preserved 18th-century ambience of Florian's Cafe.

One such visitor, E.W. Phillips, observed that

> Venice had parted with her old nobility of soul, and
> enjoyment had become the only aim in life . . . It had become
> the city of pleasure . . . The convents boasted their *salons,*
> where nuns in low-cut dresses, with pearls in their hair,
> received the advances of nobles and gallant *abbes.*

A visit to the small Querini-Stampalia Gallery can provide a glimpse
into this era. Here, together with more genre works by Longhi, especially
hunting scenes around the lagoon, hang the paintings of one Gabriele
Bella, a painter of little talent but whose work—vignettes of Venice's 18th
century activities—illustrates the life of the times. Pictured are such events
as bull and bear baiting, acrobats in the piazza, fairs like that of the Sensa
(Ascension Day Festival), ritual fights between combatants from two of the
sestieri, indoor tennis, regattas, weddings, fishing expeditions, carnival scenes,
and always the Ridotto.

No one captured this atmosphere of hedonistic pleasure-seeking better

The statue of the playwright Carlo Goldoni reflects the man himself, but also his city: rather disheveled but sophisticated and resolutely determined to enjoy life.

than the city's playwrights; the best known of these was Carlo Goldoni (1707–1793). Before his time, theatre had been dominated by the slapstick and crudity of the semi-improvisational *commedia dell'arte*. But by the 18th century, that form of entertainment had become decadent and unresponsive to the more sophisticated needs of Venetian society. Under the shrewd insights of Goldoni, who followed in the vein of Molière and the English playwrights before him, minimal scenarios, spontaneous dialogue, masks and stock characters gradually gave way to carefully written, elaborate plots and more realistic characterizations, although he continued to use the Venetian dialect, satirize the classes and mirror the life of his time. His most consistent and likable quality was an optimistic and kindly attitude; he portrayed his fellow citizens and city in decline with humor, but without malice, in spite of frequent vindictive attacks from the jealousy of his rival dramatists.

Popular during his lifetime, but even more so after his death, Goldoni was honored with a statue located not far from the Rialto Bridge. It is a perfect tribute not only to the man himself, but to the Venice of his time. What a contrast to the Colleoni monument raised up when the city was pugnacious, aggressive and powerful. Now the citizen to be honored is a companionable, friendly type; his statue is on a much smaller scale, almost at eye level, his clothes somewhat rumpled, cocked hat aslant and a smile of detachment and subtle knowing humor on his face. One might say Venice had come to terms with reality—no longer the hub of a dynamic maritime empire, but rather, in a lighter vein, the sophisticated, somewhat jaded center for music, art and entertainment.

By Goldoni's time there were some 15 theatres in Venice, most producing operas, but some presenting comedies and tragedies in spoken prose. All are gone today except one relatively late construction, La Fenice (1790). The building had been preserved in almost its exact original condition, with its neoclassical architecture, rococo interior of five tiers of boxes and frescoed ceiling intact, until a fire in the mid-1990s gutted almost the entire structure. It has since been reconstructed.

Venice in the Eyes of Its Visitors

There were indeed many attractions to draw foreigners to Venice. Besides the opera, theatre, gambling, carnival, and beautiful women of diverse accomplishments and reputations—some as courtesans presiding over literary salons—there was the city itself with its unique setting, its mysterious ambience, its collections of art, its composite of architectural styles, at last in full maturity in its final form. Small wonder that a stay here was not only required but greatly anticipated by young Englishmen and others setting out on their Grand Tour. Moreover, the intellectual and cultural life of the Venetian educated class was hardly moribund despite the bankruptcy of the city's commercial, political and military institutions. Venice of the 18th century produced men like Vivaldi, the city's greatest composer, and Marco Foscarini, a shrewd ambassador, a procurator of St. Mark's and finally a doge (1762–1763). Foscarini was perhaps one of the most scholarly of the doges—he composed poetry, collected manuscripts and wrote a literary history of the Republic.[26]

Apparently the cost of living in Venice, at least compared to London, was relatively cheap as Lady Mary Wortley Montagu, living there at mid-century, described:

> All the conveniences of life are to be had at very easy rates
> . . . here are two playhouses and two operas constantly
> performed every night at exceedingly low prices . . . it is the
> fashion for the greatest ladies to walk the streets, which are
> admirably paved; and a mask, priced (at only) a sixpence . . .
> the greatest equipage is a gondola, that holds eight persons
> and is the price of an English (sedan) chair . . .

Even Rousseau, with whom Lady Montagu often corresponded and who spent a year in Venice in 1743, did not let his critical eye overlook the pleasures there, especially the music and the women, which, he said, the city offered so cheaply.

However, not everyone who came to Venice was equally impressed. Both Horace Walpole and Edward Gibbon complained about "the stinking ditches" that pass for canals, and there were many other negative comments by writers like Edward Lear and D. H. Lawrence. They and other 18th-century visitors repeatedly noted the filth in the canals, the noisome smells and the piles of uncollected rubbish at street corners. Goethe, for example, was disappointed that "there is no regularity or strictness" about garbage

---

[26] In fact there were many celebrated Venetian men of letters and scientists who contributed to the growing store of knowledge in the 18th century: Gaspari Gozzi, Apostolo Zeno, Francesco Maffei, Francesco Algarotti and especially Giovanni Morgazini, the founder of pathological anatomy.

removal, "all the more unpardonable because Venice is as well situated for cleanliness as any town in Holland." Even the grand Piazza San Marco was often cluttered with the stalls and claptrap of hucksters and peddlers.

The English traveler, Joseph Addison, writing in 1705, perceived a more profound problem—a hardening conservatism among the upper classes: "They are tenacious of old laws and customs to their great prejudice, whereas a trading nation must be for new changes and expedients as different junctures and emergencies arise." He went further and accused the Senate of encouraging "idleness and luxury in the nobility, ignorance and licentiousness in the clergy . . . viciousness and debauchery in the convents . . . ." Again, while someone like Casanova, a rogue and libertine, could hardly criticize the amorality or self-indulgence of his fellow citizens, he did complain about their resistance to change, whether they be "important or trifling things, however absurd." For instance, they were reluctant to give up oared galleys, by then obsolete and largely manned by prisoners, "because they would not know what to do with the many men sentenced to hard labor."[27] But most visitors, even the critics, inevitably concluded that despite its shortcomings, its disrepair and dereliction, the city had an incomparable and persistent hold on the imagination and an impact on the senses that was unique in this world.

Internal Tensions

In fact, Venice had assumed two contrasting aspects of itself that were captured by its two greatest *vedutisti*. The one, Canaletto, concentrated on the exterior façades and material remains of the city's former triumphs, from the sweeping views of the Piazza to the magnificent buildings and monuments to the waterways. A well-ordered, sunny and prosperous-looking place appears, perhaps somewhat polished up, in his architectural paintings. The other, Guardi, with greater insight and imagination, reveals in his work the melancholy, hollow, lost soul of the city as it gradually crumbles both physically and morally amidst the panoply of Carnevale and other antiquated rituals.

---

[27] This comment may not have been very objective as Casanova had been imprisoned, unfairly he claimed, and roughly treated by the Republic. He was fortunate not to have been sent to the galleys but instead was incarcerated in the "leads," those stifling cells in the attic of the Doges Palace from which he later escaped.

Still, as it had always been, Venice continued as a center for the exchange and mingling of ideas, old and new. Traditionalist and conservative on the whole, it was yet cautiously receptive to new and divergent concepts as well. This was a place where, for example, the congealed, oligarchic institutions of an ancient government could tolerate the radical writings of Rousseau and Voltaire; where indigenous art forms could blend with both an imported rococo style and in turn with neoclassical motifs from France; where the older and simpler forms of theatre and music could evolve into more sophisticated structures; where the façade of Catholic morality could live with an underlying nonconformity and licentiousness. Occasionally, one of the more outspoken intellectual publications, of which 18th-century Venice had many, would be suppressed (for example, one called Frusta Letteraria—the Literary Whip—was shut down in 1765), but most enjoyed relative freedom from censorship, which permitted the expression of unconventional political ideas.

The ever-present contrasts between the poor and the rich also became more pronounced as thousands of beggars rubbed shoulders with other thousands of elaborately uniformed servants and their even more gorgeously attired employers. When much commercial enterprise wasted away and productive jobs with it, many youths were forced into monastic orders, domestic service or artisan trades. Large-scale building projects, including the continual remodeling of existing churches, monasteries and palaces, demanded a vast army of craftsmen—stonemasons, stonecutters and carvers, woodworkers and painters—as everything turned to show and extravagance. The patrician's country villas, originally modest farmhouses built for the purpose of supervising agricultural production, were now the objects of careful renovation and embellishment and became as important to social and cultural life as the city itself. So much so that holdings on the mainland were soon to become a source of concern when the turmoil of the French Revolution, no longer confined to France, spilled over into the rest of Europe, including Northern Italy. The buffer state of Milan had been in Austrian hands since the War of the Spanish Succession and Venice optimistically gambled that Hapsburg troops there would serve as a barrier. This hope proved futile when in May 1796 the French army, under the young general Napoleon Bonaparte, unexpectedly drove the Austrians out of Milan and threatened the Veneto.

The whole environment of the French pre-revolutionary period, the theories of Rousseau and the Philosophers, had been anathema to the Venetian patricians, who reacted to these intellectual probings and warnings with disdain and contempt, but did nothing about them. For years the government had neither voted significant funds for the military nor formed any alliances with its neighbors. It had been afraid to sign a proffered treaty with the new French regime for fear of offending Austria, and vice versa, so it did neither. Now, in the person of Napoleon, a remote threat had suddenly become a stark reality.

The End of the Republic

With Milan conquered and the Austrians on the defensive and in retreat, the French moved against the cities north of the Po River—Bergamo, Crema, Brescia, even Verona—on the pretext that they were hindering the army's advance toward the Brenner Pass and the Tyrol. Most offered little resistance and were taken one by one through the remainder of 1796 with the exception of Mantua, a Hapsburg possession, which defiantly held out. Meanwhile, the Venetians belatedly attempted to negotiate with Napoleon, but their entreaties fell on deaf ears. He accused them of working with the Austrians and the British and of maintaining an antiquated government in the age of enlightenment. He blamed them for widespread local resistance in the countryside of the Veneto that interfered with his army. Finally in April 1797 an incident occurred that provided him with a convenient excuse, if one were needed, to justify his scorn and loathing for the Venetians. A French gunboat seeking refuge near the Lido was fired upon and her captain killed. Napoleon was enraged—whether genuinely or contrived it didn't matter. He sent an ultimatum[28] and then a declaration of war.

When Mantua finally fell that spring, panic gripped the Venetian nobles. Not only were their properties on the mainland threatened, but the city itself was now vulnerable to attack and destruction. In spite of the fact that the lagoon was most difficult to invade, Doge Ludovico Manin and the other leaders had little heart to resist. Venice had grown weak, and like Constantinople before it, was ripe for plucking. As French troops

---

[28] Some of his demands: disband mercenary troops, pay a large indemnity, expel all British envoys, publish a manifesto creating a democracy, erect a "tree of liberty" in the Piazza, free all political prisoners. To Napoleon's chagrin when the jails were finally opened, there were none.

swept across the Veneto, the Great Council hastily assembled, its members confused, helpless and without direction. The debate was short. Napoleon had ordered, among other things, that the patricians renounce "their hereditary rights of nobility" and that the government dissolve itself. On May 12, 1797, it did just that. After some 11 centuries as a triumphant and independent state, the last of the doges joined with the other nobles and voted the Council and the oligarchy out of existence. La Serenissima's long history had come to a sudden and abject end.

Afterward, while a cease-fire was being negotiated by Napoleon with the Austrians, arrangements were made in June 1797 for some 4,000 French troops to occupy Venice. At the same time, to further emphasize the finality of the defeat, on the young general's command, all reminders of the old regime were burned in a great bonfire in the Piazza: the Golden Book, symbols and banners from the Bucintoro, all insignia of the Lion of St. Mark, the doge's mantle, robe and jeweled crown. On the same day, the French Tricolors, symbols of a new era, were hoisted on the three red masts standing before San Marco, where the flags of Cyprus, Crete and the Morea had proudly flown before. Then, just months later on October 17, 1797, the treaty of Campo Formio imposed a further humiliation. The French ceded the city and most of the Veneto and Dalmatia to the Austrians in return for undisputed sovereignty over the rest of Northern Italy. Napoleon also took the Venetian fleet and Ionian Islands, assets he needed in his continuing war against Britain. Finally, before the Austrians took over, insult was added to injury as many of the city's art treasures were systematically confiscated, including the famous bronze horses of Byzantium, which on Napoleon's instructions were unceremoniously shipped off to Paris.

Epilogue

Once did She hold the gorgeous east in fee;
And was the safeguard of the west: the worth
Of Venice did not fall below her birth,
Venice, the eldest Child of Liberty.
She was a maiden City, bright and free;
No guile seduced, no force could violate;
And, when she took unto herself a Mate,
She must espouse the everlasting Sea.
And what if she had seen those glories fade,
Those titles vanish, and that strength decay;
Yet shall some tribute of regret be paid
When her long life hath reached its final day;
Men are we, and must grieve when e'en the Shade
Of that which once was great is passed away.
(Wordsworth 1807)

Thus ended the independent Republic of Venice. The city's story after 1797 must be briefly told, but nothing of any positive nature was added to the sum total of traditional Venetian culture, art, architecture or ambience. On the contrary, the intervening years have left certain scars on that ultimate work of art that was the fully developed 18th-century city. The earliest modernizations, if not vandalisms, were the work of Napoleon, who, soon after the Austrian occupation, took back the city and the Veneto in 1805 following his victories at Ulm and Austerlitz. Besides closing a number of convents and monasteries and demolishing scores of churches, he further violated the city by deciding to fill in several canals in order to facilitate traffic. An important one became the wide street now known as the Via Garibaldi. The Public Granary, an old Gothic landmark on the Molo behind the Procuratie Nuove, was swept away to provide a useless garden for Napoleon's viceroy to walk in, while the Procuratie Nuove itself was redone inside as the new governor's residence.[29] At the same time, it was decided that the old structures at the far western end of the Piazza must go, including the ancient church of San Geminiano, with its fine Renaissance façade connecting the two differing but complimentary wings of the Old and New Procuratie. The asymmetrical arrangement—the church was located slightly to the north of the piazza's central axis—and the contrasting stylistic juxtaposition at this end were too much for the rationalist French mind to accept, so even in the very heart of old Venice things had to be tidied up. Accordingly, between 1807 and 1814 the church was pulled down and uniformity was imposed by a two-story attempted copy of the Libreria Sansoviniana, while inside a grand staircase and antechambers were fitted out as suitable approaches to the vice-royal residence itself.

Although the Napoleonic occupation, which soon included the entire Italian peninsula, may have brought long-term benefits to the people as a whole—land reform, better roads, a more modern legal system (the Code Napoleon) and a powerful step toward unity—it was as well for Venice that its duration was short. After Waterloo (1815), the city and the Veneto were restored to Austria by the Congress of Vienna, and an attempt was made to turn back the clock and revert to the old ways. Not surprisingly, this was impossible. The ancient government was only a memory; independence, the fleet and the empire were all gone; the aristocracy was fast disappearing. Industry and commerce had dwindled and taxation by Vienna was heavy. The city reconciled itself to a less ambitious role—chemical, glass- and lace-making, precious metal and leather working, printing, fishing and, of course, local trade. To further cement commercial ties with the Veneto, studies for building a causeway to link the city to the mainland were commenced in the 1820s, though not carried out until 1846, when a railway bridge was built between Mestre and the Santa Lucia district. At the time the Venetians saw it as a means to enlarge the city's trade and population, but it seems to have had the opposite effect of siphoning off workers and business to

---

[29] Occupied successively to the present by the French viceroy, Austrian governors, the Kings of United Italy and now the Correr.

the mainland. No doubt this link was inevitable and only one among many factors contributing to the city's gradual decay.

But the loss of affluence and liberty did little to interrupt Venice's long-standing appeal to foreigners. Far from discouraging visitors, the city's congealed and insubstantial condition, a fragile mystery that seemed to float suspended in the hazy distance between sea and sky, only served to attract poets, artists and other romantics from across the continent. The English, especially, sensed the unique fascination of the place and the almost unreal, theatrical anachronism that had managed to survive. They poured forth their feelings and perceptions—expressed in ecstatic poetry, dramas, tragedies and sometimes by personal impressions or political commentary, as well as a profusion of sketches, engravings and paintings—all through the years of the Austrian occupation to a responsive, sympathetic audience,.

One of the earliest such champions was Lord Byron. He was enamored of the Mediterranean world and liberal causes and lived in and around Venice for many years while writing his historical dramas and poetry of rebellion against tyranny. Many other poets and writers of the time—Percy Shelley, John Keats, Samuel Rogers, Walter Savage Landor, Arthur Hugh Clough—and the painter, William Turner, were there. Especially influential was the art critic John Ruskin, who studied the city and its architecture for some two decades before publishing his three-volume survey, *The Stones of Venice,* the culminating and definitive 19th-century assessment of the Republic and all its works.

The uprisings of 1848 against established regimes that occurred all over Italy, including a Venetian revolt that took the Austrians most of a year to put down, only brought more repressive measures and economic retaliation. In particular, Vienna commenced an all-out effort to build up the port at Trieste in order to deprive Venice of any remaining commercial opportunities. As a result, many businesses left the city and dozens of *palazzi* fell vacant. But there was little real oppression and on the whole the Austrians tried to conduct an efficient administration. Nevertheless, resentment against them increased and the ideals of the mid-19th century that stirred the middle classes—democracy, liberalism, nationalism—would not go away. By 1860, the rest of Italy at last achieved unification and the Austrian emperor gradually became reconciled to the ultimate need to release Venice. This was reluctantly accomplished after a plebiscite in 1866, when foreign troops finally withdrew and Venice found her modern role as a not insignificant part of United Italy.

Venetian Doges, 726-1797

Orso Ipato	726-737	Domenico Flabanico	1032-1043
Teodato Ipato	742-755	Domenico Contarini	1043-1071
Galla Gaulo	755-756	Domenico Selvo	1071-1084
Domenico Monegario	756-764	Vitale Falier	1084-1096
Maurizio Galbaio	764-787	Viatle Michiel I	1096-1102
Giovanni Galbaio	787-804	Ordelafo Falier	1102-1118
Obelario degli Antenori	804-811	Domenico Michiel	1118-1130
Agnello Participazio	811-827	Pietro Polani	1130-1148
Giustiniano Participazio	827-829	Domenico Morosini	1148-1156
Giovanni Participazio I	829-836	Vitale Michiel II	1156-1172
Pietro Tradonico	836-864	Sebastiano Ziani	1172-1178
Orso Participazio I	864-881	Orio Mastropiero	1178-1192
Giovanni Participazio II	881-887	Enrico Dandolo	1192-1205
Pietro Candiano I	887	Pietro Ziani	1205-1229
Pietro Tribuno	888-912	Giacomo Tiepolo	1229-1249
Orso Participazio II	912-932	Marin Morosini	1249-1253
Pietro Candiano II	932-939	Renier Zeno	1253-1268
Pietro Participazio	939-942	Lorenzo Tiepolo	1268-1275
Pietro Candiano III	942-959	Jacopo Contarini	1275-1280
Pietro Candiano IV	959-976	Giovanni Dandolo	1280-1289
Pietro Orseolo I	976-978	Pietro Gradenigo	1289-1311
Vitale Candiano	978-979	Marino Zorzi	1311-1312
Tribuno Memmo	979-991	Giovanni Soranzo	1312-1328
Pietro Orseolo II	991-1008	Francesco Dandolo	1329-1339
Otto Orseolo	1008-1026	Bartolomeo Gradenigo	1339-1342
Pietro Centranico	1026-1032	Andrea Dandolo	1343-1354

Marin Falier	1354-1355	Pasquale Cicogna	1585-1595
Giovanni Gracdenigo	1355-1356	Marino Grimani	1595-1605
Giovanni Dolfin	1356-1361	Leonardo Dona	1606-1612
Lorenzo Celsi	1361-1365	Marcantonio Memmo	1612-1615
Marco Corner	1365-1368	Giovanni Bembo	1615-1618
Andrea Contarini	1368-1382	Nicolo Dona	1618
Michele Morosini	1382	Antonio Priuli	1618-1623
Antonio Venier	1382-1400	Francesco Contarini	1623-1624
Michele Steno	1400-1413	Giovanni Corner I	1625-1629
Tommaso Mocenigo	1414-1423	Nicolo Contarini	1630-1631
Francesco Foscari	1423-1457	Francesco Erizzo	1631-1646
Pasquale Malipiero	1457-1462	Francesco Molin	1646-1655
Cristoforo Moro	1462-1471	Carlo Contarini	1655-1656
Nicolo Tron	1471-1473	Francesco Corner	1656
Nicolo Marcello	1473-1474	Bertucci Valier	1656-1658
Pietro Mocenigo	1474-1476	Giovanni Pesaro	1658-1659
Andrea Vendramin	1476-1478	Domenico Contarini	1659-1675
Giovanni Mocenigo	1478-1485	Nicolo Sagredo	1675-1676
Marco Barbarigo	1485-1486	Alvise Contarini	1676-1684
Agostino Barbarigo	1486-1501	Marcantonio Giustinian	1684-1688
Leonardo Loredan	1501-1521	Francesco Morosini	1688-1694
Antonio Grimani	1521-1523	Silvestro Valier	1694-1700
Andrea Gritti	1523-1538	Alvise Mocenigo II	1700-1709
Pietro Lando	1539-1545	Giovanni Corner II	1709-1722
Francesco Dona	1545-1553	Alvise Mocenigo III	1722-1732
Marcantonio Trevisan	1553-1554	Carlo Ruzzini	1732-1735
Francesco Venier	1554-1556	Alvise Pisani	1735-1741
Lorenzo Priuli	1556-1559	Pietro Grimani	1741-1752
Girolamo Priuli	1559-1567	Francesco Loredan	1752-1762
Pietro Loredan	1567-1570	Marco Foscarini	1762-1763
Alvise Mocenigo I	1570-1577	Alvise Mocenigo IV	1763-1778
Sebastiano Venier	1577-1578	Paolo Renier	1779-1789
Nicolo da Ponte	1578-1585	Lodovico Manin	1789-1797

Glossary

Acqua alta, high tide inundations
Androne, ground floor entrance hall
Bottega, workshop
Bucintoro, doge's ceremonial galley
Calle, side street
Campo, square, open area
Chiaroscuro, contrasting light and dark
Colleganza, trading partnership
Condottiere, mercenary captain
Contrada, parish
Cortile, courtyard
Cupola, dome
Fondaco, merchant's business and living quarters
Fondamenta, canal embankment or road along it
Iconostasis, railing between nave and sanctuary
Libro d'oro, directory of Venetian nobles, the Patriciate
Loggia, open gallery of a palace
Maggior consiglio, Venice's Great Council
Morea, the Peloponnesus in Greece
Motoscafo, sleeker, faster waterbus
Oltremare, overseas, the levant
Orto, garden or orchard
Piano nobile, principal floor of a palace
Plutei, marble panels in front of an altar
Portego, main hall of a palace
Pozzo, water well

Predela, smaller painting below an altarpiece
Procuratie, residence of the San Marco trustees
Rio, canal
Riva, street along a quay
Ruga, shopping street
Scuola, lay confraternity
Sensa, Ascension Day
Sestiere, one of the six quarters of Venice
Sotto portego, arcaded street under a building
Squero, boatyard
Terrafirma, the mainland
Tessera, piece of marble or glass in a mosaic
Traghetto, gondola ferry
Vaporetto, waterbus, once steam powered

Index

(Page numbers of illustrations are in bold type)